A BEGINNER'S GUIDE
TO THE New
Testament

A BEGINNER'S GUIDE
TO THE New
Testament

Arthur E. Zannoni

ThomasMore®
– An RCL Company –
Allen, Texas

NIHIL OBSTAT:
Rev. Msgr. Glenn D. Gardner, J.C.D.
Censor Librorum

IMPRIMATUR:
† Most Rev. Charles V. Grahmann
Bishop of Dallas

May 1, 2002

The Nihil Obstat and Imprimatur are official declarations that the material reviewed is free of doctrinal or moral error. No implication is contained therein that those granting the Nihil Obstat and Imprimatur agree with the contents, opinions, or statements expressed.

Acknowledgments

The Scripture quotations contained herein are from the *New Revised Standard Version Bible: Catholic Edition* copyright © 1993 and 1989 by the Division of Christian Education for the National Council of the Churches of Christ in the U.S.A. Used by permission. All rights reserved.

Send all inquiries to:
Thomas More® Publishing
An RCL Company
200 East Bethany Drive
Allen, Texas 75002-3804

Telephone: 800-264-0368 / 972-390-6300
Fax: 800-688-8356 / 972-390-6560

Visit us at: **www.thomasmore.com**
Customer Service E-mail: **cservice@rcl-enterprises.com**

Printed in the United States of America

7491   ISBN 0-88347-491-3

1 2 3 4 5   06 05 04 03 02

ACKNOWLEDGMENTS

There are many who deserve thanks for helping with this book. The original idea for this volume came as the result of a conversation I had with my friend and fellow writer Bill Huebsch. Bill encouraged me to explore writing something for beginners about the Bible. In turn, he introduced me to John Sprague, of Thomas More Press, who liked the idea and refined the project into two volumes, and offered to publish them. I am deeply grateful to both of them for their support and encouragement throughout the writing process.

While composing the book, invaluable support and suggestions were given to me by Kevin Perrotta, David Haas, Jeffrey Judge, and Matthew Linn, S.J. Special thanks goes to Leslie Carney for typing the entire manuscript and for her wonderful editing suggestions and attention to every detail of layout and design that goes into desktop publishing.

My entire family supported me with encouragement, prayer, and time to write. To my older children, Laura and Luke, I offer thanks for their constant love and care of their dad; and to my younger son, Alessandro, for helping me to keep a sense of wonder and exploration in my life, which only a toddler can do. Finally, words cannot even begin to express all the care, love, support, encouragement, and challenges that my spouse, Kathleen, provided during the composition of this book. A poet and fellow writer, she is my beloved and companion on the road of life. She has stayed the course, and together we have embraced life's challenges, weathered every storm, and enjoyed many a moonrise and sunset.

CONTENTS

INTRODUCTION

Everyone WANTS TO READ THE BIBLE FROM COVER TO cover, but no one does it because the task becomes overwhelming and confusing. The size of the Bible is daunting. The time, places, characters, vocabulary, and events are different from everyday modern life. Without a guide, touring the Bible can be confusing, laborious, and for some downright scary.

This book is the first volume of a two-volume series that I am preparing to help guide "beginners" through the library of books known as the Bible. In this first volume I explore the New Testament. At a later date, a companion volume will be published in which I deal with the Old Testament.

If you are new to the study of the Bible and unacquainted with the twenty-seven books of the New Testament, I have given myself the task of guiding you through all the books. And I present a selection of themes with which you need to be familiar in order to better grasp the greatest story ever told. Since I am aiming this book primarily at Catholics and their use of the Bible in the practice of their faith, I make every effort to show how the church acts as a guide for the believer—you the reader—as you explore the "Good Book." I intend this volume to be a basic introduction that provides both information and material for reflection on the New Testament.

In chapter 1, I provide a concise summary of the Catholic Church's teachings on how to read and use the Bible along with some basic tools. In chapter 2, I begin an exploration of the four gospels and how they came to be faith literature, who wrote them, where, when, why, to whom they were written, and what they contain. I emphasize the similarities and differences found in the gospels and how, in their own unique way, they reveal the Jesus of the gospels.

Since Jesus is the most important person in the gospels, I examine in chapter 3 how the gospels portray him, who he was, what he taught, how he functioned, and how people responded to his lifestyle and teachings. All four of the gospels portray Jesus as a storyteller of God who made use of a particular type of story known as the parable. I reflect upon these parables, the stories Jesus left behind, in chapter 4.

According to the gospels, Jesus' disciples were the first audience to hear his stories. Their selection by Jesus and their response to his call, as well as the price of discipleship, I examine in chapter 5. Then, in chapters 6 and 7 I focus on the gospel narratives of Jesus' passion and resurrection. My goal is to provide you with the insights I feel are necessary to explore the meaning of Jesus' death and resurrection.

The remaining books of the New Testament, the Acts of the Apostles, the Pauline letters and other epistles, as well as the Book of Revelation, I cover in chapters 8 through 10. There is a treasure trove of knowledge and insight on these remaining books of the New Testament. I outline them for you as concisely as I can.

Occasionally through this book you will find helpful maps of the Bible. On the inside of the front and back covers (for easy access) you will find a time line to help you position personalities and events vis-à-vis the Bible. In the appendix I will highlight the various translations of the Bible available to us in English today. (The English translation I use throughout is the *New Revised Standard Version*.) I provide all this as supplementary tools to read and interpret the Bible.

To enhance your use of the material I present, I include detailed information, diagrams, and illustrations within each chapter. I conclude each chapter with discussion questions to help you evaluate your understanding and a list of books for further reading. Those of you who wish to delve further into a particular topic will find ample resources. I strongly encourage you to keep a Bible at hand as you read so that you can look up the biblical passages I refer to throughout.

I sincerely hope that this book helps you to better understand, interpret, and live the challenges of Jesus as presented in the New Testament. May your reading help you develop a newfound respect for the books of the New Testament and the transmission of our faith. May it help you to realize that, "Indeed, the word of God is living and active, sharper than any two-edged sword, piercing until it divides soul from spirit, joints from marrow; it is able to judge the thoughts and intentions of the heart" (Hebrews 4:12).

Soli Deo Gloria

1

THE CHURCH AS A GUIDE TO READING THE BIBLE

Of ALL THE BOOKS IN THE WORLD, THE BIBLE IS THE MOST read. It has been translated into just about every language on the face of the earth. Millions of people use it as a guide for their life and for inspiration in times of tragedy and joy. The Bible is present when people take an oath at baptisms, marriages, and funerals.

The Bible is so much a part of our English language that people quote it without even realizing what they are quoting. For example, if you call someone the "apple of your eye" (Deuteronomy 32:10), the "salt of the earth" (Matthew 5:13), a "fleshpot" (Exodus 16:3), or a "painted woman" (2 Kings 9:30), or say that he "has gone out of his mind" (Mark 3:21), you are quoting the Bible. And if you mention any one of these phrases: a "drop in the bucket" (Isaiah 40:15), the "fat of the land" (Genesis 45:18), the "handwriting on the wall" (Daniel 5:5), an "olive branch" (Genesis 8:11), the "potter's field," (Matthew 27:7), the "powers that be" (Romans 13:1), a "scapegoat" (Leviticus 16:8), "sour grapes" (Ezekiel 18:2), the "straight and narrow" (Matthew 7:14), the "twinkling of an eye" (1 Corinthians 15:52), "wheels within wheels" (Ezekiel 1:16), you are quoting the Bible. Expressions like "the blind leading the blind" (Matthew 15:14), "face to face" (Exodus 33:11), "give up the ghost" (Mark 15:39), "holier than thou" (Isaiah 65:5), "hope against hope" (Romans 4:18), or "keep the faith" (2 Timothy 4:7), all come from the Bible.

Finding Your Way Around the Bible

For some people, finding their way around in the Bible can be a daunting and at times disconcerting task. What follows are some basic suggestions.

The minute you open your Bible, look at the table of contents and the introductory sections. Often the editor or publisher will explain where the various books of the Bible are found or have them indexed. Further, there will be a chart or a visual that lists and explains all of the abbreviations for the various books of the Bible.

In addition to these introductory materials, many modern English-language Bibles have notes at the bottom of each page. These will often explain terms or situations, and at times will provide cross-references to other texts (books) of the Bible. These notes are quite helpful. Often there is also a brief introduction to each book of the Bible printed just in front of the particular book.

Study Bibles have time lines, maps, glossaries of terms, charts of weights and measures, and possibly an index of Lectionary readings for the various Sundays of the liturgical year. These are all useful tools and will prove to be quite helpful.

Finally, a person needs to be familiar with the way in which a biblical citation is to be deciphered.

UNDERSTANDING A BIBLICAL CITATION

Reference	Meaning
Mark 6 (or Mk 6)	The Gospel of Mark, chapter 6
Mark 6:3	The Gospel of Mark, chapter 6, verse 3
Mark 6:3–11	The Gospel of Mark, chapter 6, verses 3 through 11
Mark 6:3, 11	The Gospel of Mark, chapter 6, verses 3 and 11
Mark 6:3–11:1	The Gospel of Mark, chapter 6, verse 3 through chapter 11, verse 1
Mark 6:3a	The Gospel of Mark, chapter 6, the first part of verse 3
Mark 6:3b	The Gospel of Mark, chapter 6, the second part of verse 3

The Bible is part of the very fabric of our lives, and while used and quoted by many, its interpretation requires a good deal of work and a helpful guide.

The Church as a Guide to Reading the Bible

Whenever we visit a foreign country or a museum, we have a guide who helps us better understand the place we are visiting. Catholics have a well-trained guide in the church who helps us better read, understand, and pray the Sacred Scriptures. Unfortunately, not all of us are acquainted with the church as a guide. A short history lesson might help.

The church's teachings on the Bible are contained in a variety of documents that stem from the mid-sixteenth century through the end of the twentieth century. What follows is a brief summary of the *most* important documents.

CHURCH TEACHINGS ON THE BIBLE

- **Council of Trent.** The fourth session of this council (1546) settled the canon (official list) of Sacred Scripture that Catholics would use.

- **Vatican Council I.** In a constitution of this council entitled *Dei Filius* and promulgated in 1870, the council affirmed the inspiration of the Bible and the fact that God is ultimately the author of the Sacred Scriptures.

- *Providentissimus Deus.* An encyclical letter of Pope Leo XIII issued in 1893 which presents a plan for Catholic scholars to study the Bible using some of the modern methods of biblical study that were emerging in the nineteenth century.

- *Spiritus Paraclitus.* An encyclical letter of Pope Benedict XV issued in 1920 on the fifteen hundredth anniversary of the death of Saint Jerome, the great biblical scholar of fourth to fifth centuries C.E. A rather conservative encyclical that commended biblical scholars who were following the guidelines set down by Pope Leo XIII.

- *Divino Afflante Spiritu.* An encyclical letter of Pope Pius XII issued in 1943 which is the most important official document that inaugurated modern Catholic critical (analytic) exegesis (analysis) of the Bible. The encyclical affirms that the Bible contains no errors in faith and morals, but it also respects the human dimension of the Word of God.

- **Instruction of the Pontifical Biblical Commission,** *On the Historical Truth of the Gospels.* Issued by the commission in 1964, it acknowledges the multilayered traditions that are found in the canonical gospels. It explains the threefold stages by which the gospels developed: oral, written, and edited (redacted) traditions. Each of these corresponds to particular time frames: the time of Jesus and the apostles, the time of preaching and collecting traditions of later disciples, and the time of the evangelists who finally collected and edited the tradition into written form for their individual faith communities.

- **Vatican Council II,** *Dei Verbum, Dogmatic Constitution on Divine Revelation.* Issued in 1965 by an ecumenical council, this document provides extensive teaching about the Bible. It affirms basic Catholic doctrine on the Bible, e.g., inspiration, lack of error in matters of faith and morals, the human dimension of the Sacred Scriptures that nonetheless communicates the divine message as God intended, and the fact that Scripture is "the soul of theology." It also articulates the complex relationship of Scripture and tradition as the sources and channels of divine revelation which give life to the church.

- **Instruction of the Pontifical Biblical Commission,** *The Interpretation of the Bible in the Church.* Issued by the commission in 1993, this document treats extensively the many methods of modern scientific biblical study that are prevalent today, both historical-critical methods and newer and more varied approaches. It carefully reviews each of them, affirming what is positive and warning against what is negative in each method. The only method that is sharply criticized and deemed incompatible with a Catholic approach to Scripture is fundamentalism.

- **Catechism of the Catholic Church,** *101 to 141.* Published in 1997, this resource is the easiest accessible, most convenient, and most succinct summary of the Catholic Church's teaching on the Bible.

  Even though the above list of documents does not do justice to all of the nuances in the church's teaching about the Bible, it does show a development in the tradition and the fact that the church has not taken a monolithic view of how one is to approach Sacred Scripture for discerning God's revelation.

Prior to the Second Vatican Council (1962–65), most Catholics had little first-hand contact with the Bible. Indeed, they were not even encouraged to read the Bible lest such reading might lead to "private interpretation," which might well be erroneous or heretical.

This fear of "private interpretation" originated in the sixteenth-century controversies between the emerging Protestant churches and the Catholic Church. The Protestant churches claimed that the Bible *alone* was the norm of faith and that its plain meaning was accessible to any believing reader, while the Catholic Church insisted that divine revelation came through two sources, the Bible and church tradition, both of which could only be interpreted by the Magisterium, the teaching office of the church. Consequently, most Catholics prior to the Second Vatican Council only encountered the Scriptures on Sundays by means of brief Latin passages, usually read out of context, and preached on only occasionally.

In the first part of the twentieth century, the Holy See severely restricted Catholic biblical scholars from participating in the rapidly developing field of biblical scholarship. In 1943, however, in a landmark encyclical entitled *Divino Afflante Spiritu,* Pope Pius XII encouraged Catholic scholars to undertake serious study of the Bible using all appropriate modern critical analytical methods. Then in 1964, the Roman Pontifical Biblical Commission issued a document entitled *On the Historical Truth of the Gospels.* In it the commission held that the gospels, while retaining the sense of the sayings of Jesus, were not necessarily expressing them literally. The truth and historicity of the gospels must be judged from the fact that the teachings and life of Jesus were not reported for the purpose of being remembered but were preached so as to offer the church a basis of faith.

CHURCH TEACHINGS ON AND ABOUT THE BIBLE

"Easy access to Sacred Scripture should be provided for all the Christian Faithful."   Vatican Council II, *Dogmatic Constitution on Divine Revelation*, 22

"The treasures of the Bible are to be opened up more lavishly, so that a richer share in God's word may be provided for the faithful."
Vatican Council II, *Constitution on the Sacred Liturgy*, 51

"Those divinely revealed realities which are presented and contained in Sacred Scripture have been committed to writing under the inspiration of the Holy Spirit." Vatican Council II, *Dogmatic Constitution on Divine Revelation*, 11

"Ignorance of the Scriptures is ignorance of Christ."   Saint Jerome

"Sacred Scripture changes the heart of whoever reads it from earthly desires to embracing spiritual things."   Saint Gregory the Great

"The scholar, the student of the Bible, is first of all an ardent and fearless listener to the divine message. He knows that it is not a dead letter locked away in archival documents, but rather the living and still intact message that comes from God and is to be welcomed in its entirety."
Pope John XXIII

"In the view of the church, the Bible is not merely a literary work but also a religious work put together with a religious motive, chosen and constituted according to a religious criteria. . . . It differs from all human books for it is an inspired book containing and transmitting divine revelation."
Pope Paul VI

"It is important for every Catholic to realize that the church produced the New Testament, not vice versa. The Bible did not come down from heaven, whole and intact, given by the Holy Spirit. Just as the faith and experience of Israel developed its sacred books, so was the early church the matrix of the New Testament. . . . The Bible, then, is the church's book. The New Testament did not come before the church, but from the church."
United States Catholic Bishops,
A Pastoral Statement for Catholics on Biblical Fundamentalism (1987)

Catholics and a Renewed Enthusiasm for the Bible

In the wake of the Second Vatican Council, many Catholics took up the Bible with enthusiasm and fell in love with this beautiful story of God's engagement with humanity: the creation, formation, and liberation of a chosen people recounted in the Old Testament, and the coming of God among us in Jesus and the spread of the Gospel throughout the whole world recounted in the New Testament.

Catholics flocked to lectures and summer courses on the Bible, made biblical retreats, formed Bible study groups, and prayed fervently with the biblical text. The Lectionary was revised so that large portions of the Scriptures were read, sequentially when possible, during the liturgy. Younger clergy were formed in contemporary biblical methods and trained to preach on the Lectionary readings.

Many Catholics in their enthusiasm for Scripture were attracted by the (biblical) fundamentalist approach of some charismatic Protestant groups. We cannot trace the history and development of fundamentalism here. But it can be described briefly as a position that claims that the Bible is the literal word of God, virtually dictated by God to the sacred authors and therefore to be taken literally as completely free of error of any kind (historical, scientific, theological, moral, social, etc.) and absolutely authoritative for the reader. Such fundamentalism has never been the approach of the Catholic Church.

As a matter of fact, the 1993 Pontifical Biblical Commission's statement entitled *The Interpretation of the Bible in the Church* is quite clear about the inadequacy of fundamentalism. The document states:

> *Fundamentalism thus misrepresents the call voiced by the Gospel itself. The fundamentalist approach is dangerous for it is attractive to people who look to the Bible for ready answers to the problems of life. It can deceive these people, offering them interpretations that are pious but illusory, instead of telling them that the Bible does not necessarily contain an immediate answer to each and every problem. Without saying as much, . . . fundamentalism actually invites people to a kind of intellectual suicide. It injects*

into life false certitude, for it unwittingly confuses the divine substance of the biblical message with what are in fact its human limitations.

This is a powerful and sober statement to all Catholics.

Here are some of the myriad of problems with a fundamentalist interpretation of the Bible.

Fundamentalism refuses to accept the historical character of biblical revelation. It does not admit that the inspired word of God has been expressed in human language by human authors who had limited capacities, resources, and knowledge. Thus the fundamentalist reader:

- treats the biblical text as if it had been dictated word-for-word by God, and
- fails to recognize that the Bible was formulated in language conditioned by various times.

Fundamentalism pays no attention to the literary norms and human ways of thinking found in the biblical text. Further, it unduly stresses the inerrancy of certain details in the biblical texts, most especially in what concerns historical events or scientific truth. Thus the fundamentalist reader:

- often historicizes material that, from the start, never claimed to be historical; and
- considers historical everything reported or recounted with verbs in the past tense, failing to take account of the possibility of symbolic or figurative meaning.

In addition, biblical fundamentalism does not consider the development of the gospel tradition. Fundamentalist interpretation naively confuses the final stage of gospel development (what the evangelists wrote) with the initial stage (the words and deeds of Jesus).

Biblical fundamentalism tends to adopt extremely narrow points of view. Thus the fundamentalist reader:

- accepts the literal reality of an ancient, out-of-date cosmology, simply because it is found in the Bible; and
- relies on a nonreflective, noncritical reading of certain texts of the Bible to reinforce political ideas and social attitudes marked by a variety of prejudices (such as racism) contrary to the teachings of the Gospel.

Biblical fundamentalists' attachment to the principle of "Scripture alone" produces an antichurch attitude. Thus the fundamentalist reader:

- separates the interpretation of the Bible from tradition;
- fails to realize that the New Testament took form within the Christian church, whose existence preceded the composition of the texts;
- gives little if any importance to the creeds, doctrines, and liturgical practices of church tradition, as well as the church's teaching function; and
- does not acknowledge that the church is founded on the Bible and draws its life and inspiration from Scripture.

In effect, fundamentalism so overemphasizes the divinity of the biblical text that it denies the text's real human character. By contrast, the theological position of the Catholic Church on the character of the Bible parallels its position on the identity of Jesus Christ, the Word of God incarnate. Just as Catholics believe that Jesus is fully human and fully divine, so Catholics believe the Bible is fully human and fully divine. It is the Word of God purveyed through the words of humans. As such it has both God and humans as its authors. The bishops of Vatican II put this quite well when they state: "To compose the sacred books, God chose certain men who, all the while [God] employed them in this task, made full use of their powers and faculties so that, though he acted in them and by them, it was as true authors that they consigned to writing whatever God wanted written, and no more" (*Dogmatic Constitution on Divine Revelation,* 11).

The Bible, although a witness to divine revelation, is a human text, not an oracle. God did *not* literally dictate the Bible any more than God literally created the universe in seven calendar days. As a book, the biblical revelation must be read and interpreted through our human efforts.

Biblical texts, then, bear all the marks of human composition: historical conditioning, prejudice, factual error and moral limitation, as well as deep theological and religious insight into the mystery of God's relationship with humanity. It is this twofold character of the biblical text, its mysterious divine depths expressed in humanly fallible language, which makes interpretation necessary.

As we all know, all meaningful human expression must be interpreted to be understood. This is true of a film, a novel, a cartoon, a letter from a friend, and even the Bible. The church has given us some guidelines and procedures for interpreting biblical texts.

The way Catholic biblical scholars and, by extension, all Catholics read biblical texts is stated concisely in paragraph 12 of the *Dogmatic Constitution on Divine Revelation (Dei Verbum):* "The exegete [biblical scholar] must look for that meaning which the sacred writer, in a determined situation and given the circumstances of his time and culture, intended to express and did in fact express, through the medium of a contemporary literary form." This sentence is very dense. Put in simpler terms, it means that Catholic biblical study has three aspects: theological, historical, and literary. This means that every time we look at a biblical text we need to consider its literary form, its historical context, and its theological or religious meaning. We will attempt to follow this guideline throughout this book.

A similar teaching is found in the *Catechism of the Catholic Church:* "In order to discover *the sacred authors' intention,* the reader must take into account the conditions of their time and culture, the literary genres in use at the time, and the modes of feeling, speaking, and narrating then current" (110).

The *Catechism* goes on to summarize succinctly how one is to approach a biblical text.

- *Be especially attentive "to the content and unity of the whole Scripture."*
- *Read the Scripture within "the living Tradition of the whole Church."*
- *Be attentive to the analogy of faith . . . ([i.e.,] the coherence of the truths of faith among themselves and within the plan of Revelation) (112–14).*

The effect of these principles is to broaden the context of interpretation. It includes the context of interpretation. It includes the contexts of the canon as a whole, and the church's teachings through the ages. Context is vitally important. From the Catholic perspective, the Scriptures should not be read outside the larger context of the church's tradition and the entire biblical canon itself. The late eminent and premier American Catholic biblical scholar Sulpician Father Raymond E. Brown was fond of telling his students and audiences, "A passage is biblical only when it is *in the Bible.*" In other words, interpreting passages by considering them individually and removing them from their context within the Bible can lead to misinterpretation.

How to Handle a Biblical Text

When encountering a biblical text, here are some hands-on suggestions:

- Pray to the Holy Spirit for guidance and the gift of discernment.
- Read, preferably aloud and at least three times, the text (chapter and verses) that you are studying.
- If possible, read more than one modern English translation of the Bible. Check for variations. Ask if the variations help or hinder your understanding and interpretation of the text.
- Read all cross-references in the Bible that relate to the text you are reading.

- Read all notes (usually found at the bottom of the page) that your translation of the Bible provides on the text you are studying.
- Ask the following questions of the text:
  —What is the historical context?
  —What is the literary form of this text?
  —What is the context or setting of the text?
  —How do the responses to these questions help you to better understand the biblical text?
- Ask the theological/spiritual question of the text, namely, what is God revealing to you and to his people through this text?
- Every biblical text exists in three distinct worlds of meaning: the world of the author behind the text, the world within the text itself, and the world of the reader who is encountering the text.

THE THREE WORLDS OF THE BIBLICAL TEXT

1. **The world behind the text.** This is the world of the author and the original audience. This is the historical and cultural situation in which the author(s) composed the text as a response to some particular problem or need of the audience.

2. **The world within the text.** This is the world described and portrayed within the text itself. This world can be self-contained, but normally readers connect this world with their own world in order to apply its meaning to their own situation.

3. **The world encountering the text.** This is the present circumstances and situation of the person who is reading the text. Since a text endures through time, once it is written down, this world changes with each historical situation of later readers.

The World Behind the Text

This is the historical and cultural world in which the author and the original readers lived and in which the text originated. Exploring this world helps readers understand the situation of both the author and the original readers, in particular the specific problems and issues that motivated the author to write the text. Every biblical text is some kind of response or answer in a particular situation.

We explore this world using historical methods to answer questions about what was going on at the time of the writing—for example, the identity of the author and audience, the date and location of composition, the historical situation, the reasons for the text's composition, etc. Since answers to these questions depend upon the methods and procedures of historical scholarship, they are always open to further revision whenever the results of scholarship are updated or the methods of inquiry improved.

For the Old Testament, the world behind the text is the ancient Near Eastern world and the Hebrew people during the twelve hundred years before Christ. Such a long period of history reveals many different social, political, and religious situations in which the various biblical books were written. Knowing the general framework of this historical development is profoundly helpful for situating the various books in their proper historical contexts.

For the New Testament, the world behind the text is the first-century Mediterranean world. The gospels and epistles describe various situations in the Hellenistic Roman world, especially in the areas of Palestine, Syria, Asia Minor (modern-day Turkey), Greece, and Rome. Some New Testament authors give important clues about their location and their audience, as does Paul in his letters and the author of the Book of Revelation. For others, scholars must sift through their texts to tease out clues about their original historical situations.

The World Within the Text

Texts create worlds of meaning. When we read them they invite us to enter into these worlds. Biblical texts also create worlds of meaning, and when we step inside we are confronted by people, settings, and theological claims that are often strange and always challenging. Readers discover the textual worlds by a careful and analytical reading of the text itself. We are all familiar with textual worlds by reading novels or science fiction in which the story world describes a situation that is different from ours or the author's.

The textual world of the Old Testament Book of Exodus, for example, is set in Egypt, most likely in the thirteenth century before Christ. The story describes the conflict between God's agent, Moses, and Pharaoh, which leads to the liberation of the oppressed Hebrews from their bondage. Although the story as we have it in our Bible was written down long after the events, the story world retains its integrity because everything in it fits together.

The textual world of the gospels is that of Jesus' lifetime during the first third of the first century. The story takes place almost entirely in the Jewish homeland in Galilee and its surrounding areas in Judea and Jerusalem around the years 27–30 C.E. This world is not the same as that of the gospel authors, who wrote forty to sixty years later in greatly different circumstances. Yet the world of Jesus is consistent and coherent for any reader approaching the text.

THE COMMON ERA AND BEFORE THE COMMON ERA

Most people are accustomed to dating ancient events as either A.D. (which does *not* stand for "after death," but for *anno Domini,* Latin for "year of our Lord") or B.C. ("before Christ"). This terminology may make sense for Christians, for whom A.D. 2002 is indeed "the year of our Lord 2002." It makes less sense, though, for Jews, Muslims, Buddhists, and others for whom Jesus is not "Lord" or the "Christ." Scholars have, therefore, begun to use a different set of abbreviations as more inclusive of others outside the Christian tradition. Throughout this book, we will follow the alternative designations of C.E. ("common era," meaning common to people of all faiths who utilize the traditional Western calendar) and B.C.E. ("before the common era"). In terms of the older abbreviations, C.E. corresponds to A.D. and B.C.E. to B.C.

Scrutinizing the world within the text utilizes all our familiar reading skills. Although literary scholars have developed very sophisticated techniques for appreciating the intricacies of textual communication, a simple method for exploring a text is to ask some basic questions:

- Who (the author) addresses whom (the audience) in what circumstances (the situation) in what way (literary form) with what message (content) for what reason (function)?
- What kind of writing is this?
- How does the writing fit together (structure)?
- Who is doing what, where, when, and why (story)?

These questions lead to an initial appreciation of the message (content) that the text communicates, and the context in which it was formulated.

The World Encountering the Text

This is the world of the reader or audience. Because a text becomes permanent through writing, it is available to other audiences besides the immediate community for whom it was composed. The world of the reader shifts constantly as the text is read in many different historical times and social circumstances.

When we read the Bible now, two thousand years after its last books were written, like the original audience, we are reading for clues about who God is and for cues about how to respond to our own experience of God's transforming presence. But the world encountering the text is now our own everyday reality, along with the various modern presuppositions and expectations we bring to our reading.

Reading for meaning connects the three worlds of the author, the audience, and the text. A healthy interpretation of any biblical text demands some attention to each of these three worlds or our understanding will be incomplete.

EXAMPLES OF BIBLICAL TEXTS AND THEIR THREE WORLDS

Text	World Within Text	World Behind Text	World Encountering Text
Mark's gospel	Galilee, circa 30 C.E.	Rome, 70 C.E.	Original audience and all subsequent audiences
Paul's letters to the Corinthians	Corinth, 50s C.E.	Corinth, 50 C.E.	Same
Book of Revelation	Asia Minor, circa 95 C.E.	Patmos and Ephesus (Roman Province of Asia), 95 C.E.	Same

Lectio Divina

In addition to studying Sacred Scripture within its historical context, there is a method for prayerful reading of the Bible. The early monks of the church living in monasteries developed this method. It is known as *Lectio Divina.*

Lectio Divina (Latin for "divine reading") is a term used to describe a meditative reading of Sacred Scripture leading to prayer. Such reading enjoyed an important place in Christian and monastic practice until the Middle Ages. It is still valid today for those who want to use Scripture in prayer. There are four steps in *Lectio Divina:*

- The first step is *reading.* The goal is to be clear about what the text says. The central question is: What does the text say? This step is facilitated by a slow, thoughtful, and reverent reading of the text itself—at first silently and then out loud.
- The second step is *meditation,* in which we consider what the text says to me (or us) and to the people of God today. The central question is: What is God saying to me or to the community through this text?

- The third step is *prayer.* What do I want to say to God on the basis of this text? I might want to thank God for all God's gifts to me or for healing or for faith. I might want to praise and glorify God. I might ask God for greater trust or for compassion toward those who suffer chronic diseases or who are "outsiders."

- The final step is *action.* What difference can this text make in how I act? In how I live? What possibilities does it open up? What challenges does it pose? Does the text move me to change? Does it make me reflect on my own relationship to God and how I might become more thankful to God, more confident in God's mercy, and more compassionate toward the sick and toward the "outsiders"?

Lectio Divina is not a method for serious interpretation and understanding of Sacred Scripture so as to better understand its meaning within the historical, cultural, theological, and literary context. Rather, its purpose is spiritual formation of the reader(s) from the biblical text and as a starter for prayer with and from the text.

Both *Lectio Divina* and the historical-critical method are upheld by the church for our use. These two methods are not at war with one another but they have different outcomes. The historical-critical method leads to better understanding of the biblical text whereas *Lectio Divina* leads to a viable way of living one's faith from the text and praying with the text.

For Discussion

1. How does the church function as a guide in your life, in your practice of faith, and in your reading of the Bible?

2. What in your view is the difference between a fundamentalist approach and a Catholic approach to the Bible?

3. Why is context so important for the interpretation of a biblical text?

4. How do the three worlds of a biblical text help you better understand it? Explain.

5. How do you react to the method of Bible reading known as *Lectio Divina?* Do you think it could help you in your reading and interpretation of the Bible?

For Further Reading

Brown, Raymond E. *Reading the Gospels with the Church.* Cincinnati, Ohio: St. Anthony Messenger Press, 1996.

Kodell, Jerome. *The Catholic Bible Study Handbook* (Second Revised Edition). Ann Arbor, Mich.: Servant Publications, 2001.

LaVerdiere, Eugene. *Fundamentalism: A Pastoral Concern.* Collegeville, Minn.: Liturgical Press, 2000.

Lysik, David A. *The Bible Documents.* Chicago: Liturgy Training Publications, 2001.

Mueller, Steve. *The Seeker's Guide to Reading the Bible: A Catholic View.* Chicago: Loyola Press, 1999.

Pontifical Biblical Commission, *The Interpretation of the Bible in the Church.* Washington, D.C.: U.S. Catholic Conference, 1994.

Witherup, Ronald D. *Biblical Fundamentalism: What Every Catholic Should Know.* Collegeville, Minn.: Liturgical Press, 2001.

2

"WRITTEN SO THAT YOU MAY COME TO BELIEVE"

(JOHN 20:31)

Whenever WE PURCHASE A NEW BOOK, WE look at the table of contents. In the case of the New Testament, the table of contents consists of twenty-seven books, written by different authors at different times, and addressed to different audiences. These books were written in *koine* Greek, the vernacular Greek of the first century of the common era. They constitute the canon of the New Testament (see the diagram below), that is, they are seen as authoritative by Christians for religious belief.

THE CANON OF SACRED SCRIPTURE

The English term *canon* comes from a Greek word that originally meant "ruler" or "measuring rod." A canon was used to make straight lines or to measure distances. When applied to a group of books, it refers to a recognized list (body) of literature. Thus, for example, the canon of Shakespeare refers to all of Shakespeare's authentic writings.

With reference to the Bible, the term *canon* denotes the collection of books that are accepted as authoritative by a religious body. Thus, for example, we can speak of the canon of the Jewish Scripture or the canon of the New Testament.

THE LAYOUT OF THE NEW TESTAMENT

Gospels: The Beginning of Christianity

Matthew	Luke
Mark	John

Acts: The Spread of Christianity

Acts of the Apostles

Epistles:
Letters Addressed to Early Christian Communities

Pauline Epistles	General Epistles
1 and 2 Corinthians	James
Galatians	1 and 2 Peter
Ephesians	1, 2, and 3 John
Philippians	Jude
Colossians	
1 and 2 Thessalonians	
1 and 2 Timothy	
Titus	
Philemon	
Hebrews	

Apocalypse: Literature to Inspire Hope to Christians During Times of Persecution

Revelation

The gospels have as their purpose to evoke faith (see John 20:31). They do not provide detailed and accurate information but, rather, present revelations about Jesus and his followers that are directed at inspiring readers to appropriate such a lifestyle.

The gospels are faith literature, written by people of faith to inspire faith. They are not video camera recordings of events. Rather, they are proclamations of belief.

The gospels went through three stages of development, as outlined by the Roman Pontifical Biblical Commission in its instruction *On the Historical Truth of the Gospels.* In this document, biblical scholars of the Catholic Church present the first stage of gospel development as "Public Ministry or Activity of Jesus of Nazareth" (the first third of the first century of the common era). He did things of note, orally proclaimed his message, and interacted with others, namely John the Baptist, Jewish religious figures, and his disciples. Their memories of his words and deeds are what the gospels record. These memories were selective and do not include such trivia as Jesus' weight and height or the color of his eyes and hair.

The second stage of gospel development is "(Apostolic) Preaching About Jesus" (the second third of the first century of the common era). Those who had seen and heard Jesus had their following of him confirmed through postresurrection appearances. And they came to full faith in the risen Jesus as the one through whom God was manifested. This postresurrection faith illumined the memories of what they had seen and heard during the preresurrection period, and so they proclaimed his words and deeds with enriched significance. These preachers are referred to as apostolic because they understood themselves as being sent forth *(apostallein)* by the risen Jesus, and their preaching is often described as *kerygmatic* proclamation intended to bring others to faith.

Another factor operative in this stage of gospel development was the necessary adaptation of the preaching to a new audience. Jesus was a Galilean Jew of the first third of the first century of the common era who spoke Aramaic. By midcentury his gospel was being preached in the *Diaspora* (Jews living outside of Palestine) to urban Jews and Gentiles in Greek, a language that Jesus did not normally speak. This change of language involved translation in the broadest sense of that term, i.e., a rephrasing in vocabulary and patterns that would make the message intelligible and alive for new audiences.

The final stage of gospel development is "The Written Gospels" (the last third of the first century of the common era). During this stage, oral traditions and preachings were collated together into a written form. The era from 65 to 100 C.E. is when all four canonical gospels were written. It was the stage of articulation. As for the evangelists or gospel writers/authors, according to traditions stemming from the second century and reflected in titles prefaced to the manuscripts of gospels circa 200 C.E. (or even earlier), gospels were attributed to apostles. Yet most modern biblical scholars do not think that the evangelists—understood as those who wrote the gospels down—were eyewitnesses to the ministry of Jesus.

This recognition—that the evangelists were not eyewitnesses of Jesus' ministry—is important for understanding the differences among the gospels. In the older approach, wherein the evangelists themselves were thought to have seen what they reported, it was very difficult to explain differences among their gospels. How could "eyewitness" John (chapter 2) report the cleansing of the Temple at the beginning of Jesus' ministry and "eyewitness" Matthew (chapter 21) report the cleansing of the Temple at the end of the ministry? This is no longer a problem if neither evangelist was an eyewitness and each had received an account from the oral tradition and preaching of the Temple cleansing from an intermediate source—neither one (or only one) may have known when it occurred during the public ministry. Rather than depending on a personal memory of events, each evangelist arranged the material he received in order to portray Jesus in a way that would meet the spiritual needs of the faith community to which he was addressing the Gospel.

In sum, the gospels are not literal records of the ministry of Jesus. Decades of developing and adapting the Jesus tradition had intervened.

For some, this calls the truth of the gospels into question. Truth, however, must be evaluated in terms of the intended purpose. The gospels might be judged untrue if their goal was strict reporting or exact biography; but if the goal was to bring readers/hearers to a faith in Jesus that opens them to God's activity, then adaptations that make the gospels less than literal—adding dimensions of faith, adjusting to new audiences—were made precisely to facilitate this goal and thus to make the gospels true. Further, by our belief in inspiration we maintain that the Holy Spirit guided the process, guaranteeing that the end product known as the gospels reflect the truth that God sent Jesus to proclaim.

The Synoptic Problem

Matthew, Mark, and Luke are often called the "synoptic gospels." This is because they have so many stories in common that they can be placed side by side in columns and "seen together" (the literal meaning of the word *synoptic*). Indeed, not only do these gospels tell many of the same stories, they often do so using the very same words. This phenomenon is virtually inexplicable, unless the stories are derived from a common literary source. Consider a modern-day parallel. You may have noticed that when newspapers, magazines, and books all describe the same event, they do so differently. Take any three of today's newspapers and compare their treatment of the same news item. At no point will they contain entire paragraphs that are word for word the same, unless they happen to be quoting from the same source, for example, an interview or a speech. These differences occur because every journalist wants to emphasize certain things and has his or her own way of writing. When you find that two newspapers have exactly the same account, you know that they have simply reproduced a feature from somewhere else. This happens, for example, when two newspapers pick up the same news story from the Associated Press.

We have a similar situation with the gospels. There are passages shared by Matthew, Mark, and Luke that are verbatim (see Matthew

13:1–9, Mark 4:1–9, Luke 8:4–8). This can be scarcely explained unless all three of them drew these accounts from a common source. But what was it? The question is complicated by the fact that the synoptics not only agree extensively with one another, they also disagree. There are some stories found in all three gospels, others found in only two of the three (see Matthew 3:7–10, Luke 3:7–9), and yet others found only in one (see Luke 3:10–14). Moreover, when all three gospels share the same story, they sometimes give it in precisely the same wording and sometimes word it differently. Or sometimes two of them will word it the same way and the third will word it differently. The problem of how to explain the wide-ranging agreements and disagreements among these three gospels is called the "synoptic problem."

Biblical scholars have offered a number of theories over the years to solve the synoptic problem. Many of these theories are extraordinarily complex. We do not need to concern ourselves with all of these solutions. We will instead focus on the one that most scholars have come to accept as the least problematic.

This explanation is sometimes referred to as the "four-source hypothesis." According to this hypothesis, Mark was the first gospel to be written. It was used by both Matthew and Luke. In addition, both Matthew and Luke had access to another source called "Q" (from the German word for "source," *quelle*). Q provided Matthew and Luke with the stories that they have in common that are not, however, found in Mark. Moreover, Matthew had a source (or group of sources) of his own, from which he drew stories found in neither of the other gospels. Scholars have simply labeled this source "M" (for Matthew's special source). Likewise, Luke had a source (or sources) for stories that he alone tells; this is called "L" (for Luke's special source). Hence, according to this hypothesis, four sources lie behind our three synoptic gospels: Mark, Q, M, and L (see the following illustration).

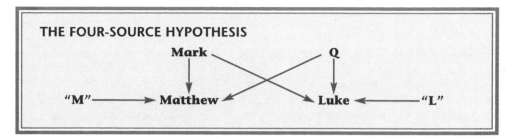

THE FOUR-SOURCE HYPOTHESIS

Mark   Q

"M" ——→ Matthew   Luke ←—— "L"

The Gospels of the New Testament

We will now turn to the four gospels and succinctly present their content. To help prepare for our study, please refer to the following timeline:

30–100 C.E. ORAL TRADITION ABOUT JESUS

4 B.C.E.——30 C.E.		50–60	65–70	80–85	95–100
Life of Jesus		Letters of Paul	Mark	Luke, Matthew	John

The Gospel of Mark

The gospel of Mark is the earliest written gospel. It is a testimony of faith. Mark was a common name at the time of Jesus; the Mark credited with writing the first gospel could have been just about anyone. None of the gospels names its author directly. All gospel authors are anonymous. The names of the authors attached to the gospels represent the opinion of the early church. The author of Mark is, at times, associated with a certain John Mark mentioned in Acts 12:12. Some believe this John Mark to be the author of the gospel. This supposition, however, would be impossible to prove.

For whom was the gospel written? Scholars traditionally accept that Mark wrote his gospel in Rome for the church there, and that it was intended for non-Jewish readers—Gentiles. Customs that Jews would have readily understood, for instance, are explained in Mark's gospel in a way that suggests the audience is not familiar with them (see Mark 3:17; 5:41; 7:3–4, 11, 34; 15:22, 34).

PAGAN AND GENTILE

Throughout this book, the terms *pagan* and *Gentile* will be used. When historians use the term *pagan,* they do not assign negative connotations to it. When used of the Greco-Roman world—the world in which the New Testament was composed—the term simply designates a person who subscribed to any of the polytheistic religions, that is anyone who was neither a Jew nor a Christian. The term *paganism,* then, refers to the wide range of ancient polytheistic religions outside of Judaism and Christianity. The term *Gentile* designates someone who is not a Jew, whether the person is pagan or Christian. It, too, carries no negative connotations.

Mark wrote his gospel sometime between 65 and 70 C.E., that is, thirty-five to forty years after the death of the historical Jesus. There is a heavy sense of suffering in Mark, with many references to trials and persecutions. This reflects the persecution of the Christians by the Roman emperor Nero, who blamed the Christians for the burning of Rome in the year 64 C.E.. For our purposes, we will settle on the years 65 to 70 as roughly the dates of the writing of the Gospel of Mark.

Why was the gospel written? Mark's gospel stresses the human suffering of Jesus and his passion and death as a way to relate to the Christians who were suffering terrible persecution under Nero at the time. The central point of Mark's gospel is to describe the suffering and death of Jesus, and everything else is by way of introduction. Mark's intention was to explain to the members of the early church that suffering is an essential part of Christian life and to give them the courage to endure it as Jesus did. Taken literally, following Jesus is the path of martyrdom.

There is also stress on Jesus' humanity in Mark's gospel. We see Jesus expressing strong emotions. Mark was trying to counter the claim some made during his day that Jesus was not truly human, but a divine being who simply pretended to be a man. Mark's account makes it clear that Jesus was truly human—one who embraced human suffering.

Before leaving the gospel of Mark it is important to realize that names for a number of groups of religious authorities among the Jews (see Mark, chapter 12) are mentioned throughout his gospel and the other three. Since the reader may not be familiar with these groups, here is a brief sketch of what each of these groups represented:

JEWISH GROUPS AND THE GOSPELS

Jewish scribes in the first century represented the literate elite, those who could read, write, and study the sacred traditions of Israel and, presumably, teach them to others. Recall that most Jews, as well as most other people in the ancient world, were not highly educated by our standards; those who were educated enjoyed a special place of prominence.

Pharisees were Jews who were reformers strongly committed to maintaining the purity laws set forth in the Torah and who developed their own set of more carefully nuanced laws to help them do so. They appear as the chief culprits in the Jewish opposition to Jesus during much of his ministry in Mark's gospel, as well as the other gospels.

Herodians were a group of Jews whom Mark mentions but does not identify (3:6, 12:13; see also Matthew 22:16). They are described in no other ancient source. Mark may understand them to be collaborationists, that is, supporters of the Herods, the rulers intermittently appointed over Jews in Palestine by the Romans.

Sadducees were Jews of the upper classes who were closely connected with and strong advocates of the Temple cult in Jerusalem. They were largely in charge of the Jewish Sanhedrin, the council of Jews that advised the high priest concerning policy and served as a kind of liaison with the Roman authorities.

Zealots were a group of Jews characterized by their insistence on violent opposition to the Roman domination of the Promised Land. A group that had been centered in Galilee fled to Jerusalem during the uprising against Rome in 66–70 C.E., they overthrew the reigning aristocracy in the city and urged violent resistance to the bitter end.

Essenes were a group of Jews whose name may come from an Aramaic word meaning "pious." They withdrew from Jerusalem and active participation in the Jerusalem Temple. They settled in the Judean wilderness in isolated monastic communities where they studied the Scriptures and developed their rule of life. Essenes were known for their piety, such as daily prayer, prayer before and after meals, strict observance of the Sabbath, daily ritual bathing, emphasis on chastity and celibacy, wearing white robes as a symbol of purity, communal meals, and sharing all property in common.

Chief priests were the upper classes of the Jewish priesthood who operated the Temple and oversaw its sacrifices. They would have been closely connected with the Sadducees and would have been the real power players in Jesus' day, the ones with the ear of the Roman governor in Jerusalem and the ones responsible for regulating the lives of the Jewish people in Judea. Their leader, the high priest, was the ultimate authority over civil and religious affairs when there was no king in Judea.

This basic information about Jewish groups should make us curious about certain aspects of Mark's gospel and the gospels in general. We know from other sources that the Pharisees were not numerous in the days of Jesus; there certainly were not enough to stand at every wheat field to spy out itinerant preachers on the Sabbath. Nor evidently were they influential in the politics of Palestine at the time, or even concerned that everyone else (i.e., non-Pharisaic Jews) conform to their own rules and regulations for purity. And yet they appear as Jesus' chief adversaries in Mark's narrative as well as the other gospels, constantly hounding Jesus and attacking him for failing to conform to their views. Can this be historically accurate?

Scholars have long known that some decades after Jesus' death, nearer the end of the first century, the Pharisees did become more important in Jewish life. After the destruction of Jerusalem in 70 C.E., they were given authority by the Romans to run the civil affairs of Palestinian Jews. Moreover, the Pharisees interacted frequently with Christian churches after the death of Jesus. Indeed, the one Jewish persecutor of the church about whom we are best informed was Paul, a self-proclaimed Pharisee.

Is it possible that the opposition leveled against the church by Pharisees after Jesus' death affected the ways that Christians told stories about his life? That is to say, because of their own clashes with the Pharisees, could Christians have narrated stories in which Jesus himself disputed with them (usually putting them to shame), even though such disputes would have happened only rarely during his lifetime? The scholarly consensus is that this was the case.

The Gospel of Matthew

The gospel of Matthew is the second written gospel. It was composed by a Christian community in Antioch of Syria around the mid-80s of the first century of the common era, and attributed to Matthew. The language of the gospel is Greek, but it reflects a knowledge of Hebrew and Aramaic as well.

The core of Matthew's gospel is derived from a collection of Jesus' sayings. According to ancient tradition, this collection of sayings was ascribed to the apostle Matthew. It is possible that it could have been written in Aramaic and is commonly referred to as the "M" source.

The gospels of Matthew and Luke have a source common to both of them, but not found in Mark or John. This source is referred to as "Q" from the German word for "source," *quelle*. An unknown Greek-speaking Christian scribe in Antioch took the material from "M" and "Q" as well as another source, the gospel of Mark, and composed the gospel of Matthew from it. Modern biblical scholars follow the ancient custom in referring to this final author as Matthew.

The gospel was not written all at once. The scribe who composed it was perhaps a catechist who may have prepared certain texts for special occasions. He may have composed the sermon on the mount, for instance, to give a comprehensive view of Jesus' new moral principles (Matthew 5–7). Further, he gathered seven parables to express Jesus' view of the kingdom of heaven (Matthew 13). In addition, a string of ten miracles proved Jesus' role as the messianic healer (Matthew 8–10).

Such texts were presented to the community, reflected on, discussed, and improved upon. Then Christian scribes well versed in the Old Testament refined the scriptural references. Gentile Christians sharpened the universal implications. Only at the end did the final compiler, technically known as a redactor, sit down and construct the whole gospel, putting various sections into their present places, linking them, integrating, weaving them into a tapestry of rich material.

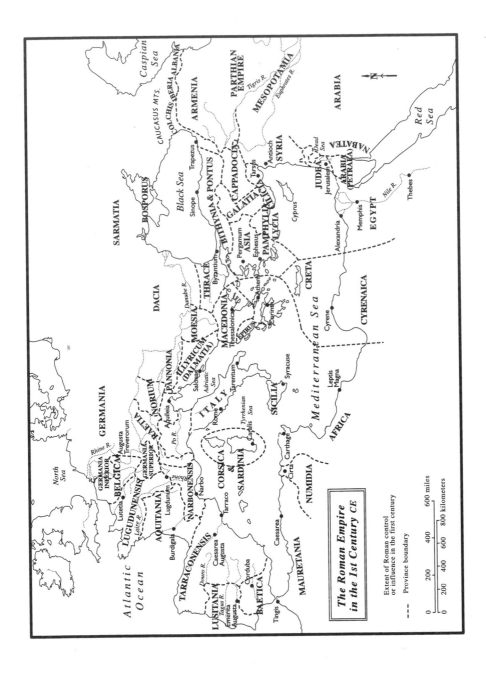

The Roman Empire
in the 1st Century CE

Extent of Roman control
or influence in the first century

--- Province boundary

The gospel's place of composition, Antioch, ranked as the third largest city in the Greco-Roman empire. Antioch also contained large Jewish populations surpassed in size only by those in Jerusalem and Alexandria. Life for these Jews revolved around the Torah, the word of God as contained in the five books of Moses (Genesis through Deuteronomy), also called the Pentateuch. All sects within Judaism accepted the Pentateuch. These five books were God's Law, revealed by God and conveyed to the people through Moses. They determined worship, ritual practice, and everyday morality. Those who listened to a reading from any of these five sacred scrolls knew they were listening to God.

Accordingly, the gospel of Matthew was constructed around five collections of sayings, sometimes referred to as discourses, of Jesus: the Sermon on the Mount (Matthew 5–7), the sermon to the apostles (Matthew 10), the sermon on the kingdom (Matthew 13), the sermon on leadership (Matthew 18), the sermon on the last things (Matthew 22–23).

This construction is not a coincidence. In Matthew's plan for his gospel, Jesus' five sermons replaced the five scrolls of the Pentateuch. By his presentation of Jesus' teaching in five books, the author presents Jesus as the new Moses or, even more, as the new Law (Torah), the revelation of God.

The Sermon on the Mount

The most famous of the discourses is the Sermon on the Mount (chapters 5–7). The sermon is a collection of the teachings and sayings of Jesus brought together by Matthew. It ranks among the most famous and universally revered pieces of religious literature in the world. In it, Jesus is compared to Moses. Just as Moses went up the mountain to bring down the law, so now Jesus climbs the mountain to fulfill the law.

One of the great insights of the sermon is on the importance of interior conversion in the heart, reaching beyond the minimal demands of the law. Jesus seems to belong to a liberal tradition within

43

Judaism that believed not only in the written Law but in the oral interpretation of the law (a position consistent with the Pharisees). Throughout chapter 5, Matthew contrasts the written law with Jesus' interpretation. For example, "You have heard that it was said to those of ancient times, 'You shall not murder'; and 'whoever murders shall be liable to judgment.' But I say to you that if you are angry with a brother or sister, you will be liable to judgment" (Matthew 5:21–22). Or again, "You have heard that it was said, 'You shall not commit adultery.' But I say to you that everyone who looks at a woman with lust has already committed adultery with her in his heart" (Matthew 5:27–28). Jesus does not say that the law (the Torah) is unimportant or wrong. But his interpretation of the Torah demands more than simple outward conformity. It demands that the law be written in one's heart as love.

THE GOLDEN RULE

The most familiar form of the golden rule is "[D]o to others as you would have them do to you" (Matthew 7:12). Many people think that Jesus was the first to propose this ethical principle; but, in fact, it was given in a variety of forms by moral philosophers of the ancient world.

The rule was found, for example, among the Greeks many centuries before Jesus. One of the characters described by the Greek historian Herodotus (fifth century B.C.E.) said, "I will not myself do that which I consider to be blameworthy in my neighbor," and the Greek orator Isocrates (fourth century B.C.E.) said, "You should be such in your dealings with others as you expect me to be in my dealings with you." The saying was present in Oriental cultures as well, even on the lips of Confucius (sixth century B.C.E.): "Do not do to others what you would not want others to do to you."

Closer to Jesus' time, the golden rule is found in various forms in a number of Jewish writings. In the book of Tobit, we read, "And what you hate, do not do to anyone," and in rabbinic interpretation of the book of Leviticus, we find, "Don't do to him [your neighbor] what you yourself hate."

Possibly the best expression of the rule in Jewish circles comes from the revered rabbi of Jesus' day, Rabbi Hillel. A pagan approached the rabbi and promised him that he would convert to Judaism if Hillel could recite the entire Torah to him while standing on one leg. Hillel's reply sounds remarkably like the statement of Jesus in Matthew 7:12: "What is hateful to you do not do to your neighbor; that is the whole Torah, while the rest is commentary. Go and learn it."

In short, Jesus was not the only teacher of his day who taught the golden rule, or who thought the essence of the Law of Moses could be summed up in the commandment to love.

The Mission of the Church

The second discourse, chapter 10, clearly reflects Matthew's understanding of the church. In it, Jesus gives his apostles instructions for their mission, yet much of it mirrors the situation of the first-century church: ". . . they will hand you over to councils and flog you in their synagogues ["their" synagogues reflects the fact that Christians were expelled from them]. You will be dragged before governors and kings because of me, as a testimony to them and the Gentiles" (Matthew 10:17–18). This passage reflects what did, in fact, happen in the early church, although Matthew makes it appear that the words are addressed by Jesus to the apostles to help them in their mission while Jesus was still alive. The apostles are the legitimate witnesses of faith in the early church: "Whoever welcomes you welcomes me" (10:40) but the leaders of the church are to expect conflict. When Matthew writes, "Do not think that I have come to bring peace to the earth; I have not come to bring peace but a sword" (10:34), he is aware of the great conflicts that have taken place in order to give birth to the church—namely, Jew versus Jewish-Christian and Jewish-Christian versus Gentile Christian, to name only two.

Parables of the Kingdom

The third discourse (chapter 13) is made up of seven parables of the kingdom. Each of the parables is adaptable to the situation of Matthew's readers. The parable of the seed when originally told by Jesus probably was meant to emphasize the overbounding generosity of the Father who sent his grace everywhere. In Matthew's interpretation (13:18–23), however, it is turned into an allegory concerning the different trials of the life of faith. This interpretation is Matthew's creative adaptation of the story to the needs of his community.

Advice to the Community

The fourth discourse (chapter 18) is Matthew's advice column. The section is addressed to a community (church) struggling with divisions and questions of authority and lifestyle. Matthew gives five pieces of advice:

1. Power and authority in the church is not to be modeled on the notion of power and authority in the world. Rather, "Whoever becomes humble like this child is the greatest in the kingdom of heaven" (18:4).
2. Scandalous behavior by members of the church is even worse than such behavior by the pagans, because it can lead others astray. Church members are to live holy lives.
3. The Christian community is to be one of reconciling love: "Then Peter came and said to him, 'Lord, if another member of the church sins against me, how often should I forgive? As many as seven times?' Jesus said to him, 'Not seven times, but I tell you, seventy-seven times' [a metaphor for infinity]" (Matthew 18:21–22).
4. Christians are not to take each other to court over their problems but should be able to solve them among them-selves in the spirit of charity (Matthew 18:15–17).
5. The Christian community must be guided by a life of prayer: "For where two or three are gathered in my name, I am there among them" (Matthew 18:20).

The End Time

The fifth and final discourse (chapters 24 and 25) have to do with the end time and the judgment of God. The early church believed that the end time was near. After the death and resurrection of Jesus, it was commonly believed that he would return to establish the kingdom in its fullness. By the time Matthew was written, this belief had become a problem. The church had to reinterpret the meaning of the end time and the coming of the kingdom. Matthew uses imagery and language from the Book of Daniel to talk about the impending judgment (Matthew 25:31–40). He uses the image of the "Son of Man" which is found in Daniel, chapter 7, to refer to the Messiah as he ushers in the final kingdom. Yet Matthew remains extremely humble about when the end will occur. According to him, only the Father knows this, not even the Son (24:36). In the meantime, Christians are to lead lives of vigilance, always attentive to the possible coming of the Lord. Ultimately, however, judgment will depend on how we have treated our brothers and sisters (parable of the judgment of the nations, also known as the parables of the last judgment, Matthew 25:31–40).

The Gospel of Luke

The gospel of Luke is part of a two-volume set; the other part is the Acts of the Apostles. Both volumes were composed by the same author. They were intended to be read in sequence. Luke presents the good news of Jesus, the gospel; and Acts of the Apostles presents the good news of the church and what people did in response to this gospel. In the gospel of Luke, Jesus moves from Galilee to Jerusalem, toward the center of the Jewish world. In the Acts of the Apostles, the "way"—a synonym for the followers of Jesus—moves from Jerusalem to Rome, the center of the Greco-Roman world.

There are three brief references to "Luke" in the New Testament. Philemon mentions a "Luke" as Paul's fellow worker (verse 24), and 2 Timothy 4:11 notes that a "Luke" was alone in staying with Paul in the days of Paul's imprisonment. Finally, Colossians 4:10–14 mentions a "Luke," a physician and Gentile. Are these references to Luke the evangelist? It is unclear!

Who was this highly gifted and reflective evangelist? The only thing that can be said with certainty is that Luke was a Gentile Christian. No ancient tradition suggests a place of composition for the gospel. Luke's view of Jerusalem, his literary conventions, and his vocabulary make it probable that he wrote outside Palestine in a Christian community with strong Gentile and female membership. Further, because the gospel of Luke has special concern for the poor and oppressed, it is suggested that its community was one that had both very wealthy and seriously marginalized as well as downright poor members. Parables like the rich fool (Luke 12:13–21) and the rich man and Lazarus (Luke 16:19–31), told only by Luke, suggest that Luke's community had rich members who needed to be reminded about their obligation to the poor in their midst. This concern for affluence further suggests and supports an urban origin for the Lucan gospel—possibly Antioch.

Luke's gospel comes from the middle period of gospel writing (83–90 C.E.); it was written after Mark (on which it depends) and before John.

Luke writes with an eye toward influencing Rome positively toward Christianity. The primary audience for Luke's writing were Gentiles, some of whom were Roman citizens. For these people, a literary approach that would not jar educated tastes was required. And so, using the *Septuagint* (the Greek translation of the Old Testament) as his stylistic model, Luke writes in the mode of a Roman historian, using literary forms and designs drawn from that world. Luke is a classic defender of the faith. To Romans who have viewed Christianity as having sordid origins (it sprang from the suspect Jews), Luke demonstrates Christianity's universality. The salvation offered by Jesus is available to everyone, not just Jews: ". . . and all flesh shall see the salvation of God" (Luke 3:6).

Dedicated to a Gentile, the Theophilus of Luke's prologue (1:1–4; see Acts of the Apostles 1:1–5) the two-volume set commends Christianity to a Gentile world; Luke argues that church and state can live peaceably together. His writings were not only a defense to the empire but a tool for its evangelization. Further, since *theophilus* means "God lover" some scholars suggest that Luke is writing to all God lovers, not just a particular historical person.

Characteristics and Themes in Luke's Gospel
In Luke's gospel, women have a prominent role, one that at times puts them on a par with men. There are ten named and unnamed

women in Luke's gospel. In Jesus' teaching in Luke, women are mentioned eighteen times and speak fifteen times; and in ten of these instances their words are given. In Luke, there are women disciples who provide for Jesus and his disciples out of their financial means (Luke 8:1–3). Two of Jesus' closest friends are Martha and Mary of Bethany (Luke 10:38–42). Further, women follow Jesus to Calvary (23:27–31), are present at the crucifixion (23:49; and see 23:55–56), and discover the empty tomb after Jesus' resurrection (24:1–12).

In Luke's gospel, the role of the Holy Spirit is underlined. Often known as the "Gospel of the Holy Spirit," Luke provides more references to the Holy Spirit than any other of the synoptic gospels (see Luke 1:15, 35, 41, 67; 2:26–27; 3:16, 21–22; 4:1–14, 18–19; 12:12).

Luke's gospel is also known as the "Gospel of the Poor," and the "Gospel of Mercy and Forgiveness of God." Luke sees Jesus as friend and advocate of those whom society ignores or turns from in distaste, the poor, handicapped persons, public sinners, and all who found themselves related to the fringes of the community. The Lucan Jesus has great compassion for all of these. In Luke's day, none bore the brunt of ostracism more than the Samaritans. Only Luke tells the story of the good Samaritan (Luke 10:30–37) and the story of the cleansing of the ten lepers by Jesus, in which the only leper to return with gratitude to thank Jesus is a Samaritan (see Luke 17:11–19). The most famous of Jesus' parables on forgiveness—the parable of the prodigal son (Luke 15:11–32)—is so familiar that many think it was related by all the gospel writers. It is, however, Luke's alone.

Luke's gospel stresses prayer. Jesus is portrayed in Luke as praying "without ceasing." Jesus prays seven times in the gospel of Luke (see 3:21; 5:16; 6:12; 9:18, 28–29; 11:1; 22:40–46). In Luke, Jesus prays at every major decision-making moment in his life. Luke provides this as a model for all who would be followers of Jesus.

Luke's gospel contains the largest number of parables, the two most famous being the parable of the good Samaritan (Luke 10:29–37) and the prodigal son (Luke 15:11–32). Luke's gospel alone contains three parables about poverty and riches: the rich fool

(Luke 12:13–21), the shrewd manager (Luke 16:1–13), and the rich man and Lazarus (Luke 16:19–31). Luke records three parables on prayer: the friend at midnight (Luke 11:5–8), the parable of the persistent widow (Luke 18:1–8), and the parable of the Pharisee and the tax collector (Luke 18:9–14). Further, Luke provides parables on being a disciple: the parable of the two builders (Luke 6:47–49), the tower builder and the warring king (Luke 14:28–33), and the parable of the unworthy servant (Luke 17:7–10).

Luke is also known as the "Gospel of Table Fellowship." There are ten meal stories in Luke. Often, when Jesus dines, an outcast or socially unacceptable person becomes included in Jesus' table fellowship. Further, the risen Jesus is recognized in Luke in the "breaking of the bread" (24:13–35).

The Gospel of John

Many people simply assume that the author of the gospel of John is the apostle. Scripture scholars today do not believe this. In biblical times, it was common to ascribe authorship to a great person in order to give a work greater authority. There is, however, good reason to believe that much of the gospel was written by one of John's followers. The gospel has also gone through a second stage of editing, in which new passages were added (most notably the beginning and the end). So when we talk about the authorship of John, we are really talking about a complex sequence of events that includes preaching, writing, and, later, editing.

It is commonly accepted that John's gospel is the last of the four to be written, probably near to the end of the first century (90–100 C.E.). It is written to a community that has its own unique problems and questions. They were dealing with the animosity and hostility of Jewish leaders who had expelled Christians from the synagogues. For this reason, there is an anti-Jewish polemic within John's gospel. It should be noted, however, that whenever Jesus uses the term *Jews* in a negative sense, he is always referring to their leaders and not to the Jews as a people (see below).

THE TERM *THE JEWS* IN THE GOSPEL OF JOHN

In the fourth gospel, even though Jesus himself says, "[S]alvation is from the Jews" (4:22) and some Jews, like Nicodemus, are sympathetic to Jesus (3:1–11, 7:50–52, 12:42), the gospel often uses the expression "the Jews" as a symbol of all those who oppose Jesus. They display a murderous desire to kill God's envoy and will be condemned by the founders of their own tradition, who testify to Jesus (Moses, 5:41–47; Abraham, 8:48–59). The hostility in the Johannine account may have had its roots in the expulsion of Christian Jews from the synagogues referred to in John 9:27 and 16:1–4a.

The animosity between synagogue and church produced bitter and harsh invective, especially hostility of the religious authorities toward Jesus— Pharisees and Sadducees—who are combined and referred to frequently as "the Jews." These opponents are even described in 8:44 as springing from their father the devil, whose conduct they imitate in opposing God by rejecting Jesus, whom God has sent.

If you read the gospel of John carefully, you will notice that the author often does not bother to include the various groups within Judaism of Jesus' day, such as Sadducees, Herodians, scribes, lawyers, Pharisees. He often speaks of "the Jews" as though summarizing a story in which Jesus is facing "the bad guys." This habit creates a huge tension between the fact that Jesus and his followers were also Jews and the way in which the gospel writer is using "the Jews" as a term for a role in his story. John 18:35ff. clearly illustrates this tension. Pilate treats Jesus with scorn because he is a Jew, handed over by fellow Jews. Jesus' answer distinguishes himself and his followers from "the Jews," that is, the group opposed to him. The author of the fourth gospel is not making a statement about all Jewish people at all times when he uses "the Jews" to fill the role of "the bad guys." He is using a literary device, not a racial slur. *Throughout the gospel of John, "the Jews" does not refer to the Jewish people as a whole in either Jesus' day or today, but to the hostile authorities, both Pharisees and Sadducees, particularly in Jerusalem, who refuse to believe in Jesus. The usage reflects the atmosphere at the end of the first century, of bitter arguments between church and synagogue, both of which were made up of Jews.*

We must acknowledge that in the past people have not distinguished between John's use of "the Jews" as characters and the Jewish people from whom Jesus came. Today we must be very careful to not continue this misreading, for it is a disservice to our Jewish brothers and sisters and a sacrilege to use the gospel of John as a means of condoning racism.

Differences Between the Gospel of John and the Synoptics

We have seen how Matthew, Mark, and Luke share a great deal of material in common. They certainly have their own characteristics, but, on the whole, their similarities outweigh their differences. John is aware of the synoptic tradition but makes very little use of it. His style, language, theology, structure, and sources have contributed to this gospel's uniqueness.

It is not necessary to read any further than the first verse to realize that the language of John's gospel is very different from that of the synoptics. John uses language much more symbolically. The opening line, "In the beginning was the Word . . ." (John 1:1), contains language not found elsewhere in the gospels. Light and darkness, life, sign, glory, flesh, spirit, and eternal life are all typical of Johannine language that is filled with figurative meaning.

The Teaching About Jesus in the Gospel of John

John's gospel emphasizes themes that are only implicit in the synoptic gospels. The message of Jesus himself is transformed into a new expression of Christian faith. Two major themes can be discerned in Jesus' teaching in John:

Jesus and the Father are one. As we have seen, the synoptics present the teaching of Jesus in terms of the coming of the reign of God. In the gospel of John, this reign, or kingdom, goes virtually unmentioned. Instead, Jesus speaks mostly about himself. Why? Because for John, Jesus is the kingdom of God in the flesh. There are a whole series of "I Am" sayings in which Jesus reveals himself:

"I am the bread of life" (John 6:35).
"I am the light of the world" (John 8:12).
"I am the gate for the sheep" (John 10:7).
"I am the good shepherd" (John 10:11).
"I am the resurrection and the life" (John 11:25).
"I am the way, and the truth, and the life" (John 14:6).
"I am the true vine" (John 15:1).

In Hebrew, the verb "I Am" forms the root of the word Yahweh, the divine name for God, revealed to Moses at the burning bush (see Exodus 3:13–15). John uses certain "I Am" passages to identify Jesus with God.

Eternal life. In addition to talking about himself, Jesus also speaks often of "eternal life," and this can be confusing because he does not use it in the same sense that it is used today concerning the immortality of the person. Eternal life, for John, has more to do with the quality of life than the length of life, "And this is eternal life, that they may know you, the only true God, and Jesus Christ whom you have sent" (John 17:3). In this sense, eternal life has begun in the earthly life of the believer and continues beyond death. From John's perspective, the enemy of eternal life is not death but sin. Put simply, this means that Christian fulfillment begins on this side of the tomb. This is in contrast to a future notion that looks to the next life as the source of God's salvation and human fulfillment. John's gospel is the strongest of the four in its emphasis on what's technically called "realized eschatology"—that salvation begins here on earth and not in the hereafter.

John's Unique Style

Jesus' message in John differs not only in content but in style. In the synoptics, Jesus teaches, often using parables and short sayings. In John, there are, instead, long, symbolic, theological discourses. None of the synoptic parables can be found in John.

The evangelist also makes great use of double meaning and irony. Jesus often says something only to be misunderstood by his listeners because they have missed the figurative meaning. His advice to Nicodemus that a man be "born from above" is met with the response: "How can anyone be born after having grown old? Can one enter a second time into the mother's womb and be born?" (John 3:4). He has taken the literal meaning and missed the symbolic one. Jesus is talking about spiritual rebirth. John often uses these misunderstandings as the basis for explaining the true meaning of Jesus' message. Likewise, there are quite a few ironic passages in John in which a true statement about Jesus is unknowingly spoken by a character. For example, when Jesus promises the Samaritan woman "living water," she replies, "Are you greater than our ancestor Jacob, who gave us the well?" (John 4:12). The reader, of course, knows the ironic answer to that question.

Touring the Gospel of John

In the remainder of this chapter, we will take a brief tour through the gospel of John so as to become better acquainted with this unique gospel.

Prologue: John 1:1–18

¹In the beginning was the Word, and the Word was with God, and the Word was God. ²He was in the beginning with God. ³All things came into being through him, and without him not one thing came into being. What has come into being ⁴in him was life, and the life was the light of all people. ⁵The light shines in the darkness, and the darkness did not overcome it.

⁶There was a man sent from God, whose name was John. ⁷He came as a witness to testify to the light, so that all might believe through him. ⁸He himself was not the light, but he came to testify to the light. ⁹The true light, which enlightens everyone, was coming into the world.

¹⁰He was in the world, and the world came into being through him; yet the world did not know him. ¹¹He came to what was his own, and his own people did not accept him. ¹²But to all who received him, who believed in his name, he gave power to become children of God, ¹³who were born, not of blood or of the will of the flesh or of the will of man, but of God.

¹⁴And the Word became flesh and lived among us, and we have seen his glory, the glory as of a father's only son, full of grace and truth. ¹⁵(John testified to him and cried out, "This was he of whom I said, 'He who comes after me ranks ahead of me because he was before me.'") *[16]From his fullness we have all received, grace upon grace. [17]The law indeed was given through Moses; grace and truth came through Jesus Christ. [18]No one has ever seen God. It is God the only Son, who is close to the Father's heart, who has made him known.*

This prologue was originally an early Christian hymn, adapted to serve as an introduction to the gospel. In it, we find many of the central theological ideas in the fourth gospel.

The prologue begins with the same words that begin the Book of Genesis: "In the beginning." Immediately, the reader is being introduced to a highly developed understanding of Jesus. He was "in the beginning." He is the preexistent Word of God, present from the dawn of creation. Christians today may take this picture for granted, but at the time it represented a new and creative insight into the person of Jesus. Whereas Mark introduces the divinity of Jesus at his baptism ("You are my Son, the Beloved" [Mark 1:11]), in Matthew and Luke at his birth (the infancy narratives and the virginal conception), John traces the divine nature of Jesus back to the dawn of time.

John uses "the Word" to represent Christ. The expression "the Word of the Lord" has a rich tradition in the Old Testament as God's communication to his people through his prophets. Jesus, as the Word, is the communication and self-revelation of the Father. He is the source of all creation and is present to all creation as light in the midst of darkness. Wherever God makes his presence known, the Word takes shape. The hymn explains that the Word was always in the world, but the world did not know him. Finally, the climax of this hymn is described in verse 14: "And the Word became flesh and lived among us, and we have seen his glory, the glory as of a father's only son, full of grace and truth" (John 1:14).

At the heart of this gospel is a theology of the incarnation: God has become a human being. The word *glory,* used to describe the Son is an important one in John's gospel. In the Old Testament, it refers to the visible manifestation of the power of the invisible God. In John, "the glory of God" can be seen in Jesus throughout his public ministry and his "signs" (miracles), but it is his death and resurrection that fully reveal the glory of the Father. As Jesus is facing his death, he prays: "Father, the hour has come; glorify your Son so that the Son may glorify you . . . the glory that I had in your presence before the world existed" (John 17:1, 5b).

In the midst of this hymn, the gospel editor injects two passages concerning John the Baptist (1:6–9, 15). They seem somewhat out of place, but have a very practical purpose. Both of the passages emphasize the superiority of Jesus over the Baptist, and the fact that the Baptist is not the Messiah. Scholars believe that this was done to combat a group still following the Baptist and awaiting the Messiah. These passages make it clear that the role of the Baptist was to point to Jesus: "He [John] came as a witness to testify to the light, so that all might believe through him. He himself was not the light, but he came to testify to the light" (John 1:7–8).

The Book of Signs (John 1:19–12:50)

The next major division within John's gospel is the "Book of Signs." This section of the gospel contains the public ministry of Jesus, in which he reveals himself as the revelation of the Father through his words and "signs." These signs are miracles. In many ways, they are similar to the synoptic miracle stories. The major difference comes about in their function in the gospel of John. Miracles in the synoptics signify the power of the reign of God breaking into history. In John, there is no theme concerning God's reign. The signs have a largely symbolic and christological meaning. Like most of this gospel, they point beyond themselves to Jesus. There are seven signs in John which reveal the glory of Jesus. (The number seven symbolizes fullness or perfection or totality.)

The Wedding at Cana (John 2:1–11)

We need to understand that this miracle symbolizes Jesus ushering in the new messianic era, symbolized by the abundance of wine and the banquet, and his replacement of the former Jewish traditions, symbolized by the stone jars full of water.

Jesus Heals an Official's Son (John 4:46–54)

The key to this story is that the miracle occurs for a Gentile pagan, and his whole household is converted. This symbolizes the fact that Jesus has come for Gentiles as well as Jews. He is the savior of all humankind.

Jesus Heals on the Sabbath (John 5:1–15)

This sign points to Jesus' power over the Sabbath. The theme can also be found in the synoptics (see Mark 3:1–6). However, John wants to show that the source of Jesus' power over the Sabbath is his union with the Father. His rebuttal to the accusations of the Pharisees in this matter reveal the meaning of the miracle: "Very truly, I tell you, the Son can do nothing on his own, but only what he sees the Father doing; for whatever the Father does, the Son does likewise" (John 5:19).

Feeding the Five Thousand (John 6:1–13)

This miracle is linked with the bread of life discourse and reveals Jesus as the fulfillment of the Exodus, replacing the manna with his own body and blood. The miracle, in particular, has strong eucharistic overtones. In the Eucharist, the one body of Christ is miraculously given to thousands (today, millions).

Jesus Walks on the Water (John 6:16–21)

This miracle seems to bring together a number of different traditions about Jesus walking on water. For John, the key to this sign may lie in the words of Jesus: "It is I" (John 6:20), literally, "I Am." As we have seen, this may be John's way of identifying Jesus with God. Also, John understands water to be the symbol for chaos. Jesus walking on it shows he conquers chaos just as God conquered chaos in the creation story (see Genesis 1).

A Man Born Blind Receives Sight (John 9:1–7)

This miracle echoes some of the symbolism found in the prologue. Jesus is the light that has come into the world. In John, light is a symbol for truth; and darkness, a symbol for sin or confusion. This miracle points beyond the physical darkness of blindness to the spiritual darkness of sin. The story is followed by a conflict with Jewish leaders who represent the spiritual darkness and their unwillingness to accept Jesus as the light.

The Death of Lazarus (John 11:1–44)

The key to this sign is in its timing. Jesus is on his way to Jerusalem where he will be put to death. The death and raising of Lazarus is meant as a prefiguring of the death and resurrection of Jesus. Likewise, faith in Jesus allows the believer (in this case represented by Martha) to share in his death and resurrection. Again, the point of the miracle is to teach us about Jesus: "I am the resurrection and the life" (John 11:25).

The Book of Glory (John 13:1–20:31)

This section of John's gospel reveals the glory of Jesus in his death, resurrection, and ascension. It includes the story of the Last Supper, the last discourse, the arrest and trial of Jesus, and his death and resurrection. Since other sections of this book will be devoted to the death and resurrection of Jesus, we will focus here on the Last Supper and the last discourse.

The Last Supper in John

By the time this gospel was written, the Eucharist had been celebrated by Christians for roughly over fifty years. The synoptics tell the story of the final meal by Jesus and his apostles that became the basis for the Eucharist. John, however, leaves out the details of the meal. In fact, his readers would have been familiar with those events already. Instead, he portrays the Last Supper in highly symbolic terms, with the story of Jesus washing the feet of the apostles.

On the night before his death, at the meal he celebrated with his apostles, Jesus rose and washed their feet. This custom was part of Palestinian hospitality. When a guest arrived, the servant of the host would wash the guest's feet, which would have been dirty and filthy from the walk, since often the city streets were the latrines. Jesus, thus takes on the role of the servant. Obviously, the meaning of the act was symbolic and John explains it:

> *12After he had washed their feet, had put on his robe, and had returned to the table, he said to them, "Do you know what I have done to you? 13You call me Teacher and Lord—and you are right, for that is what I am. 14So if I, your Lord and Teacher, have washed your feet, you also ought to wash one another's feet. 15For I have set you an example, that you also should do as I have done to you"* (John 13:12–15).

There are several layers of meaning to this story: first, by connecting it to the Last Supper, John has implicitly tied the meaning of the story to the Eucharist. The Christian community is not only to celebrate the Eucharist—they are to live it. The ritual without the service to each other is empty. Second, the washing of the feet has baptismal symbolism as well. Baptism is a sharing in the death and resurrection of Jesus. By situating this story right before the passion, death, and resurrection, John is also teaching about baptism. This is why Jesus says to Peter, "Unless I wash you, you have no share with me" (John 13:8). Baptism unites us with Christ. Further, this story has meaning on the level of ministry in the church. Leadership in the church is not power in the normal understanding of the word. Christian power lies in service and humility, as exemplified by Jesus. Finally, this story fits as the prominent lead-in to the "Book of Glory." As we shall see, Jesus' glory lies in his love unto death; this story symbolizes exactly that.

The Last Discourse
Chapters 14–17 of the gospel of John comprise the last discourse. These four chapters are fashioned in the style of a farewell address from Jesus to the disciples in the context of the Last Supper. Farewell addresses were very common in the Old Testament, and can be associated with Abraham, Joshua, David, and Moses. In fact, the entire Book of Deuteronomy is composed of Moses' farewell address to the

people of Israel. For many, these four chapters in John represent the height of New Testament spirituality. They have consistently been the favorites of the great spiritual writers and mystics of Christianity because of their constant return to the theme of unity between the Father and the Son and those who believe in the Son.

The Vine and the Branches

On unity between the Father and the Son, Jesus is at his most explicit in these chapters: "Whoever has seen me has seen the Father. . . . Do you not believe that I am in the Father and the Father is in me?" (John 14:9, 10a). Likewise, those who believe in Jesus will be united with him and the Father. The sign of the true believer is love. John develops this theme through the image of the vine and the branches (John 15:1–17):

> *"I am the true vine, and my Father is the vinegrower. . . . Just as the branch cannot bear fruit by itself unless it abides in the vine, neither can you unless you abide in me. I am the vine, you are the branches. Those who abide in me and I in them bear much fruit, because apart from me you can do nothing"* (John 15:1, 4–5).

The image of the vine to represent Israel is a common one used by the prophets in the Old Testament (see Hosea 10:1, Jeremiah 6:9, Ezekiel 15:1–6). In the vineyard song of Isaiah (5:1–7), God laments that he has planted the choicest of vines only to have them yield wild grapes. However, in John the vine is no longer Israel. Jesus is the true vine. Here again we see the theme of replacement in John. Jesus has replaced Israel as God's means of salvation. In the allegory, the father is the vine grower, just as he is in Isaiah.

What is the connective between Father, Son, and disciple? John answers it this way: "As the Father has loved me, so I have loved you; abide in my love" (John 15:9).

The Paraclete

Jesus also seeks to assure his disciples that his death will not mean the end of his presence to them. He does this by promising to send the paraclete (see John 14:15–17, 26; 15:26; 16:7–11, 13–15).

"And I will ask the Father, and he will give you another Advocate [paraclete], to be with you forever. This is the Spirit of truth, whom the world cannot receive, because it neither sees him nor knows him. You know him, because he abides with you, and he will be in you" (John 14:15–17).

The term that Jesus uses for the spirit *paraclete*, is a legal one meaning "advocate" or "spokesperson." The spirit is God's spokesperson. He is "another" paraclete because Jesus is the first. The spirit becomes the operating principle of faith after the death and resurrection of Jesus according to the Gospel of John. Those who live in Christ have his spirit, and the spirit continues to guide and lead the church: "I still have many things to say to you, but you cannot bear them now. When the Spirit of truth comes, he will guide you into all the truth" (John 16:12–13a). Jesus confers this spirit on the disciples after his resurrection: ". . . he breathed on them and said to them, 'Receive the Holy Spirit'" (John 20:22).

Jesus Prays for the Apostles

Often in farewell addresses of the Old Testament, the speaker would end with a prayer for the people he is to leave behind. This is precisely what we find at the end of the last discourse. Jesus prays for his disciples. There are two key elements to his prayer: first, they are to be protected by God's name, which he has given them; second, they are to be consecrated in truth. In the Hebrew mentality, the name denotes the whole person and the meaning of that person. Thus, Christians pray in the Lord's Prayer, "Hallowed be thy name." This means a lot more than not saying, "God damn it." It means that God will be the number one priority in my life. Thus, to be protected by "God's name," means to be protected from the power of sin by giving God authority in one's life. When Jesus prays that the apostles be consecrated in truth, they are to be holy because they will be God's representatives and God is holy. Being consecrated in truth means being consecrated in God's word, "Your word is truth" (John 17:17) and thus it means being consecrated in Jesus who is God's Word.

Summary of John's Gospel

In sum, John's gospel was the last of the four written and, unlike those in the synoptic tradition, much of it is based on unique sources. The language of John's gospel is symbolic. John's portrait of Jesus is that of a preexistent Son of God who reveals the Father. Many of the claims made about Jesus reflect a postresurrection understanding of Jesus' divinity on the part of John's church. Jesus does not speak about the reign of God in John, but speaks mostly about himself and eternal life. None of the narrative parables of the synoptics are found in John. One of the main themes of John's gospel is replacement. Jesus replaces the feasts and traditions of Israel. The prologue is an early Christian hymn that is used as an introduction to the gospel and describes Jesus as the Word made flesh. The "Book of Signs" contains the public ministry of Jesus, in which he reveals himself through the highly symbolic miracles of hope ("signs"). The "Book of Glory" is the revelation of the glory of Jesus through his death and resurrection. It also contains the last discourse, which is Jesus' farewell address to the apostles.

Finally, the Gospel of John, like all of the gospels, has as its ultimate purpose to draw readers of every age to faith. "Now Jesus did many other signs in the presence of his disciples, which are not written in this book. But these are written so that you may come to believe that Jesus is the Messiah, the Son of God, and that through believing you may have life in his name" (John 20:30–31).

For Discussion

1. How do the three stages of gospel development help in your understanding of their origin?
2. Is the "synoptic problem" still a problem for you? Explain.
3. Which one of the four gospels is your favorite?
4. How does the Gospel of John differ from the synoptic gospels?
5. What have you learned as a result of reading this chapter?

For Further Reading

Brown, Raymond E. *The Gospel According to John* (Anchor Bible 30). Garden City, N.Y.: Doubleday, 1966–70.

———. *An Introduction to the New Testament.* Garden City, N.Y.: Doubleday, 1997.

Griffith-Jones, Robin. *The Four Witnesses.* San Francisco: Harper Collins, 2000.

Harrington, Daniel J. *The Gospel of Matthew.* Collegeville, Minn.: Liturgical Press, 1991.

———. *How to Read the Gospels.* New York: New City Press, 1996.

Hooker, Morna D. *The Gospel According to St. Mark.* Peabody, Mass.: Hendrickson, 1993.

Johnson, Luke T. *The Gospel of Luke.* Collegeville, Minn.: Liturgical Press, 1991.

Zannoni, Arthur E. *Jesus of the Gospels: Teacher, Storyteller, Friend, Messiah.* Cincinnati: St. Anthony Messenger Press, 1996.

3

"WHO DO PEOPLE SAY THAT I AM?"
(MARK 8:27)

In THREE OF THE FOUR GOSPELS, JESUS ASKS HIS DISCIPLES who people think he is (see Mark 8:27–33, Matthew 16:13–23, Luke 9:18–22). Interestingly, each gospel writer responds, but not in the same way; in fact, the gospels present us with different portraits of Jesus. Drawn with words instead of an artist's lines and colors, these portraits are sometimes intriguing, sometimes perplexing, but always interesting. How can four such diverse descriptions characterize the same person? It may seem clearer if we recall that we ourselves are seen quite differently by various people who know us well. And public figures whose portraits are painted by four talented artists often find marked differences in each portrayal. Further, four people who witness an automobile accident narrate the story of the event a little differently from one another.

In describing Jesus, the gospel writers were faced with a unique challenge: How do you portray someone who is both completely human and completely divine? In doing this, the gospel writers also had their respective audiences to consider just as we often do when writing to coworkers or friends. The four evangelists tried to choose those words and deeds, stories and images from Jesus' life which would be most relevant to their particular audience. These audiences differed dramatically in religious background, culture, and ethnic origin.

All of this and more is reflected in the portraits of Jesus drawn by the gospel writers. Which gospel portrait is the most authentic? Which best reflects Jesus? They all do. Together, like a great prism, they refract the pure light of Christ in a manner that gives each a separate and distinct coloration. As the prism colors splash against our eyes, minds, and spirits in reading the gospels, the Jesus who emerges from the four accounts possesses greater depth, breadth, and height than any single narrative could provide.

Jesus the Jew

All four gospels agree that Jesus was a Jew. He was born a Jew, and he was raised a Jew in Galilee, one of the most beautiful, fertile areas of northern ancient Palestine. He had a Jewish mother, which means that he probably looked a lot like other Jews, i.e., dark hair and complexion, perhaps with a so-called Roman nose, not too large in stature. His earliest followers were all Jewish. In all likelihood, he was addressed as *rabbi* ("teacher"). He did not write the New Testament; it was composed after his death. Jesus studied as a Jew; he read the Hebrew Scriptures, what Christians call the Old Testament; later he taught as a Jew.

That Jesus was a Galilean Jew in the first century is neither an insignificant accident of history nor a cultural veil masking his divine nature. When Christians affirm that Jesus is Christ, they affirm his membership in first-century Israel, his rootedness in Israelite and Jewish tradition, and his fidelity to the God of Abraham, Isaac, and

Jacob, Rachel, Leah, and Rebekah, the God of all Israel at all times. Jesus' activities and teachings, along with most of the New Testament claims made about him, can *only* be understood within the context of first-century Jewish society and the ongoing tradition of Israel.

In the Mediterranean world of the first century, the world into which Jesus was born, to be a member of a people was to be part of a unified network of political, economic, social, intellectual, and religious relationships. Judaism was not just a religion in the modern sense, separate from political and social life, but a total way of life which involved daily speech, tasks, economic relationships, rituals, cultural symbols, and fundamental outlooks on life. The Jewish people were not just a group of people who happened to live in the Roman Empire, but a national group which stretched back over the centuries to their kings and founders, to David, Moses, and Abraham, and looked forward to the Day of the Lord, when Israel would once more live in peace under God's direct rule. Jews also stretched outwardly geographically throughout the Roman Empire and the Middle East. These are known as Jews of the dispersion *(diaspora)*. They existed in ancient Babylon, and other Jews subsequently traveled to Egypt, North Africa, Asia Minor, Greece, Italy, and beyond.

Despite this dispersion in place and in time, and the varieties in their practice of Judaism, to be a Jew was to be different from a Roman, or a citizen of Antioch or Syria, or a Galatian farmer in Asia Minor. And to be a Jewish carpenter in Nazareth, Lower Galilee, who became a popular preacher, was to be a certain kind of Jew in the first century. What, then, was Jesus' way of life and what was the context within which he lived it?

Jesus Within Israel

Jesus was a popular preacher and teacher in northeastern Lower Galilee during the first half of the first century. The lower region where Jesus dwelt was a very rich valley that extended from the Mediterranean to the Sea of Galilee, a distance of about twenty-five miles.

Palestine in the 1st Century CE

☐ Extent of Herod's kingdom
■ Herodian fortress city
○ Decapolis city (time of Herod)
● Other city

Among the important villages of this region in Jesus' day were Nazareth and Capernaum. Nazareth, Jesus' hometown, was a small agricultural village in the very heart of rural Galilee. The village's population was made up of farmers and a few artisans. We know from Luke's gospel that Nazareth had a synagogue, which Jesus attended. It was there that he read from the Isaiah scroll (Luke 4:16–30).

Capernaum, located north of Nazareth on the Sea of Galilee, appears to have been the center of Jesus' activity during most of his public life (Matthew 4:12–13). Capernaum had a synagogue in which Jesus both healed and taught (Luke 4:31–37).

These villages were made up of the *am ha aretz* (known in those days as "the people of the land"), the farmers and the poor who were the primary receivers of the Galilean Jesus' preaching, teaching, and healing. This area was overwhelmingly Jewish. It was both the soil Jesus trod and the home of his original apostles.

Jesus was a layman, a reformer who taught many things drawn from the common fund of Jewish tradition. He sought, as did others, to increase his fellow Jews' adherence to their traditions and to enliven their relationship with God. The central symbol for this reform was the image of the kingdom of God, a symbol which connotes God's rule over Israel in the present, and God's eventual triumph over all evil powers, including the oppressive Roman Empire. The ideas which governed this renewed Israel were drawn from biblical tradition and given a particular emphasis and application for the Galilean community. Some of the themes which appear often are care for the poor and needy, reliance on God, an emphasis on honor and human authority, and just social relations.

Jesus' ministry offered healing for the sinfulness and weakness of humans, and hope for the Galilean peasants who had no control over their government or life. His program was based on faith in God's active presence as protector of Israel. As such, his teachings were quintessential Jewish. Jesus' emphasis on God's rule, God's reign, implies that the current human rulers are illegitimate or seriously deficient. Thus, Jesus' religious reform program was profoundly political and social.

Jesus was a challenge to the local Jewish authorities, especially Herod Antipas, the Tetrarch of Galilee, whose duty was to keep order, collect taxes, and see that the living of Judaism was consistent within Roman imperial policy. The *scribes,* who were the local officials charged with keeping records, administering justice, and educating the people, came into conflict with Jesus' growing popular influence and authority. In Jerusalem, the *priests* who sought to bolster the people's loyalty to the Temple, its worship, sacrifices, and tithes, also saw Jesus as a threat to political stability and the traditional way of life. The Pharisees were, like Jesus, Jewish lay reformers. They promoted a different program for the reform of Jewish life and the reinvigoration of the covenant with God and society.

At the time of Jesus, Pharisees dwelt mainly in Palestine. In Hebrew, the name *Pharisee* means "separate one," which refers to their ritual observance of purity and tithing; *Pharisee* can also mean "the interpreter," which refers to their unique interpretations of the Hebrew Scriptures, what Christians call the Old Testament.

As lay reformers, the Pharisees did not oppose Roman occupation, but they wanted more from the Jerusalem Temple, especially from its liturgical practices and priests. They turned their attention to strengthening the people's devotion to Torah, the first five books of the Bible, the heart and soul of the original covenant with God. Believing that for many the written Torah had become a dead letter, they introduced the notion that the interpretation of Torah had to be continually renewed and readjusted within the framework of the changing experience of the Jewish covenantal community. They called this interpretation "Oral Torah."

The priests who were contemporaries of the Pharisees looked upon the precepts of the Torah more literally and primarily in terms of sacrificial observances at the Jerusalem Temple. These observances were seen as the primary means of relating to God and becoming holy. The Pharisees, on the other hand, believed that the Torah had to provide for the way human life was to be lived. In this way, the Pharisees hoped that every ordinary human action could become sacred—an act of worship. Doing "a good deed" for another human, in Hebrew what is termed a *mitzvah,* was given a status in some ways surpassing Temple worship. This was truly a revolution in religious thinking.

In addition, a new religious figure in Judaism—the teacher— emerged within the Pharisaic movement. This position of teacher, or *rabbi,* differed from that of the earlier prophetic and priestly roles in Judaism. Prophets were understood as spokespersons for God, whereas priests functioned as presiders or celebrants at the liturgies in the Jerusalem Temple. Rabbis, however, fulfilled a twofold role in the community: interpreting Torah and, even more important, making it concrete and relevant to the people of their day. Their principal task was instructional, not liturgical. Significantly, a nonpriestly figure, a rabbi, gradually replaced the Temple priest as the chief religious representative of Judaism's faithfulness to Torah.

Another aspect of the Pharisaic reform was the emergence of what was later called the *synagogue* ("assembly of people"). The synagogue became a centerpiece of this reform movement, spreading throughout Palestine and the cities of the Jewish diaspora (Jews living outside the land of Israel). Unlike the Jerusalem Temple, the synagogues were not places where priests presided and sacrifices were offered; rather they were places where Torah was studied, rabbis/sages offered their interpretations, and prayers were offered. They became not merely "houses of God," but far more, "houses of the people of God."

A further characteristic of this Pharisee movement was its emphasis on *table fellowship*—a way of strengthening relationships within the community. The Pharisees intended to extend to all the people the duties previously prescribed only for the Temple priests. In the eyes of the Pharisees, the Temple altar in Jerusalem could be replicated at every table in the household of Israel. A quiet but far-reaching reform was at hand. There was no longer any basis for assigning the priestly class a unique level of authority.

The Pharisees saw God not only as creator, giver of the covenant, an all-consuming presence, and much more, but in a special way, as the *father* of each individual. Everyone had the right to address God in a direct and personal way.

The Pharisees also believed in the resurrection of each individual from the dead. Those whose lives were marked by justice would rise once the Messiah had come. They would enjoy perpetual union with God, the Father.

Convictions That Jesus and the Pharisees Shared

In light of the aforementioned, there is little doubt that Jesus and the Pharisees shared many central convictions in common. It is to these that we now turn.

Their first common point was their basic approach to God. The Pharisees elevated the notion of God as *Father* to a central place in their theological outlook. So did Jesus! Story after story in the gospels have Jesus addressing God with this title, and Jesus' central prayer begins by invoking God as "Our Father" (Matthew 6:9–13). In the Gospel of Mark, when he is praying to God, Jesus addresses God as *Abba,* a term of intimacy, roughly equivalent to "daddy" (Mark 14:36). The overall effect of this stress on divine fatherhood was fundamentally the same for Jesus as for the Pharisees. It led both to an enhanced appreciation of the dignity of every person and ultimately to the notion of resurrection—perpetual union with God.

Jesus' own public stance in the community also closely paralleled the evolving role of the Pharisaic teacher. On numerous occasions in the gospels Jesus was called teacher or rabbi. Also, the gospels are filled with examples of Jesus teaching in synagogues (see Matthew 4:23, 9:35; Luke 4:15–18; John 18:20).

Jesus also shared with the Pharisees a general reluctance to antagonize the Roman authorities occupying Palestine. When the disciples of the Pharisees ask him about the lawfulness of paying taxes to Caesar, Jesus' response is an example of a position he shared with the Pharisees: "Give therefore to the emperor the things that are the emperor's, and to God the things that are God's" (Matthew 22:21).

Besides the new role of the teacher (rabbi) and the synagogue, Jesus clearly picked up on another central feature of Pharisaism, "oral Torah." Oral Torah refers to interpretations given by the Pharisees to various Torah texts. Throughout the gospels we find Jesus offering interpretations of the Scriptures that were often quite similar to those of the Pharisees (see the Sermon on the Mount, Matthew 5–7).

Jesus also employed Pharisaic use of Sacred Scripture by employing a method known as "proof texting." In the gospels, Jesus often argued his position by using so-called "proof texts," quoting from the Old Testament to *prove a point* or to refute a critic. A good example of this is when Jesus is tempted by the devil and Jesus refutes every temptation by quoting a text from the Old Testament (see Luke 4:1–13). As the gospel writers present him, Jesus was drawing on a technique used by the Pharisees.

The "proof texting" that Jesus used at times pitted him against the Pharisees—such as when he challenged certain claims they made about the written law and called them hypocrites for placing higher value on the teachings of humans than the teachings of God (Matthew 23:1–36), and when Jesus used Scripture to refute the Pharisaic teachings prohibiting the plucking of grain on the Sabbath (Matthew 12:1–8) or unwashed hands (Matthew 15:20).

At other times, Jesus' "proof texting" placed him on the side of the Pharisees. One example of this is when, in an impressive debate with the Sadducees, he used the Old Testament to reinforce his belief, and that of the Pharisees, in resurrection and an afterlife. Jesus was so impressive he won the Pharisees' applause (Matthew 22:23–33).

In sum, many of Jesus' teachings were either literally biblical or filtered through the Pharisaic use of Scripture, or both.

Finally, the New Testament provides us with plenty of support on how deeply Jesus embraced the table fellowship notion of Pharisaism. The meal narratives in the New Testament are an example of this. In the end, he selected this setting—table fellowship—for one of the most critical moments of his entire ministry, the celebration of the first Eucharist (Matthew 26:26–30, Mark 14:22–26, Luke 22:14–20).

While all four gospels understand Jesus to be Jewish, nonetheless they all have their own unique portrayals of him, and it is to these that we now turn.

Mark's Jesus

Mark's Jesus is a man in a hurry. If this gospel were dramatized, Jesus would hit the stage running and never stop! It has been said of this first description of Jesus' public life that if Jesus ever sat down, Mark failed to record it. There is no mention of Jesus' birth or childhood and none of his young adulthood. The curtain in Mark's drama opens to introduce a no-holds barred John the Baptizer who baptizes Jesus prior to his forty-day desert experience—all this in the first thirteen verses of the first chapter. Things don't slow down much from there. Before the first chapter ends, Jesus has called his first disciples, performed his first cure (followed by two more), and set off for Capernaum.

Reading Mark often leaves one out of breath. All too frequently, this impression of Jesus' style is lost or considerably diminished by hearing the gospel read in short excerpts during the Sunday liturgy. The way to assimilate Mark is in a single gulp: sit down and read all sixteen chapters of his gospel as you would any other book. Simply read it whole and entire in one sitting and you'll be introduced to a Jesus whom you may not have met before.

You'll meet a Jesus who is earthy and easy to relate to, a Jesus with whom most of us would be very comfortable, a Jesus who is quite approachable providing you can catch up with him, a Jesus constantly hemmed in by crowds: "That evening, at sundown, they brought to him all who were sick or possessed with demons. And the whole city was gathered around the door" (Mark 1:32–33); "He told his disciples to have a boat ready for him because of the crowd, so that they would not crush him" (Mark 3:9); "Then he went home; and the crowd came together again, so that they could not even eat" (Mark 3:19b–20). The word *crowd* or *crowds* is used forty-two times in the *New American Bible* translation of Mark's gospel.

74

In Mark we meet a human Jesus. We identify with him readily because his feelings are obvious and much like our own. When a leper totally ostracized from society came to Jesus, he was exceptionally bold—bold enough to approach and bold enough to remind Jesus that he could make him clean if he so wished. "Moved with pity, Jesus stretched out his hand and touched him, and said to him, 'I do choose. Be made clean!'" (Mark 1:41). But if he could turn soft at the sight of suffering, Mark's Jesus could turn a flinty eye toward those who lacked his compassion, as in the case of the Pharisees who questioned Jesus about healing on the Sabbath: "He looked around at them with anger; he was grieved at their hardness of heart and said to the man, 'Stretch out your hand.' He stretched it out, and his hand was restored" (Mark 3:5). This is one of the very few passages in the gospels where the emotion of anger is applied to Jesus.

As Jesus' earthly life drew near to close and he and his closest friends were assembled at Gethsemane, "he took with him Peter and James and John, and began to be distressed and agitated. And he said to them, 'I am deeply grieved, even to death'" (Mark 14:33–34). The range of emotions shown in the gospel of Mark endears Jesus to those of us who see the same emotions in ourselves and those whose lives touch ours every day. Finally, Mark's Jesus is a man who suffers. He does his very best to embrace his suffering and death, for he knows that suffering and dying are not ends in themselves but a means of reaching God. Mark's Jesus is adamant that the Son of Man must suffer (8:31–33) and that his disciples are to embrace suffering in their own lives.

Matthew's New Moses: Jesus the Teacher

If Mark wrote for Roman followers of Jesus, most of whom had come to Christianity from pagan backgrounds, Matthew had a different audience entirely. His audience was Jews who had become Christians. Matthew takes full advantage of his peoples' extensive Hebrew background to proclaim the good news that Jesus is, without doubt, the long-awaited Messiah, the fulfillment of all that is written in the Old Testament.

Jesus emerges here as the new Moses. Unlike Mark, Matthew is very interested in Jesus' Jewish origins and launches into his account with a rundown of Jesus' family tree, a tree whose more illustrious branches include names such as Abraham, Isaac, Jacob, Judah, Ruth, David, Solomon, and Joseph. Joseph personifies the faithful and observant Jew and seems to be the central figure in the infancy narrative of Matthew's gospel.

With the stories of Jesus' birth, Matthew begins to draw a parallel between Jesus and Moses. Only Matthew tells how Herod's jealousy and hatred forced Joseph and his family into Egyptian exile. Matthew thereby establishes that, just as Pharaoh feared and loathed the Hebrews in Moses' time, so Herod treated Jesus and his family. Herod's phobia is seen spilling over onto the innocent young boys of Bethlehem in another episode found only in Matthew, the slaughter of the innocents (Matthew 2:16–18). Just as male Hebrew infants were doomed under Pharaoh (Exodus 1:15–22), so these young Jews fell victim to Herod. Jesus, like Moses, is safe from such authoritarian wrath and, in due time, will come forth, like Moses, from Egypt.

Gentiles were also entering Matthew's church, requiring the author to pave the way among Jewish converts with accounts of the magi, who were certainly of Gentile origin (Matthew 2:1–12), and with Jesus' comment, ". . . many will come from east and west and will eat with Abraham and Isaac and Jacob in the kingdom of heaven" (Matthew 8:11).

Matthew's comparisons of Jesus to Moses continue in his account of Jesus' most famous discourse, the Sermon on the Mount (see Matthew, chapters 5–7). In reporting this sermon, Matthew places the stamp of divinity on Jesus, situating him above Moses by having him quote from the Law Moses brought down from Mount Sinai and expand its meaning by his own authority from a mountain site of his own. "You have heard that it was said to those of ancient times, 'You shall not murder'; and 'whoever murders shall be liable to judgment.' But I say to you that if you are angry with a brother or a sister, you will be liable to judgment" (Matthew 5:21–22).

If Mark's is the action gospel, presenting an on-the-go Jesus and what he does, Matthew's is a more thoughtful gospel, spotlighting a more reflective Jesus and what he says. To make his teaching easier to follow, Matthew organized it into five major components. This is Matthew's way of showing that Jesus' teachings surpass those of the five books of Moses. So successful has Matthew been that his gospel has sometimes been referred to as a catechism. On almost every page we meet Jesus the teacher, the rabbi.

Matthew is most concerned about Jesus' teachings. In five principal areas Matthew has assembled much of what Jesus had to say on a given topic and made a single discourse of it. Each of the five is preceded by a narrative section that focuses on the same theme, and each discourse is neatly concluded by some variation on the phrase, "Now when Jesus had finished saying these things . . ." (Matthew 7:22, 11:1, 13:53, 19:1). In wrapping up the fifth and last discourse, the ending is slightly different: "When Jesus had finished saying *all* these things . . ." (Matthew 26:1). The discourses are as follows: the sermon on the mount (Matthew 5:3–7:27), the missionary discourse (Matthew 10:5–42), the parable discourse (Matthew 13:3–52), the church community discourse (Matthew 18:3–35), the eschatological (last things) discourse (Matthew 24:4–25:46).

In this gospel, Jesus is frequently addressed as rabbi or teacher. Often, this form of address is used by his opponents. Jesus instructs the entire community as Moses did before him, but he does not go to the mountain to receive authority from God as Moses did; he preaches sometimes from the mountain by his own authority. Where Mark's Jesus has much to show us, Matthew's Jesus has much to teach us.

Luke's Jesus

The portrait of Jesus that may come closest to the one most people envision is given us by Luke. Luke, like Mark, sought out others in compiling his portrait, for he himself was not one of the Twelve. He opens his account with the admission that he was not an eyewitness

77

(Luke 1:1–3). Luke was a Greek convert who wrote for an audience of Gentiles much like himself. In Luke, we encounter the most masterful writer of the New Testament—some would say, of the entire Bible. His skill allows him to balance a diversity of themes without confusing his readers.

One way to grasp the gospel of Luke's understanding of Jesus is to look at the various titles applied to Jesus. These titles help the reader to better grasp the identity and function of Jesus in this gospel.

Jesus as Prophet

The Lucan Jesus identifies himself as a prophet (Luke 4:14–44), a spokesperson for God who is sent by God to the disadvantaged and has a universal mission, yet will be rejected by his own people. Other individuals view Jesus as a prophet. Those who witness the raising of the son of the widow of Nain so identify him, as do the ordinary people (Luke 9:18–19). In the Emmaus story (Luke 24:19), Luke intends his readers to regard the disciples' hope in Jesus the prophet as well founded.

The gospel of Luke often portrays Jesus as aware that he shares the fate of those prophets who were killed by people who would not accept them as messengers of God. Nowhere is this more vividly artic-ulated than in Jesus' lament over Jerusalem: "Jerusalem, Jerusalem, the city that kills the prophets and stones those who are sent to it! How often have I desired to gather your children together as a hen gathers her brood under her wings, and you were not willing!" (Luke 13:34).

Luke draws many parallels between Jesus and Moses, who was also seen as a prophet, and thus shows the continuity of God's salvation. The most important of these parallels are found in the transfiguration story (Luke 24:19; Acts 3:22–23, 7:17–44); and the following aspects are stressed about Moses and Jesus: both are heads of communities, and Jesus is a prophet mighty in deed and word who, like Moses, is sent by God and has an exodus to achieve (Luke 9:31), which includes the journey to Jerusalem (see 9:51–19:28). Luke is willing to designate Moses "Redeemer" (Acts 7:35), mainly as a prototype of Jesus, "the Redeemer" (see Luke 1:68, 2:38, 21:28, 24:21).

Jesus as Savior

Luke understands Jesus to be the universal savior of humankind. Even before Jesus is born, Luke's readers know that through him God is now going to save his people (Luke 1:69, 71, 77). Jesus' salvation is universal, "and all flesh shall see the salvation of God" (Luke 3:6) and belief in Jesus' name realizes this salvation and the forgiveness of sins. Jesus can forgive sins, and some of his miracles and his welcoming of sinners and tax collectors pertain to this theme.

For Luke, Jesus is especially savior of the disadvantaged—he naturally recognizes their need—and very likely the universality of salvation relates strongly to this theme. Jesus cures the sick and frees those oppressed by evil spirits. He associates with and forgives sinners. Women are his companions and benefit from his saving activity (Luke 8:14); moreover, the Lucan parallels between men and women suggest an appropriate equality. Jesus the Savior saves all regardless of gender. Jesus promises persecuted Christians that he will be with them and he is with them. In short, all the disadvantaged receive favorable treatment from Jesus, who is their savior.

Jesus as Servant of God

Jesus as the servant of God does form part of Luke's understanding of Jesus, but Luke does not limit himself to the four servant hymns which we now recognize in the Book of Isaiah. Actually, many of the direct or indirect references to Jesus as this figure are unique to Luke (e.g., 2:29–32; 4:18–19; 7:21; 9:51; 20:20; 22:19, 37, 48; 23:9, 35; 24:7, 20; cf. Acts 3:13–14, 26; 4:27, 30; 8:32–33; 13:47; 25:23). Servant terminology can summarize Jesus' mission, and Jesus is God's chosen one. As the servant, Jesus sets his face firmly for the task (9:52; cf. Isaiah 50:7) and is probably the stronger warrior who takes away the armor of his opponents (Luke 11:21–22; cf. Isaiah 49:24–25, 53:12). The servant tradition particularly enabled Luke to explain Jesus' suffering and passion and to underline his innocence. Jesus' silence

79

during his passion also becomes understandable. Moreover, the theme of the servant allows Luke to picture salvation as "light" and to justify Jesus' mission to the Gentiles. Finally, the image of servant also relates to the risen Jesus (cf. Acts 3:13, 26; 4:30; 8:33).

Jesus as the Christ

As opposed to the other evangelists, Luke shows a preference for the title *"the* Christ" or *"the* Messiah." The title means "the anointed one" and must be studied in association with Jesus' being "king" and related concepts. (The ancients believed that just as olive oil penetrated into the skin of the one being anointed, so did God's spirit.) Twice, "the Christ" is the equivalent of "Son of God" (Luke 4:41; cf. Acts 9:19b–22), which we will see can convey much more. Luke underlines that Jesus, as "the Christ," is the descendent of David who fulfills the prophecy of Nathan (2 Samuel 7:11–17) and must suffer (be rejected) but brings salvation. As "the Christ," Jesus is surely superior to John the Baptist and associated with Christian baptism and the Holy Spirit (also with fire and judgment). Most likely, through his use of "anointed," which comes from the same Greek stem as "Christ," Luke (4:18) presents Jesus as the Messiah. However, his mission will also be prophetic. Jesus the Christ will work miracles and have a universal mission; he will be rejected, yet will be raised from the dead. During the crucifixion, Luke by means of irony stresses that Jesus is the Christ, "the King of the Jews" who saves. At the end of the gospel, the apostles are instructed that in Christ's name, repentance for the forgiveness of sins is to be proclaimed to everyone.

Jesus, as "the Christ," is greater than David. Jesus is a king of both heavenly and earthly peace whose coming results in praise of God and joy; yet his is a kingdom of service. For Luke, the eucharistic meal is an anticipation of the heavenly messianic banquet. Jesus' presence and actions relate to the kingdom, as does following him. Jesus and the things about him can be interchanged with "the kingdom of God." Whoever refuses his inevitable kingship acts foolishly.

Jesus as Son of Man

Luke surely seems aware that this title partially depends on Daniel 7:13–14 (cf. Luke 21:37, 22:69; Psalm 109:1), which explains its heavenly nuance. "Son of Man" can be Jesus' identification of himself and reveal his human limitations. Jesus behaved like any other human being, but did not have anywhere to lay his head. However, Jesus as the Son of Man will be rejected and handed over, suffer and be crucified.

On the other hand, the Son of Man has power; for instance, he forgives sins and is Lord of the Sabbath. Jesus as Son of Man "came to seek out and to save the lost" (Luke 19:10) and is a heavenly being who sits or stands at God's right hand and so has an intimate relationship with God. On the Day of the Lord, he will come again in power and glory, and there will be fear and foreboding and the judgment. Although not predictable, the actual day will be obvious to everyone. However, the faithful believers who have confessed the Son of Man will find in him a defender.

Jesus as Son of God

For Luke, the title "Son of God" is more exalted than most other titles and on the same level as "Lord"; but at least twice "Son of God" is the equivalent of "the Christ." Luke sees Jesus as Son of God primarily in terms of his mission. Surely, the child Jesus knows that he has to be in his Father's house or about his Father's business; and Jesus as Son of God is twice tempted to change the nature of his mission. However, Luke's clear elimination of any earthly father through Mary's virginity reveals the radical relationship he sees between God and Jesus. There are, at least, three passages (Luke 1:34–35, 9:35 [cf. vv. 18–20], 22:66–71) in which "Son of God" looks to Jesus' divinity. In each of these passages, Jesus is first called Christ; this designation is followed by a clarification or a number of verses and then Jesus is identified as Son of God, at apparently a more exalted level and in a context where a reference to his divinity is quite reasonable.

Jesus as Lord

The title "Lord" (*kyrios* in Greek) originally referred to God in the Greek (Septuagint) translation of the Old Testament, and Luke applies it to Jesus as a postresurrection title. The title can imply divinity. It can also be a respectful form of address to an important or higher ranking individual who exercises authority or power (*kyrios* can mean "sir"). However, in any passage in the Gospel of Luke where the risen Jesus is addressed as "Lord," the title carries the nuance of divinity (see Luke 12:35–48, 13:25, 14:15–24, 19:11–27, 24:3).

Jesus as a Person of Prayer

In the gospel of Luke, Jesus prays more often than he does in any other gospel. He prays at every major transition in his life. There are seven references to Jesus praying in Luke. He prays at his baptism (3:21), when he retreats into the wilderness (5:16), when he chooses the apostles (6:12), as he starts his ministry in Gentile territory (9:18), at his transfiguration (9:28), when he teaches the disciples how to pray the "Our Father" (11:1), and during the agony in the garden (22:40–46). Prayer, and Jesus as a man of prayer, is a central theme in the Gospel of Luke. As these passages make clear, Jesus is described as being at prayer mostly during times of decision and important transitions in his life. The reader of Luke's gospel is challenged to live life as Jesus lived, praying at the crucial points in his or her life.

The gentle, forgiving, compassionate Jesus who emerges from the pages of Luke is given greater emphasis by Luke's own writing style. Repelled by violence, strong language, and raw emotion, Luke often softens these when he uses Mark as source material. Toning down Mark's blunter media style gives Luke's gospel an aura of kindness and peace even amid tumultuous events, such as Jesus' crucifixion and death, where he forgives his persecutors and commends his spirit back to God.

John's Noble, Majestic, Divine Jesus

The first three gospels dealing with Jesus' life and teaching have a certain commonality resulting in their being termed the "synoptic gospels," meaning "seen together" but the gospel of John is like entering a whole new world. Gone is Mark's hurried, tired, and probably sweaty Jesus, hemmed in by crowds. In his place, John sets a Jesus of great nobility, who deals with individuals instead of crowds: Nicodemus (John 3:1–21), the Samaritan women (John 4:4–42), the man born blind (John 9:1–41), and Lazarus (John 11:1–44).

John's Jesus inspires awe from the opening verse of chapter 1. Not for John are stories of mangers and shepherds, stars and magi. John wants his audience to see Jesus' origins as divine, coexistent with the Father: "In the beginning [reminiscent of the opening of Genesis] was the Word [Jesus], and the Word was with God, and the Word was God" (John 1:1). From this point on, John makes it clear that he is speaking of someone whose humanity is undeniable, but who possesses another great nature: divinity. The oneness of Jesus and his Father is a theme returned to again and again by John. Jesus says at one point to the Pharisees, "You know neither me nor my Father. If you knew me, you would know my Father also" (John 8:19). And to Philip at the Last Supper, Jesus says, "Whoever has seen me has seen the Father" (John 14:9).

Interestingly, a series of titles are applied to Jesus in John, chapter 1, especially in verses 29–51: "Lamb of God," "Messiah," "Anointed," "King of Israel," "Son of God," "Son of Man." Examined individually, these titles provide an insightful view of John's Jesus.

The Lamb of God

Twice John the Baptist heralds Jesus as "the Lamb of God" (John 1:29, 35). The exact phrase "Lamb of God" is not found anywhere else in Scripture, but the figure of the lamb is rich in symbolism in Judeo-Christian thought.

In the Old Testament, the sacrifice of a lamb provided atonement for sin. Further, the Passover lamb, though not a sacrifice for sin, symbolized deliverance from evil. In the Gospel of John, Jesus died on the afternoon before the feast of Passover, as the Passover lambs were being slain in the Temple—thus presenting Jesus as the lamb of the Passover sacrifice. Still yet another relevant image is the lamb to which the suffering servant of the Lord is likened (Isaiah 53:7). Finally, in certain Jewish circles, the Messiah was described as a powerful horned lamb, or ram, who would bring about the judgment of the wicked and the salvation of the righteous in a decisive way to end the present age and begin the new age. Thus, in John, chapter 1, several concepts of the lamb are combined into a picture of Jesus, the Messiah, who brings judgment and deliverance by offering himself to remove our sin.

Messiah, the Anointed, the King of Israel

Other designations of Jesus in John, chapter 1, are "Messiah" (John 1:41), "Anointed" (John 1:41), "him about whom Moses in the law and also the prophets wrote" (John 1:45), and "King of Israel" (John 1:49). These should all be regarded as messianic claims. They each refer to the same figure, but in varied ways, according to different Jewish messianic expectations. There is an emphasis on God's choice of Jesus, the fulfillment of Old Testament promises, and royal rule; but the reader of the gospel is not allowed to linger with any one of these ideas, as if they were the only one applied to Jesus.

THE JEWISH MESSIAH

The term *messiah* comes from a Hebrew word that means "anointed one," the exact equivalent of the Greek word *Christos* (thus *Messiah* and *Christ* mean the same thing). In the Old Testament, the term is applied to the Jewish king who was anointed with oil at his inauguration ceremony as a symbolic expression of God's favor; he was called "the Lord's anointed" (see 1 Samuel 10:1, Psalm 2:2). The idea for the ancients was that just as the oil penetrated the skin of the one being anointed, so did God.

The term *messiah* came to refer to a future deliverer of Israel only after the Babylonians overthrew the nation of Judah in 587 B.C.E. and removed the Jewish king from the throne. From that time on, there was no anointed one (Messiah) to rule for several centuries. But some Jews recalled a tradition in which God had told David, his favorite king, that he would always have a descendant on the throne (2 Samuel 7:14–16). This is probably the origin of the idea that there would be a future messiah to fulfill God's promises, a future king like David who would rule the people of God once again as a sovereign nation in the Promised Land.

By the time of the New Testament, different Jews had different under-standings of what this future ruler would be like. Some expected a warrior-king, like David; others, a more supernatural cosmic judge of the earth; still others (such as the community that produced the Dead Sea Scrolls), a priestly ruler who would provide the authoritative interpretations of God's Law for his people. (All of these figures are designated "messiah" in the ancient Jewish sources.)

In no source prior to the writing of the New Testament, however, is there any reference to a future messiah who is to suffer and die for the sins of the people. The notion appears to be a Christian creation. It may represent a combination of the belief in a future messianic deliverer with the notion that the one who is truly righteous suffers, a notion expressed in such biblical passages as Psalm 22 and 69, and Isaiah 53.

Son of God

When both John the Baptist and Nathanael (John 1:49) call Jesus "Son of God," we have the paramount designation for Jesus in John's gospel. Many statements throughout the New Testament indicate that the sonship of Jesus is unique, and so the fourth gospel is not innovative in this respect. However, John's claim that Jesus is the "only" (*monogenes*) Son of God is conspicuously explicit. The term is used of Jesus by John alone (John 1:14, 18; 3:16; 1 John 4:9), and literally means "of a single kind." No one but Jesus is God's Son in the sense that he is. This may explain why John does not say that we can become "sons of God." Instead, we become "children of God" (John 1:12 and 11:52).

Son of Man

In the final scene of John, chapter 1, Jesus responds to Nathanael's confession of him as Son of God and King of Israel: ". . . you will see heaven opened and the angels of God ascending and descending upon the Son of Man" (John 1:51). This statement serves as a conclu-sion to the list of messianic titles. Significantly, this is the one term

Jesus himself uses. John 1:51 demonstrates that of all the messianic titles offered for Jesus, "Son of Man" least suits him.

This term—"Son of Man"—is first used messianically in Daniel 7:13 and from that point it was developed in a number of directions, although it did not have great significance outside Jewish circles until Jesus adopted it for his own use. In so doing, Jesus accepts the title of Messiah, but his use of "Son of Man" implies something special about how his hearers are to regard his messiahship. Jesus' own preference for the title "Son of Man" may be due to the mystery of the term itself (John 12:34). The messianic title "Son of Man" allowed Jesus to reeducate his hearers about the Messiah.

After the introduction of the "Son of Man" in John 1:51, later chapters expand upon his origin, function, and destination. In addition to isolated references to the "Son of Man" (John 5:27; 6:62; 8:28; 12:23, 34; 13:31), the gospel of John presents extended discourses on Jesus as the "Son of Man" in 3:12–36 and 6:25–59. Jesus makes the explicit claim that he is the "Son of Man" (John 9:35–38) and he is unique (3:13–31).

In the Gospel of John, the picture of Jesus as the "Son of Man" develops: Jesus the unique Son of Man is sent down from heaven to save and to judge. Once his earthly work of deliverance is accomplished, God will exalt him by means of the cross. In this act he returns to the Father, leading the way for those who believe.

This majestic Jesus portrayed by John is totally in control of the situation at all times, even his own death: ". . . I lay down my life in order to take it up again. No one takes it from me, but I lay it down of my own accord. I have power to lay it down, and I have power to take it up again" (John 10:17–18). Aware of the thoughts and plans of others, the stately Jesus neatly sidesteps or challenges them: "When Jesus realized that they were about to come and take him by force to make him king, he withdrew again to the mountain by himself" (John 6:15); "Then Jesus, knowing all that was to happen to him, came forward and asked them, 'Whom are you looking for?' They answered, 'Jesus of Nazareth.'

Jesus replied, 'I am he.' . . . they stepped back and fell to the ground" (John 18:4–6).

In formulating his answer with these two terse but powerful words, Jesus again proclaims his divinity. The "I am" passages sprinkled throughout John's gospel are intended to remind the reader of Moses' encounter with God at the burning bush centuries before. When Moses asked who God was, the answer came from the bush, "I AM WHO I AM" (Exodus 3:14). As was mentioned earlier, there are seven "I am" statements that are spoken by Jesus in the gospel of John (John 5:35, 51; 8:12; 9:5; 10:7, 9, 11, 14; 11:25; 14:6; 15:1, 5).

At his trial in John's gospel, Jesus displays his dignity yet again. Bewildered because Jesus refuses to answer his questions, Pilate says, " 'Do you not know that I have power to release you, and power to crucify you?' Jesus answered, 'You would have no power over me unless it had been given you from above' " (John 19:10–11). Sublime to the end, Jesus' final words from the cross as recorded by John are simply, "It is finished" (John 19:30).

Which gospel portrait of Jesus do we choose? Can all of these be representative of the same Jesus? They can and they are. Jesus, the God-man, is more than any one person can adequately describe. That each evangelist chose to bring certain of Jesus' attributes to the fore is totally understandable. Each was aware of those facets of Jesus' personality, teachings, and deeds that would draw his community into deeper faith in the Christ, the Messiah, the Son of God. And so the gospel accounts form a prism, a clear medium through which the pure light of Christ can be refracted in diverse and beautiful ways.

For Discussion

1. How do you respond to Jesus' question: "Who do people say that I am?"
2. Has your discovery of Jesus as a Jew steeped in his Jewish religious tradition altered your understanding of Jesus? Explain.

3. Why is it impossible to capture in any one title who Jesus was?

4. Of the four portraits of Jesus found in the gospels, which one is your favorite? Why?

5. Are you more comfortable with some of the titles applied to Jesus in the gospels than with others? Why?

For Further Reading

Chilton, Bruce. *Rabbi Jesus.* New York: Doubleday, 2000.

Harrington, Daniel. *Who Is Jesus: Why Is He Important?* Franklin, Wisc.: Sheed & Ward, 1999.

Meier, John P. *A Marginal Jew: Rethinking the Historical Jesus.* New York: Doubleday, 1991.

Vermes, Geza. *Jesus the Jew.* Philadelphia: Fortress Press, 1986.

Wright, N.T. *Jesus and the Victory of God.* Minneapolis: Fortress Press, 1996.

Zannoni, Arthur E. *Jesus of the Gospels: Teacher, Storyteller, Friend, Messiah.* Cincinnati, Ohio: St. Anthony Messenger Press, 1996.

4

HE BEGAN TO TEACH THEM MANY THINGS IN PARABLES

(MARK 4:2)

All OF US ENJOY HEARING AND READING GOOD STORIES, for they both capture our imagination and cause us to reflect on life. Jesus' disciples and the crowds that followed him also enjoyed stories. Jesus himself was a master storyteller. He was God's storyteller, who could capture his audience by spinning his yarn and simultaneously cause them to reflect on God's activity in their life. The stories Jesus told and left behind are parables. They are found in three of the four gospels—Matthew, Mark, and Luke.

Parables

The English word *parable* has its origin in two Greek words: *para*, meaning "beside," and *ballo*, meaning "to throw." In its root and origin, the word means something that is "thrown beside." Parables are stories with meanings ("things") thrown beside them. Another way of saying this is to say that parables are stories with a meaning that runs alongside them.

When Jesus taught in parables, he illustrated ideas about the kingdom of God by examples ("thrown beside"), drawn from the everyday experiences of his hearers. "The kingdom of God is like . . ." a woman who mixed yeast into dough, a fig tree, a pearl, a treasure buried in a field, a sower sowing seed, a mustard seed.

Parables are the recounting of a common incident of daily life in concise, figurative form to illustrate a spiritual truth. Put another way, a parable is simply a story with a religious meaning drawn from ordinary life, or a story with a moral. For example, when Jesus wanted to teach about the forgiveness of God, he told the story of the prodigal son. When he wanted to teach about who is our neighbor, he told the parable of the good Samaritan.

Parables almost by definition are puzzling. They are figurative speech, symbolic language, with more than one level of meaning. The word *parable* has a wide range of meanings. It can refer to a proverb, such as "Doctor, cure yourself!" (Luke 4:23), or a wisdom saying or riddle, such as "It is not what goes into the mouth that defiles a person, but it is what comes out of the mouth that defiles" (Matthew 15:11). A parable can also be a similitude, that is, a slightly developed comparison, such as, the parable (lesson) of the fig tree (Matthew 24:32–35).

Commentators on the gospels quite often divide the parables of Jesus into three somewhat distinct categories: similitude, parable, and exemplary story. Similitudes are very concise narratives that make a comparison between an aspect of God's realm and a typical event in life, for example, seed growing in the ground (Mark 4:26–29) or yeast in bread dough (Matthew 13:33).

Parables are usually longer and more detailed. They tell a story about a one-time fictitious but true-to-life event such as that of a farmer whose enemies sow weeds in his wheat field (Matthew 13:4–30) or a king who forgives a servant when settling accounts (Matthew 18:21–35).

An exemplary story (e.g., the good Samaritan in Luke 10:29–37; the good shepherd in Luke 15; and the woman who searches the house for a lost coin, also in Luke 15) presents a specific example that illustrates the general principle.

Regardless of what form a parable takes, it is not an entertaining story that confirms the status quo. Nor are parables humorous stories designed to have the listener laugh, like a joke. Rather, parables have as their purpose to persuade the hearer to adopt the particular view of God and of life in God's world. Their aim is to convert the hearer, to prick away at his or her conscience, to cause one to pause and reflect. Parables turn the world upside down by challenging presumptions, reversing expectations, and proposing a different view of God and of life with God. The fact that parables often have open endings makes it necessary for the hearers of every age to grapple with their implications. In other words, parables are not first-century period pieces that are to be treated as antiques but, rather, stories that impinge on current events and the living of life.

Parables in the Gospels

The three synoptic gospels (Matthew, Mark, and Luke) all contain parables. Luke has the largest number, followed by Matthew, and then Mark. Biblical scholars do not universally agree on the number of parables found in these three gospels. What they do agree on is that we have the texts of the parables and these are what we will have to wrestle with as we approach the gospels. In other words, we can't get back to the raw experience behind the parable, when it was told by Jesus. We can, however, go to the biblical text which narrates the parable.

Reading a parable requires a certain amount of work. Here are some suggestions that may help. Obtain a good, critical copy of the

Bible. Read the parable out loud, preferably twice. Check to see if there is a parallel to this parable. If there is, read it. Then ask the following: To whom is Jesus speaking? What is the topic or central point of the parable? With which person or event in the story does the reader identify? What lesson is drawn from this comparison? How is the reader being asked to change as a result of hearing or reading the parable?

When we encounter parables in the gospels, we are looking at narratives. They are short stories or, more precisely, teaching stories. Stylistically, as pieces of literature, the parables are characterized as follows: There is a narrator or storyteller—in this case, Jesus. The narration is concise; only necessary people appear and much information is communicated by suggestion. Groups of people tend to be treated as single characters. Usually only two characters interact at the same time. And, finally, the listener is asked to focus on only one perspective or character at a time.

You will also note that in the gospel parables there is little description in terms of attributes, feelings, or emotions of the characters involved. What people do indicates their character. Another way of saying this is that motivations are rarely given.

All parables need to be read within their context. Jesus' parables existed first in the social context of his ministry and the religious context of his mission and proclamation. But a parable also exists in a literary context—it appears in a certain section of a particular gospel. In a sense, the original context of the parables is irretrievable, since we can never be in the historical position of Jesus' audience. Thus, the original context is always a reconstruction, and this reconstruction requires a whole series of judgments about the life and ministry of Jesus on the part of the interpreter.

Parables That Cause Us to Reflect on Ourselves

In the gospels, the parables are mirrors that we place in front of our face. They often cause us to reflect on our own behavior. A good example of this is the parable of the good Samaritan (Luke 10:25–37), in which Jesus takes the experience of a fellow human being in need and shows that help knows no boundaries.

The Parable of the Good Samaritan

²⁵Just then a lawyer stood up to test Jesus. "Teacher," he said, "what must I do to inherit eternal life?" ²⁶He said to him, "What is written in the law? What do you read there?" ²⁷He answered, "You shall love the Lord your God with all your heart, and with all your soul, and with all your strength, and with all your mind; and your neighbor as yourself." ²⁸And he said to him, "You have given the right answer; do this, and you will live."

²⁹But wanting to justify himself, he asked Jesus, "And who is my neighbor?" ³⁰Jesus replied, "A man was going down from Jerusalem to Jericho, and fell into the hands of robbers, who stripped him, beat him, and went away, leaving him half dead. ³¹Now by chance a priest was going down that road; and when he saw him, he passed by on the other side. ³²So likewise a Levite, when he came to the place and saw him, passed by on the other side. ³³But a Samaritan while traveling came near him; and when he saw him, he was moved with pity. ³⁴He went to him and bandaged his wounds, having poured oil and wine on them. Then he put him on his own animal, brought him to an inn, and took care of him. ³⁵The next day he took out two denarii, gave them to the innkeeper, and said, 'Take care of him: and when I come back, I will repay you whatever more you spend.' ³⁶Which of these three, do you think, was a neighbor to the man who fell into the hands of the robbers?" ³⁷He said, "The one who showed him mercy." Jesus said to him, "Go and do likewise" (Luke 10:25–37).

The parable of the good Samaritan is preceded by a lawyer's question. The lawyer here is understood to be not a lawyer in the modern, secular understanding but, rather, a lawyer of the Jewish law, one who had great knowledge about the Law of Moses—the Torah. What we have here is a question from an expert in the Law of

Moses. The question is hostile, designed to "test" Jesus (Luke 10:25). It seeks to put him in some way over against the law, to draw out from him a teaching suggesting that one can "inherit eternal life" while bypassing the law.

Jesus will not have this for a moment. As so often, he throws the question back on the questioner (verse 26) and draws from him a perfectly satisfactory answer in terms of the law (verse 27). The lawyer cites as a single commandment the injunction to "love the LORD your God with all your heart, and with all your soul, and with all your might" from Deuteronomy 6:5, and the command to "love your neighbor as yourself" from Leviticus 19:18. "Do this," says Jesus, "and you will live" (verse 28b). In other words, the law itself, understood holistically with the separate commandments to love God and love one's neighbor brought into unity and mutual interaction, provides the path of life. Jesus is not outside or bypassing the law. In addition, the lawyer has answered correctly.

But the expert in the law—the lawyer—is not satisfied. He suspects—rightly, as it turns out—that Jesus may be pushing the term *neighbor* further than the conventional understanding, where it was restricted basically to fellow Israelites/Jews. So he presses his case. "Who is my neighbor?" (verse 29).

The lawyer's persistence prompts Jesus to tell one of his most famous parables. It is traditionally known as the parable of the "good Samaritan," a title that immediately blunts its impact for the reader. Centuries of holding together the adjective *good* and the noun *Samaritan* have dulled us to the explosive tension of the phrase in the world of Jesus. The hostility between Jews and Samaritans at the time makes the phrase an oxymoron—as phrases like "good terrorist" or "good drug dealer" would be for us. A better title for the parable is that of the "compassionate Samaritan."

As masterfully told by Jesus, the parable draws the hearer into the perspective of the wounded, half-dead traveler. The passing parade of three persons sets up a pattern that cumulatively builds up expectation. A certain class of persons on a journey arrives at that place, sees the wounded traveler, and responds. In the first two cases, that of the priest and the Levite, the response is "to see" and then "pass by on the other side." This is to avoid defilement by contact with the dead—or soon to be dead—which would prevent them, according to the law, from carrying out their religious duties. Who does the audience expect the third passerby to be? Probably a Jewish layperson, one who is righteous before the law—someone who will do the right thing, pick up the dirty work from which the law exempts the other two. So the audience is probably expecting something of an "anticlerical" ending at the expense of the religious functionaries (priest and Levite).

That the third person arriving on the scene should be a Samaritan creates a shudder in the hearers. Surely this alien will also "see" and "pass by on the other side"! Instead, when he "sees" he is "moved with pity." The Greek word used here for *compassion* communicates the sense of a great wave breaking over one. The same word describes Jesus' reaction to the plight of the widow of Nain who has lost her son (see Luke 7:13). The Samaritan sets about fulfilling in a most extravagant way the duties of mercy and hospitality that the other two had ignored (Luke 10:33–34). Moreover, he provides not only "first aid" but an ongoing structure of rehabilitation, drawing generously on his own funds (verse 35). The Lucan narrator has peppered this section of the parable with verbs describing the behavior of the Samaritan; they include seeing, going, bandaging, pouring, taking care.

The story compels its audience to identify with the experience of the unnamed and wounded traveler. What did the traveler feel when this "enemy," instead of robbing him further and finishing him off, approached with rescue and aid? The Samaritan's action forces the wounded traveler—and the audience—to reevaluate their prejudices. If the law—or a particular understanding of it—prevented the priest and the Levite from rescuing human life in this way, then there is something flawed about this understanding. It cuts against the heart of the law as found in the single commandment binding together love of God and love of neighbor. In the parable, Jesus has not overthrown or bypassed the law. He has simply shown that to fulfill the law's true intent the notion of "neighbor" has to be drastically revised and expanded.

In Luke's textual setting (verses 36–37), when the parable proper is over, Jesus takes the offensive, as it were, and makes the lawyer draw the application (verse 36). But in so doing he changes the terms of reference. The lawyer had asked, "Who is my neighbor?" (verse 29). Jesus asks, "Which of these three . . . was a neighbor to the man who fell into the hands of the robbers?" (verse 36). At the end of the parable it is not a question of where and how far I should draw the limits of the notion "neighbor" to see how far my obligations of "love" extends. It is a question of imitating the hospitality shown by the despised alien who broke through the barriers of ethnic and religious prejudice to minister to a fellow human being in need. The point, we learn, is not who deserves to be cared for, but rather the demand to become a person who treats everyone encountered—however frightening, alien, naked, or defenseless—with compassion. The concept of "neighbor" shifts from being a tag that I may or may not apply to another, to being a quality or vocation that I take upon myself and actively live out.

This is the way to inherit eternal life. The God whom one is attempting to love with all one's heart is the God who reaches out to the world in compassion in the same way as the good Samaritan. In the ministry of Jesus, which the church has to continue, God offers extravagant, life-giving hospitality to wounded and half-dead humanity. The way to eternal life is to allow oneself to become an active instrument and channel of this same boundary-breaking hospitality.

Thus, this parable causes every hearer and reader in every generation to reflect on themselves and their own behavior toward other human beings and toward God.

Parables About Praying

Another group of parables that cause us to reflect on ourselves are those found in the Gospel of Luke that deal with persistence in prayer. They are the parable of the friend at midnight (Luke 11:5–8), the parable of the persistent widow (Luke 18:1–8), and the parable of the

Pharisee and the tax collector/publican (Luke 18:9–14). All three are masterfully told by Jesus and are profoundly challenging to anyone who encounters them. They provide models for individuals seeking to pray to God and deep meditations on prayer in the form of a story.

In the Gospel of Luke, after Jesus teaches the "Our Father" prayer to his disciples (see Luke 11:1–4), Jesus tells the first of the three parables on prayer, the friend at midnight.

> *⁵And he said to them, "Suppose one of you has a friend, and you go to him at midnight and say to him, 'Friend, lend me three loaves of bread; ⁶for a friend of mine has arrived, and I have nothing to set before him.' ⁷And he answers from within, 'Do not bother me; the door has already been locked, and my children are with me in bed; I cannot get up and give you anything.' ⁸I tell you, even though he will not get up and give him anything because he is his friend, at least because of his persistence he will get up and give him whatever he needs* (Luke 11:5–8).

The parable leaps right out of village life in Palestine in a wonderfully fresh way. To grasp its meaning, we have to appreciate that no less than three "friends" are involved. There is a central figure, whom Jesus addresses directly. This person then has friends in two "directions" as it were, a friend who is a fellow villager and a friend who suddenly turns up as a guest. The arrival of the friend from somewhere else causes a crisis in hospitality: the main character has nothing to set before the friend. So, though it is midnight, "you" go to your fellow villager friend, seeking three loaves of bread. The logic of the parable depends heavily on the sense of "shame" so powerful in such Mediterranean cultures. In effect, the story puts the suggestion to the audience: Is it really conceivable that a man would respond in the way described, "unwilling to get up and help because the door has been locked and children are in bed"? Is it not certain that even if he won't get up for friendship's sake he certainly will to avoid shame, the shame he would inevitably feel before the entire village the next day because he caused it to fail in hospitality.

As seen upon occasion in Jesus' parables in the gospel of Luke (see 16:1–8, 18:1–8), the chief character is something of a rogue, someone forced to do the right thing against personal inclination or interest. The purpose is to make the logic of the story work even better. If this rogue will most certainly act and provide what is required, how much more certainly will the God of all goodness move to hear the petitions of those who approach in prayer? So the parable becomes an instruction on the need to persevere in prayer.

Further, why can one be certain that if one searches, one will find; if one asks, one will receive; if one knocks, the door will be opened (Luke 11:10)? Because it is inconceivable that as human parents you would give your children a snake when they ask for a fish or a scorpion when they ask for an egg. If, on the contrary, "evil" as you are (that is, as human beings in comparison with the all-good God), you know how to give good and not evil things to your children, how *much more* will the God of infinite goodness give good things.

The genius of the parable and of the sequence that draws from it is that it engages in intense human feelings and draws these directly into an attitude toward God. Jesus does not tell his hearers about God but he makes them feel something very deeply. We might imagine Jesus saying: "That . . . multiplied a thousand and more times over is how God feels about you! It is in the light of this knowledge that you should come before God and be persistent in prayer."

The Parable of the Persistent Widow

¹Then Jesus told them a parable about their need to pray always and not to lose heart. ²He said, "In a certain city there was a judge who neither feared God nor had respect for people. ³In that city there was a widow who kept coming to him and saying, 'Grant me justice against my opponent.' ⁴For a while he refused; but later he said to himself, 'Though I have no fear of God and no respect for anyone, ⁵yet because this widow keeps bothering me, I will grant her justice, so that she may not wear me out by continually coming.' " ⁶And the Lord said, "Listen to what the unjust judge says. ⁷And will not God grant justice to his chosen ones who cry to

*him day and night? Will he delay long in helping them? ⁸I tell you,
he will quickly grant justice to them. And yet, when the Son of Man
comes, will he find faith on earth?"* (Luke 18:1–8).

This parable addresses that all too real temptation to give up
hope and lose heart in the midst of the evils of the time. It commends
praying to God with the kind of persistence displayed by the widow in
her dealings with the judge. The matters are not quite so simple.

The parable hardly means to suggest that God needs to be worn
down like the judge. Basically, it commends an attitude of trust in
God that will motivate such persistence. At the center of the action
(see 16:1–8) stands an unsavory character: a judge who fears neither
God nor fellow human beings, and so takes no action in defense of a
widow who had appealed to him. Lacking the support of a husband
and possibly adult sons (see 7:11–17), widows were particularly
dependent on the smooth and fair workings of the institutions of
justice—hence the plight of this woman, whose entreaties the judge so
long ignores. He stirs himself on her behalf only when he suspects
that her verbal entreaties are about to give way to actual violence.

The English translation of verse 5 does not often convey what is
said literally in Greek. The Greek reads, "Lest she come and give me
a black eye." The expression comes from the boxing arena. In a very
literal sense, the judge feared that she would batter him. He moves,
against his own previous inclination, because he realizes that a stage
has been reached where to take no action may incur serious violence
and loss.

The story is almost comical by modern standards. One could
possibly say that the widow threw a few punches to get action in her
case. The point of the parable, brought out by comments in verses
6–7, rests, once again, on a type of logic. If the unjust judge at long
last—due to base and self-interested motives—moves to grant justice
to the widow, how much more certainly and readily will the God of
all goodness move to grant justice to the chosen ones who make
entreaty to him day and night?

It is understandable that the final comment, "will he find faith on earth?" (verse 8b), has to do with faith. Faith in God, displayed in prayer that is both trusting and calm, as well as constant and persistent, is the right attitude for the time before the full realization of the kingdom. The parable also offers a sharp challenge in a world where so much injustice prevails and where the poor, like the widow, continue to cry out for justice day and night. Those whose actions or inertia allow the world to remain for the majority an unjust and inhospitable place must reckon with the truth that God is a God of justice. How long can such a God allow the situation to go on without redress?

The Parable of the Pharisee and the Tax Collector (Publican)

⁹He also told this parable to some who trusted in themselves that they were righteous and regarded others with contempt: ¹⁰"Two men went up to the temple to pray, one a Pharisee and the other a tax collector. ¹¹The Pharisee, standing by himself, was praying thus, 'God, I thank you that I am not like other people: thieves, rogues, adulterers, or even like this tax collector. ¹²I fast twice a week; I give a tenth of all my income.' ¹³But the tax collector, standing far off, would not even look up to heaven, but was beating his breast and saying, 'God, be merciful to me, a sinner!' ¹⁴I tell you, this man went down to his home justified rather than the other; for all who exalt themselves will be humbled, but all who humble themselves will be exalted" (Luke 18:9–14).

This parable continues the theme of prayer but is addressed not to the disciples in general but to those who "trusted in themselves that they were righteous and regarded others with contempt" (verse 9). "Righteousness" is Bible babble with little meaning for people today. Basically, it denotes living in accordance with the requirements of the covenant. "Being justified" is the verdict of acceptance one has or hopes to have in the eyes of God on the basis of such "righteous" behavior. In a strongly religious society, the issue as to who is righteous and who is not will always be central. In the milieu of Jesus, the gospels particularly associate such concern with the Pharisees—though we must be careful not to conclude that the kind of judgment behavior represented by the Pharisee in this parable was typical of all Pharisees in general, let alone of Judaism as a religion. It affects all religions, Christianity included.

The Pharisee prays, it is true. But, whereas in prayer the focus should be above all on God, this man's concentration is upon himself and—worse still—upon the failings of his fellow human beings (verses 11–12). Before beginning to enumerate his positive virtues—in themselves quite admirable (fasting, giving up a tenth of one's income)—he moves to detach himself from the sinful mass of humankind ("thieves, rogues, adulterers"), of which our representative is so conveniently at hand in the person of the tax collector at the back of the Temple.

The Pharisee illustrates the attitude of those who can only bolster their own self-image by putting down other people. Life is a competition in virtue, and God assesses and bestows prizes on the winners. Prayer has as its purpose keeping God informed about how successfully one is doing and also about the shortcoming of others.

In contrast, the tax collector stands at the very back, scarcely lifting his eyes to heaven, praying simply that God be merciful to him, a sinner (verse 13). In what sense does he own himself as a sinner? Is it because of personal moral failure for which he now repents? We should not immediately jump to this conclusion. Could it simply be that he finds himself trapped in an occupation that makes him a sinner in his own eyes and those of his world—an occupation that, with a family to support and no other possibilities of employment, he cannot simply abandon? All this the parable leaves open. In any case, as Jesus points out, God's view reverses both verdicts. The one who came to God's house in his own eyes a sinner went home with God's favor ("justified"); the one so sure of his virtue went home without it.

The parable admirably illustrates Luke's theme of reversal. God will one day move to align the human situation with the nature of

God as God truly is—not as persons like the Pharisee perceive God to be. That reversal will take place in the full realization of the kingdom. The task of Jesus is to summon human beings to align themselves with this new perspective so that when the reversal comes they will be in the right position to benefit from it. The parable, then, offers more than a simple instruction on prayer. It belongs to part of the preaching of the kingdom.

Prayer, as the Pharisee failed to see, consists not in our telling God how things are, but in allowing God to communicate to us the divine vision of life and reality. Two people came up to God's house to pray. Only one really found the hospitality that was there. As so often in Luke's gospel, we are left with the challenge: Which one are you going to be?

Parables That Provide Images for God

The Bible is filled with a variety of images for God. This is also the case of the gospels. Jesus often provides us with images for God within the parables that he tells. These parables are stories in which a character is a metaphor for God and God's activity in the lives of human beings and in the world.

The Parable of God the Gracious Employer

In the gospel of Matthew there is the parable of God the gracious employer.

> [1]"*For the kingdom of heaven is like a landowner who went out early in the morning to hire laborers for his vineyard.* [2]*After agreeing with the laborers for the usual daily wage, he sent them into his vineyard.* [3]*When he went out about nine o'clock, he saw others standing idle in the marketplace;* [4]*and he said to them, 'You also go into the vineyard, and I will pay you whatever is right.' So they went.* [5]*When he went out again about noon and about three o'clock, he did the same.* [6]*And about five o'clock he went out and found others standing around; and he said to them, 'Why are you standing here idle all day?'* [7]*They said to him, 'Because no one has*

hired us.' He said to them, 'You also go into the vineyard.' [8]*When evening came, the owner of the vineyard said to his manager, 'Call the laborers and give them their pay, beginning with the last and then going to the first.'* [9]*When those hired about five o'clock came, each of them received the usual daily wage.* [10]*Now when the first came, they thought they would receive more; but each of them also received the usual daily wage.* [11]*And when they received it, they grumbled against the landowner,* [12]*saying, 'These last worked only one hour, and you have made them equal to us who have borne the burden of the day and the scorching heat.'* [13]*But he replied to one of them, 'Friend, I am doing you no wrong; did you not agree with me for the usual daily wage?* [14]*Take what belongs to you and go; I choose to give to this last the same as I give to you.* [15]*Am I not allowed to do what I choose with what belongs to me? Or are you envious because I am generous?'* [16]*So the last will be first, and the first will be last"* (Matthew 20:1–16).

In this parable, the employer seeking employees is God. The employees are the faithful who are seeking to respond to God's activity in their life. Gradually, the unusual details of the story shift the parable suddenly to a deeper level of meaning. Instead of sending his manager, the landowner, who represents God, goes himself to the marketplace to hire laborers (verse 8). Throughout the day, he hires workers, even at the eleventh hour (around 5 P.M.). The reason those standing idle were not hired during his earlier recruitment visits is left completely unexplained. The first group of workers is hired with an oral contract for the normal day's wage. Although the first group has a contract and the second group of laborers has only their trust in the master's sense of justice, both groups depend on the landowner's trustworthiness. In the climax, when every worker is paid the same wage, the second group of laborers is ignored in order to focus on the first and last groups.

The final descriptive scene of the parable contains a disturbing element that causes the reader to pause. On the landowner's order, those hired last are the first paid and receive a full day's pay. Those hired first then expect to receive more money (verse 10), but receive only the agreed-upon wage. Matthew's readers share the concern of the workers who worked the longest. They too assume the same standard of justice, equal pay for equal work.

Jesus, the storyteller of God, provides in Matthew another insight. The parable deals with resentment toward others who have received the grace of God we usually affirm only in theory. Those who worked all day begin not by objecting to the grace others received but by expecting to receive more than the others. When they receive their day's pay, the just fulfillment of the contract to which they agreed, they object not to the sum paid them but to the fact that the partial-day workers were made their equals. They cannot stand God's graciousness in doing this. The first receive what they have by justice; the last receive what they have—equality—by God's graciousness.

This graciousness of God the first group finds unbearable, and it is their objection to the landowner's (God's) gracious acceptance of others as equals that alienates them. In view of this, the landowner (God) addresses the complainer from the first group by pointing out that he had paid them what they agreed upon.

The parable seems to teach that God loves the person who is faithful throughout the day as well as the one who is called into relationship with God at the last hour. The parable invites the reader to reflect upon the sovereignty of the good God with whom we cannot bargain. Likewise, the parable points out that no one can presume God's graciousness. Grace is always a gift freely accepted by those who receive it and freely given by God who bestows it. Grace is not a quantity that can be measured by wage but rather a quality that is measured by the activity of God.

Images for God in Luke's Parables

In the fifteenth chapter of the gospel of Luke there are three parables that center around the theme of loss—a lost sheep, a lost coin, and a lost son. In each of them, the shepherd who searches for the sheep, the woman who searches for the lost coin, and the father who welcomes back his lost son are images for God provided by the Lucan author's Jesus in parabolic format. We will look at each of them individually.

The Parable of the Lost Sheep

[3]So he told them this parable: [4]"Which one of you, having a hundred sheep and losing one of them, does not leave the ninety-nine in the wilderness and go after the one that is lost until he finds it? [5]When he has found it, he lays it on his shoulders and rejoices. [6]And when he comes home, he calls together his friends and neighbors, saying to them, 'Rejoice with me, for I have found my sheep that was lost.' [7]Just so, I tell you, there will be more joy in heaven over one sinner who repents than over ninety-nine righteous persons who need no repentance" (Luke 15:3–7).

The parable of the lost sheep begins with a question, "Which one of you . . . ?" It invites hearers to reflect upon what would be their own response. We should note that the response might well be: "None of us!" Or "Not if I were the shepherd!" We have to reckon with the possibility that what is being described is a rather foolish behavior and that this might be precisely where the provocation lies.

So it is in the case of the lost sheep (verses 4–6). Would a responsible, hard-working, first-century shepherd really leave niney-nine sheep defenseless in the wilderness while he goes in search of the one that is lost? Would he not run the risk of losing many more? Would he not place the flock at risk? The gesture of carrying the sheep home on his shoulders, as if in triumph, and summoning his friends and neighbors for a joyful celebration seems extravagant, "over the top." The friends and neighbors might, in fact, join in. But they might also mutter a bit among themselves: "This shepherd must be crazy about that sheep!" And this may, in fact, be the point the parable makes at the end (verse 7).

"Heaven," that is, God and the entire heavenly court, rejoices over one sinner who repents more than over ninety-nine who have no need of repentance. Why? Because God is crazy with love over each individual human being and rejoices exuberantly over finding one that had been lost in the death that is sin. God continually searches for the lost sinner without ceasing. Jesus' celebration of joyful meals with repentant sinners simply enacts on earth the exuberant heavenly joy of God. This is the image for God that Jesus provides in the parable.

The Parable of the Lost Coin

8"Or what woman having ten silver coins, if she loses one of them, does not light a lamp, sweep the house, and search carefully until she finds it? 9When she has found it, she calls together her friends and neighbors, saying, 'Rejoice with me, for I have found the coin that I had lost.' 10Just so, I tell you, there is joy in the presence of the angels of God over one sinner who repents" (Luke 15:8–10).

The parable of the lost coin is found only in the gospel of Luke and is twin to that of the parable of the lost sheep. This time, God is a poor woman searching her house for a lost coin. The house may be a metaphor for the church. The lost coin is a metaphor for the sinner, and sinners do exist in the church as well.

The activity of the woman is that of a domestic. She lights a lamp, searches the house, and sweeps—all activities of God who has lost one of his beloved. When the coin is found, the woman calls her friends in to celebrate. Before the celebration can happen, she spends the whole day turning her house upside down to find the single coin. Are the friends and neighbors summoned to rejoice with her really going to participate all that enthusiastically in her joy? Again, her behavior seems extravagant. They might well remark: "She's a bit obsessive about that coin. Surely it would have turned up one day. Why all this fuss!" But once again, the extravagance is a revelation of God.

The last sentence, verse 10, makes the point: "Heaven" (here "the angels of God") reacts like that to the recovery of a single sinner who had been lost. The challenge of the parable is why not share on earth the joy of the celebration that God is having in heaven over a returned sinner.

Both the parable of the lost sheep and the parable of the lost coin present an image of God as one who searches for human beings, one who wants to be reconciled with human beings, one who forgives human beings for their shortcomings. These images provided by Jesus in these parables would have been countercultural to the dominant images of the day. They would have provided an angle of vision on God not quickly recognized by Jesus' opponents who appear at the beginning of the chapter, namely, the Pharisees.

Like all parables, they have meaning "thrown alongside." They can't be read literally. We all know that sheep and coins do not repent. But we look for the meaning that is thrown alongside, the very meaning of parable, and discover therein both a God of forgiveness and a God who has found the lost sinner. Thus we have a parabolic imaging for God.

The Parable of the Prodigal

[11]Then Jesus said, "There was a man who had two sons. [12]The younger of them said to his father, 'Father, give me the share of the property that will belong to me.' So he divided his property between them. [13]A few days later the younger son gathered all he had and traveled to a distant country, and there he squandered his property in dissolute living. [14]When he had spent everything, a severe famine took place throughout that country, and he began to be in need. [15]So he went and hired himself out to one of the citizens of that country, who sent him to his fields to feed the pigs. [16]He would gladly have filled himself with the pods that the pigs were eating; and no one gave him anything. [17]But when he came to himself he said, 'How many of my father's hired hands have bread enough and to spare, but here I am dying of hunger! [18]I will get up and go to my father, and I will say to him, "Father, I have sinned against heaven and before you; [19]I am no longer worthy to be called your son; treat me like one of your hired hands." ' [20]So he set off and went to his father. But while he was still far off, his father saw him and was filled with compassion; he ran and put his arms around

him and kissed him. *²¹Then the son said to him, 'Father, I have sinned against heaven and before you; I am no longer worthy to be called your son.'* *²²But the father said to his slaves, 'Quickly, bring out a robe—the best one—and put it on him; put a ring on his finger and sandals on his feet.* *²³And get the fatted calf and kill it, and let us eat and celebrate;* *²⁴for this son of mine was dead and is alive again; he was lost and is found!' And they began to celebrate.*

²⁵"Now his elder son was in the field; and when he came and approached the house, he heard music and dancing. *²⁶He called one of the slaves and asked what was going on.* *²⁷He replied, 'Your brother has come, and your father has killed the fatted calf, because he has got him back safe and sound.'* *²⁸Then he became angry and refused to go in. His father came out and began to plead with him.* *²⁹But he answered his father, 'Listen! For all these years I have been working like a slave for you, and I have never disobeyed your command; yet you have never given me even a young goat so that I might celebrate with my friends.* *³⁰But when this son of yours came back, who has devoured your property with prostitutes, you killed the fatted calf for him!'* *³¹Then the father said to him, 'Son, you are always with me, and all that is mine is yours.* *³²But we had to celebrate and rejoice, because this brother of yours was dead and has come to life; he was lost and has been found'"* (Luke 15:11–32).

Of all the parables in the gospels, none is more difficult to accurately title than this one. The traditional title, "the prodigal son," reflects a long-standing tendency to concentrate totally on the first part of the story, that of the younger brother (verses 12–24), to the neglect of the second half (verses 25–32), with its far less resolved and more challenging ending. It is tempting to dub the parable simply "the lost son," which brings out well the parallel pattern across all three parables: lost sheep, lost coin, lost son. Unfortunately, it is not quite adequate, however, because it fails to bring in the older son, who is equally the focus of attention. If his father has lost a son, the older son has lost a brother, and his attitude to this is crucial. Hence, perhaps a more clumsy title might be in order, "the lost son and brother." This would give us a triangular pattern—father, younger brother, older brother—that would make for an easier modality of interpreting the parable.

The assumptive world of the parable is that of a wealthy family, with considerable household property and servants. The younger brother's request to be given the property that falls to him (verse 12) has already a callous ring about it. Strictly speaking, a share of the property should accrue to him on his father's death. His demand for it now in some sense says to the father, "You're as good as dead as far as I am concerned." Very soon, of course, his dissolute style of living squanders the entire sum.

In a few brief phrases, the parable depicts the personal degradation that then follows (verses 14–16). He is in a foreign country; his hunger forces him to become a hired laborer to one of its citizens; the work he is given to do is, for a Jew, the most degrading imaginable: feeding pigs. He even envies the pigs because the food they have to eat is not available to him.

In verse 17, the phrase "when he came to himself" signals a measure of self-knowledge, "a moment of realism," if not moral conversion—what colloquially might be expressed as an "aha" moment. The young man calculates that the hired hands on his father's farm, though only servants, have at least food enough to eat. Better to join them in their servitude than to die of hunger in this foreign place. So he prepares a set speech to win over his father and rehearses it: "Father, I have sinned against heaven and before you; I am no longer worthy to be called your son; treat me like one of your hired hands" (verses 18–19). The speech introduces a distinction between "son" and "hired hand" that from now on becomes crucial in the narrative.

As the younger son makes his return (verse 20a), the father, who represents God, reenters the story. That he should catch sight of his son while he is still "far off" gives the impression that he spends his days ever on the watch for his son's return. Then he too (like the shepherd and like the woman with the coin) "goes overboard." Filled with compassion (the same Greek word used to describe the reaction of the good Samaritan on seeing the wounded traveler [10:33; also 7:13]), he runs out, falls upon his son's neck (the literal expression), and kisses him (verse 20b).

We modern readers have to understand that this is a totally unconventional behavior for a dignified man of affairs in the Palestinian culture of the day. To leave the house to meet one of lower rank, to run rather than walk sedately, to display emotion extravagantly in public—all this involves serious loss of face and dignity. And that is not all. The speech the son has prepared is cut off by the father before the part about becoming one of the hired hands. This possibility never arises. Orders are quickly given by the father (verses 22–23): bring out the best robe, put a ring on his finger, sandals on his feet. All symbolize complete reinstatement as son and as a member of the family.

Finally, as in the earlier parables, there is to be a communal celebration. The calf that has been fattened is to be killed and eaten, and the reason: "for this son of mine was dead and is alive again; he was lost and is found" (verse 24).

We may note that the topic of "sin" and "repentance" has no place in the father's explanation—though this trajectory had certainly been in the young man's mind ("Father, I have sinned . . ." [verses 18, 21]). The father thinks only in terms of "dead" and "alive," "lost" and "found." And so the celebration gets under way.

Now the parable turns its attention to the older brother (verses 25–32), who, as he will later remind his father (verse 29), has been out in the field working all day. He is surprised at the sound of music and dancing, sure signs of a celebration. When he summons a slave to ask what it is all about, he receives a very accurate report: "Your brother has come and your father has killed the fatted calf, because he has got him back safe and sound" (verse 27). Immediately overcome with anger and resentment, the older brother refuses to go in and join the party (verse 28).

Again, the father—who in the parable represents God—forsakes his dignity and leaves the house to meet his son, this time to plead (verse 28). Patiently he listens while the son pours out his resentment, a resentment directed in the first instance against the father himself: "For all these years I have been working like a slave for you, and I have never disobeyed your command; yet you have never given me even a young goat so that I might celebrate with my friends. But when this son of yours came back, who has devoured your property with prostitutes, you killed the fatted calf for him" (verses 29–30).

Each detail here is significant. Viewed from an overview standpoint, the older son is whining. Possibly one of the only cases of whining in all of Sacred Scripture. In addition, the older son thinks of himself as a servant (for years he has "worked like a slave") rather than a son. He thinks that such work should have earned a decent reward; he is in a "contract" relationship with his father. He disowns his brother, referring to him simply as "your son" (his father, too, he bluntly addresses as "you"). What he resents particularly is that his brother has "devoured" the family property, lessening the amount that will eventually fall to him.

Once again, the father makes his explanation. He first dwells upon their own immediate relationship: "Son, you are always with me and all that is mine is yours" (verse 31). Whatever the older brother may have felt, there was never any doubt in the father's mind that he was a son and not a servant. Nor was he working for reward in a contract kind of way; the family property was shared—had he wanted a calf to celebrate with his friends he had only to ask or perhaps simply take.

Then, as regards the younger brother, comes the now familiar refrain: "We had to celebrate and rejoice, because this brother of yours was dead and has come to life; he was lost and has been found" (verse 32; see verse 23). Where the older brother sees life in terms of a contract relationship—one his brother has forfeited—for the father (God) the person is more important than what he has or has not done; he can never cease being a brother and a son. And as a brother and a son he has returned.

111

And there the story ends. We never learn whether the older brother was persuaded, whether he went in to join the music and the dancing or remained outside, stubbornly and bitterly nursing his anger.

And this is precisely where the parable makes its point. While almost from the start the older brother does not come across as an attractive character, his reaction is in many ways reasonable, one with which not a few in the audience might be inclined to agree. In several respects, the father has acted extravagantly, certainly overtolerantly. The story invites the audience of every age to feel the older brother's anger and maybe recognize in themselves several aspects of his resistance: the "contract" mentality, the concern over property squandered, the resentment that others are getting favored treatment instead of what they seem to deserve. It leaves the question, "Well, where are you in the end?" Inside joining in the celebration or stuck outside, hearing the music and dancing but too angry to go in? This is the genius of the open-ended nature of this parable.

In its Lucan setting, the story suggests that those who criticize Jesus place themselves in this last situation. Jesus is celebrating the return of the lost of God's family. They, for the reasons the parable suggests, make themselves unwilling and unable to join in. Ultimately, then, this last parable joins the others in putting to its audience the question about God. Can you cope with a God imaged by the father in this parable? Do you find in yourself some stirrings of the resistance of the older brother? Can you be part of a family whose hospitality is so extravagant, so uncalculating, so indulgent of human failing as this?

In its original setting, the parable serves to ward off criticism that the scribes and Pharisees mount against Jesus' celebration of God's acceptance. Doubtless, the early church found in it, too, an analysis of Israel's problem with accepting the gospel of the crucified messiah and the inclusion of the Gentiles in the people of God. The applications are endless. One perhaps that we should not omit considering is that of finding in ourselves and our communities the rather different patterns of sinfulness shown by the two brothers: the overt sinning of the younger, the resentment and resistance of the older—and to ask which of the two patterns the parable suggests to be the more difficult for God to deal with.

But in the end sinfulness is not the main point of this parable. Fundamentally, like all the parables, the three stories in Luke 15 ask: Are you comfortable with a God who acts with the foolishness of love displayed here?

The Parable of the Woman and the Yeast

²⁰And again he said, "To what should I compare the kingdom of God? ²¹It is like yeast that a woman took and mixed in with three measures of flour until all of it was leavened" (Luke 13:20–21; see Matthew 13:33).

In this parable, God is portrayed as a woman. This would have been shocking to the audience who lived entirely in a patriarchal world with men "on top" and women considered simply another commodity owned by men.

The portrait of God contained in the parable is that of a female baker, whose baking activity—mixing flour and yeast—is a metaphor for God's activity and God's grace. God's grace is to be seen, then, as a leavening activity in a believer's life. It is almost imperceptible, but still there. The bread eventually produced is food for the life of the spirit, which God provides for all human beings. In this parable, God is also portrayed as a nutritive mother who nurtures her children by kneading them with proper strength so as to spread the gluten of God's flour into her children, allowing them to rise to new life.

Conclusion

In this chapter, I have attempted to provide some reflections and insights on some of the parables of Jesus found in the gospels. We looked at how they challenge readers of all ages to reflect on how they relate to other human beings and to God.

The gospel parables are model stories which prick away at our consciousness in hope to expand our horizons beyond that of the dominant culture to new horizons provided by God through Jesus his storyteller.

For Discussion

1. What role do stories play in your life? Explain.
2. What steps or procedures would you follow in reading a gospel parable?
3. How do Jesus' parables about prayer help you to pray?
4. How do you relate to the parable of the good (compassionate) Samaritan? Have you ever experienced a modern-day "good Samaritan"?
5. Have your images for God been expanded or changed by Jesus' parables about the activity of God?

For Further Reading

Donahue, John R. *The Gospel in Parable: Metaphor, Narrative and Theology in the Synoptic Gospels.* Philadelphia: Fortress Press, 1988.

Fisher, Neal F. *Parables of Jesus: Glimpses of God's Reign.* New York: Crossroad, 1990.

McKenna, Megan. *Parables: The Arrows of God.* New York: Orbis Books, 1994.

Scott, Bernard Brandon. *Hear Then the Parables: A Commentary on the Parables of Jesus.* Minneapolis: Fortress Press, 1989.

Zannoni, Arthur E. *Tell Me Your Story: The Parables of Jesus.* Chicago: Liturgy Training Publications, 2002.

5

"COME AND FOLLOW ME": THE CALL TO DISCIPLESHIP

So OFTEN WHEN CHRISTIANS PONDER DISCIPLESHIP, they imagine themselves as small and weak, burdened with the cross, trudging dutifully behind the Lord. Their eyes are glued to the ground, their faces gnarled up in pain. They are all alone. This is an invalid "caricature" of the four gospels' portrayal of discipleship. Discipleship, the following of a master or teacher, can take on a wide variety of forms depending on how, why, and in what way the disciple follows. This is also true of the four gospels and their approach to Jesus and his followers.

Three concentric circles of disciples may be identified in the gospels: a large group of followers, from which the Twelve are chosen (Luke 6:13–17; see Matthew 8:21) and which, apparently, included some women (Luke 8:1–3); "the Twelve," who were designated as "apostles" and were especially called by Jesus to travel with him and learn (Mark 3:16–19); and an inner circle of Peter, James, and John, who alone accompany Jesus on certain key occasions (for example, the transfiguration [Mark 9:2–13] and the garden of Gethsemane [Matthew 26:36–46]).

Matthew, Mark, and Luke begin their accounts of Jesus' mission with dramatic calls to discipleship. In Mark (1:16–20) and Matthew (4:18–22), Jesus inaugurates his ministry not with healing or teaching, but by encountering two sets of brothers plying their fishing trade at the Sea of Galilee. Without preparation or even conversation, the unsuspecting brothers are summoned to follow Jesus and to join in his work of fishing for people. Simon and Andrew drop their casting nets; James and John leave father, hired hands, and boats. All four "immediately" begin to follow Jesus.

CALL STORIES IN THE SYNOPTIC GOSPELS

	Matthew	Mark	Luke
Call of Peter, James, and John	4:18–22	1:16–20	5:1–11
Call of Levi	9:9–13	2:13–17	5:27–32
Call of the Twelve	10:1–4	3:13–19	6:12–16

The Lucan call story (Luke 5:1–11) is more elaborate, but the same vivid elements of the call stories in Mark and Matthew are present. In Luke, Jesus has already begun his powerful mission of the word in the synagogue of Nazareth (4:16–30) and in the village of Capernaum (4:31–41). That powerful word now engulfs Simon and his partners James and John. Their frustrating night of empty nets is transformed by the potent word of Jesus; at his command they come up with a staggering haul of fish. At that moment, Simon, dumbfounded by the majesty of Jesus, is called to "catch people alive." As in Mark and Matthew's stories, these fishermen leave boat and trade and immediately follow their new master.

These eloquent stories of the beginnings of discipleship clearly signal what Christian readers of the gospels have instinctively recognized for ages: In the gospel narratives, the disciples are mirror images of the Christian. In the hopes and failures of these first followers of Jesus are sketched the essential qualities and experiences of all the followers of the risen Christ.

It should be pointed out that Matthew, Mark, and Luke do not portray the disciples in homogenized form; just as the unique circumstances and purpose of each gospel lead to a distinct portrayal of Jesus, so, too, their presentations of the disciples have special tones and emphases unique to each evangelist.

The dramatic proportions of the call stories give us a hint as to the major elements of gospel discipleship. First, the *initiative* in the stories is all on the side of Jesus; the disciples are called by him without preparation or merit. Second, the call is a call to *follow* Jesus. This is especially clear in the call stories of Mark and Matthew, but it's not absent in Luke either. Third, discipleship means *empowerment for mission.* The disciples are not called to learn the art of interpreting the law, as rabbinic disciples were. The Christian disciple is summoned "to catch people alive," to be involved in Jesus' own decisive mission of salvation. Fourth, the call demands a *response;* the disciples must leave all and set out on the journey of faith. They are called to leave the known for the unknown. This is a call to conversion. Finally, the call includes the cross. The would-be follower of Jesus must be prepared to take up the cross of Jesus (Mark 8:34, Matthew 16:24, Luke 9:23).

Discipleship in the Gospel of Matthew

Matthew tells us that all Christians are called to be disciples of Jesus, and the Sermon on the Mount (Matthew, chapters 5–7) gives us a description of what a true disciple of Jesus is like.

The Sermon on the Mount, however, can only be understood in the context of the Gospel as a whole. The sermon describes the ways in which a disciple of Jesus follows his master; the Gospel as a whole puts in perspective why he follows and how it is possible to follow.

According to the Sermon on the Mount, a true disciple of Jesus is one who is poor in spirit, turns the other cheek, loves his enemies, refrains from judging, and has a childlike trust in his heavenly Father. This revered image of Christian existence is, however, seldom, if ever, perfectly realized and is regarded by many to be an impossible ideal.

Its impossibility actually seems to be demonstrated by Matthew's portrayal of the disciples. In Matthew's account, Jesus gathers a small band of disciples and teaches them by word and deed the will of his Father. The disciples, however, throughout Jesus' life, remain weak in faith. Jesus, on the other hand, lives out the will of his Father, going all the way to the cross. Then, when the climactic moment is reached, "All the disciples deserted him and fled" (Matthew 26:56).

These disciples are hardly examples of the exalted picture of discipleship given in the Sermon on the Mount. Nevertheless, it is to these very disciples that Jesus returns and gives the great commission:

> [18]And Jesus came and said to them, "All authority in heaven and on earth has been given to me. [19]Go therefore and make disciples of all nations, baptizing them in the name of the Father and of the Son and of the Holy Spirit, [20]and teaching them to obey everything that I have commanded you. And remember, I am with you always, to the end of the age" (Matthew 28:18–20).

These words at the close of Matthew's gospel have long been recognized as the key to understanding the entire gospel. The gospel of Matthew is the good news about Jesus, the Son of God, who calls all nations to follow him. Actually, the more appropriate understanding is not a political notion but a people. Jesus is challenging his disciples to go out to all people.

As Jesus does the will of his Father, he expects no less of his disciples. A disciple of Jesus is much more than a disciple of the Pharisees or even of John the Baptist. A Jewish disciple, as such, was simply a follower, a student. A disciple learned from his master until the day when he had learned enough, became independent, and perhaps began to gather disciples of his own.

With Jesus, there are two important differences in what a disciple is. First, a disciple of Jesus never becomes independent of his master; he remains his disciple forever. Second, a disciple of Jesus does much more than learn from his master a way of life. A disciple of Jesus not only learns a way of life but actually lives that life. He lives that life because his own life has been transformed by the life of his master.

Jesus taught and did the will of his Father. His disciple takes on, in his or her own life, the very conditions of Jesus' life: sharing Jesus' destiny in submission to the will of the Father. A disciple of Jesus radically abandons his or her own ego in responding to the call: "If any want to become my followers, let them deny themselves and take up their cross and follow me" (Matthew 16:24).

Interestingly, Matthew (unlike Mark and Luke) has Jesus issue the call to discipleship only to the Twelve. In fact, whenever Matthew uses the term *disciple* (in the sense of a disciple of Jesus), he restricts it to the Twelve. The very first usage appears just after Jesus had called his first disciples and began his public ministry. "When Jesus saw the crowds, he went up the mountain; and after he sat down, his disciples came to him. Then he began to speak, and taught them" (Matthew 5:1–2). In chapters 5–7, there follows the Sermon on the Mount.

What is usually not noticed is that the sermon is addressed only to the disciples, not to the crowd, as opposed to Luke's sermon on the plain (Luke 6:17ff.). In Matthew's plan, Jesus calls his disciples, instructs them on the nature of true discipleship in his sermon, continues this instruction in word and deed throughout his public ministry, goes to his cross doing the will of his Father, and rises to a new life, opening up for all men and women the possibility of sharing in this new life.

Only after the Resurrection does Matthew extend the possibility of discipleship beyond the Twelve. His last use of the term *disciple* is remarkably similar to his first. "Now the eleven disciples went to Galilee, to the mountain to which Jesus had directed them" (Matthew 28:16). There on the mountain, Jesus speaks to the disciples alone, as he had done earlier at the Sermon on the Mount. At this final meeting, however, Jesus gives them the command, "[M]ake disciples of all nations, . . . teaching them to obey everything that I have commanded you" (Matthew 28:19–20).

The eleven disciples had heard Jesus' teachings, had witnessed his life and ministry, and had failed. Yet Jesus' invitation to discipleship was not revoked. In fact, by virtue of his death and resurrection to new life these eleven were empowered by the spirit to begin to live as true disciples and even to carry on the work of Jesus, making disciples of all nations (people). What happened with the eleven should help us understand what happens when the invitation to discipleship is extended to us.

According to the gospel of Matthew, by his death and resurrection Jesus has given to the eleven and to us the possibility of being, together with him, sons and daughters of God, that is, persons who do the will of our Father because we share his very life and because we live by a new life principle, the Spirit of God.

Discipleship is a gift. The Twelve were called first and then presented with the demands of the Sermon on the Mount. However, the possibility of their living the life described in that sermon did not appear until the death and resurrection of Jesus. It is similar with us. We are called to be disciples before we confront the "impossible" demands of the Sermon on the Mount. We receive the gift of faith by which we are truly sons and daughters of God prior to any good works on our part.

What Matthew is concerned with in the Sermon on the Mount is an ideal, but not impossible, picture of what true discipleship is like. Discipleship consists not only in receiving the gift of faith but in living out that gift as well. Christian discipleship, for Matthew, is a dynamic process by which we move like the disciples from weak faith to stronger faith, realizing ever more perfectly the condition of our sonship and daughterhood.

The Sermon on the Mount puts all of Christian existence in its proper perspective, that is, the perspective of Jesus' life. The true disciple does all that Jesus teaches; he or she does this because Jesus has given the follower the power to do it, and he or she does it by realizing in one's life the conditions of Jesus' life. In short, the true disciple loves as Jesus loved. "Love your enemies . . . so that you may be children of your Father in heaven" (Matthew 5:44–45). The life of a disciple is a life that moves in the direction of unselfish love, the love that led Jesus all the way to his cross.

The Sermon on the Mount, then, is a description of sonship and daughterhood, a description of the lives of those who do the will of their Father. The impossibility of the Sermon on the Mount becomes a possibility when we realize that Jesus has already done it. Jesus has already fulfilled the will of God. Jesus was a true son of God and has made it possible for us to be sons and daughters as well.

We are, even now, by faith, sons and daughters of God. In the Sermon on the Mount, and only there, Jesus calls his disciples children of God (Matthew 5:9, 45), and fourteen times he speaks of God as "your Father." We might not be living perfectly the Sermon on the Mount, but we can be confident that if we stand firm in our faith, after our periods of rebelliousness, we shall turn out just like Jesus, that is, sons and daughters who do the will of their Father.

Discipleship consists of finding in our lives the reality first found in the life of Jesus, and living out in our lives the gift of sonship and daughterhood made possible by the sonship of Jesus. For Matthew, discipleship consists in being as just as our heavenly Father is perfect (Matthew 5:48).

Because we have already been called to be disciples, we can already address God in the words of Matthew 6:9: "Our Father in heaven." The reality of our sonship and daughterhood, however, will be borne out in our lives if it is truly real. As Matthew says, "You will know them by their fruits" (Matthew 7:20). If we continue to follow Jesus in living the will of God, if we live out the gift of discipleship by becoming related to our heavenly Father, then one day the words of the centurion can be addressed to us: "Truly this man [person] was God's Son [Daughter]" (Matthew 27:54).

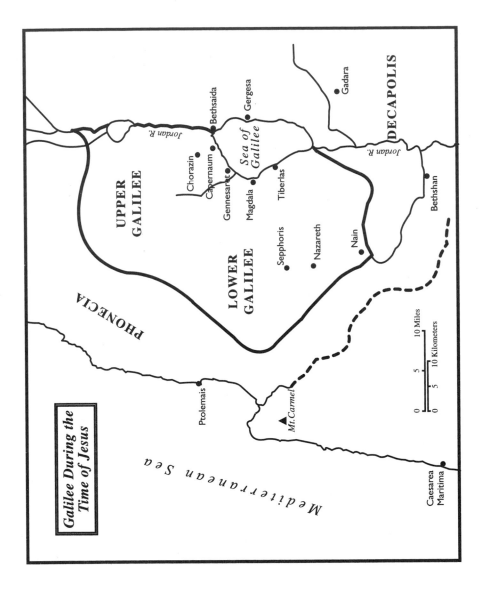

Galilee During the Time of Jesus

Discipleship in Mark

Turning our attention to the Gospel of Mark, we realize that it will not allow Christians who are disciples to hide any skeletons in the closet. Mark gives top billing to the disciples as klutzes and bunglers. Despite Jesus' best efforts to teach his disciples otherwise, they fail to understand that he has come to serve a suffering humanity and not to be served. They are dunces when it comes to Jesus' message that he has come to form a new humanity of Jew and Gentile outcasts. They see Jesus' miraculous powers as a means of self-aggrandizement and not as opportunities for restoring life to a crippled creation. When the suffering Son of Man in Mark gives up his life in service to the world, the disciples are nowhere to be found. They have abandoned their master.

While the dominant picture of disciples in Mark's gospel is bleak and sobering, there is a powerful element of hope in its ending. The young man in the tomb tells the women: "Do not be alarmed; you are looking for Jesus of Nazareth, who was crucified. He has been raised; he is not here. Look, there is the place they laid him. But go, tell his disciples and Peter that he is going ahead of you to Galilee; there you will see him, just as he told you" (16:6–7). Death has not conquered Jesus, the Son of Man. Nor has death dissolved the union between Jesus and his disciples. Jesus invites his disciples back. He extends the hand of reconciliation to those who abandoned him and his way of service. They are to see him in Galilee, the place of mission. He will go before them again, leading them, showing them what it means to follow him who "came not to be served but to serve, and to give his life a ransom for many" (Mark 10:45).

Mark's gospel presents a very realistic picture of disciples who share in Jesus' mission. But it balances that picture with that of a Jesus whose love for his disciples is stronger than death and who reconciles his weak and sinful disciples to himself. He goes before them in the mission territory of Galilee. He invites them to begin anew.

Further, in Mark, Jesus is with his followers in their suffering. Discipleship in Mark's gospel means following Jesus to the cross, to suffering and not just remaining in his glory. It means going where it is difficult and painful to go and finding Christ there, even in suffering on its most horrific scale. Mark presents Jesus as a model of fidelity to God to those in desperate need of such meaning and hope. Like the persecuted Christians of the first century in Rome, Mark's audience, we need to know that God can break through the realities of terror and violence to give meaning to the cross we bear. By so doing, Jesus is not repairing old garments and wine skins with old patches of rage, despair, or revenge, but offering a hope which is radically new (Mark 2:21–22). Mark's Jesus challenges us to believe that God has broken into our suffering and redeemed it. If we have such a belief, then we are disciples.

Discipleship in Luke

When Luke depicts Jesus gathering followers, he is in many respects dependent on his Markan source. As in Mark, the Lucan Jesus is constantly surrounded by such companions, whom he has summoned to himself and whom he sends out with instructions to preach and with power to heal (Luke 6:13, 9:1–6). They witness his wondrous and mighty deeds (Luke 4:31–44). As in Mark, the disciples are given privileged instructions (Luke 8:9–10). But more specifically, Luke uses his lengthy travel account (9:51–19:27) as a means whereby Jesus instructs those companions from Galilee who become, in time, the foreordained witnesses chosen by God (Acts 10:41), who bear testimony "to all that he did both in Judea and in Jerusalem" (10:39), beginning from Galilee (10:37). These companions fail to understand Jesus' dire forebodings about what waits for him in Jerusalem (Luke 9:45), but he tolerates them and uses them nonetheless, as in Mark's gospel, to administer his bounty to the crowds and the multiplication of the loaves (9:16).

Yet there are differences in the treatment of Jesus' immediate disciples in Mark's and Luke's accounts of his ministry. The most notable of them are the following six:

1. The Lucan Jesus sends out to preach and to heal not only the Twelve (9:1–6), as in Mark (6:6b–13), but also seventy(-two) others (10:1–16), and at the end of the commission to the latter he solemnly states, "Whoever listens to you listens to me and whoever rejects you rejects me, and whoever rejects me rejects the one who sent me" (10:16). This utterance clearly manifests the closeness of the relationship of the disciples to Jesus; it is as close as Jesus' relationship to God.

2. Luke introduces the call of Simon, James, and John in 5:1–11. It is one of the famous Lucan transpositions of Markan material in his gospel; he has transposed Mark 1:16–20 to this latter position in the ministry of Jesus, and conflated it with a tradition known to us only from the Johannine community's gospel about the wondrous catch of fish (21:1–11). The reason for all of this is clear: Luke was concerned to offer some psychological background and explanation for why such fisherman would abandon their fishing nets and follow Jesus, the teacher and healer. By recounting a bit of Jesus' ministry first, Luke has subtly prepared the reader for the call of the disciples. Luke 5:11 concludes, "When they had brought their boats to shore, they left everything and followed him." This following of Jesus is rooted in Jesus' own initiative and his invitation to followers, explicitly expressed in Mark 1:17, "Follow me!" and subtly implied in Luke 5:10b, "From now on you will be catching people."

3. The next time the Lucan Jesus calls a disciple occurs in 5:27–28, where Levi the toll (tax) collector is summoned, " 'Follow me.' And he got up, left everything, and followed him." Again, the call is expressed in terms of following; but in the sequel to it, at the banquet Levi gives in Jesus' honor, the first use of the Greek word for disciples, *mathetai,* is encountered (5:30). By the time that Luke writes his gospel and Acts of the Apostles (circa 80–85),

125

that term has become the ordinary Greek word for a Christian follower of Jesus.

4. The next significant Lucan text on discipleship is met in chapter 6 of his gospel, where Jesus chooses the Twelve. In typically Lucan fashion, he first depicts Jesus as praying during the night before summoning "his disciples" to himself, and the narrative continues, "[He] chose twelve of them, whom he also named apostles" (6:13). Only Luke has added the last clause, "whom he also named apostles." Luke equates the Twelve with the apostles and the apostles with the twelve.

5. Even though all the evangelists tell of the threefold denial of Jesus by the leader of the disciples, Simon Peter, only Luke presents Jesus at the Last Supper praying for Peter, "Simon, Simon, listen! Satan has demanded to sift all of you like wheat, but I have prayed for you that your own faith may not fail; and you, when once you have turned back, strengthen your brothers" (22:31–32). The scandal of Peter's denial is thus tempered somewhat in Luke's story. He could not gloss over the historic denial; so he makes Peter a disciple on behalf of whom Jesus has specifically interceded with his heavenly Father. He singles Peter out for the role of strengthening other disciples.

6. Luke departs from the Markan tradition that records the dereliction of Jesus by his disciples at the time of his arrest on the Mount of Olives. For Mark ominously notes, "All of them deserted him and fled" (14:50). Then to heighten the reader's sense of the absolute dereliction, Mark adds to the scene about the young man who was "following" him, clothed only in a linen cloth; when he was seized, he let go of the cloth and ran away naked (14:51–52). Letting go of the cloth thus symbolically encapsulates the utter abandonment of Jesus by those who were supposed to be his

126

followers. So runs the Markan form of the story of Jesus' arrest. But Luke has none of this. He has no counterpart of the Markan notice that they *all* fled (14:50), nor of the episode about the young man fleeing naked. Mere omission, however, is not enough for Luke, who is thus silent about the desertion of the disciples, for he even goes so far as to include them with the women from Galilee in the group that stood watching the crucifixion at a distance (see Luke 23:49).

These, then, are six of the notable details in which the Lucan picture of the immediate disciples of Jesus differs from the Markan story.

Luke's Demands of Christian Discipleship

Luke's demands of Christian involvement or discipleship can be summed up under three main headings (topics): (1) the response expected from people to the Christian *kerygma,* (2) the demands of Christian living, and (3) the community aspects of Christian life.

The Response Expected from People to the Christian Kerygma

The response expected of the disciples to the proclamation of the Good News, which *kerygma* means, consists of three things: faith, repentance and conversion, and baptism.

Faith

In Acts of the Apostles 16:31, Luke depicts Paul saying to the jailer at Philippi, "Believe on the Lord Jesus, and you will be saved, you and your household." The connection between faith and salvation is thus made clear; it is the only route for the disciple to the latter. Again, in the parable of the sower, the disciples are "the ones who, when they hear the word, hold it fast in an honest and good heart, and bear fruit with patient endurance" (Luke 8:15). Such faith involves a listening to the word proclaimed, an allegiance of openness, and a persistence that is subject to neither uprooting nor apostasy, nor worldly distraction. The link between "faith" and "salvation" is made clear in Luke 7:50: "Your faith has saved you; go in peace."

Repentance and Conversion

Another way for Luke to describe the ideal disciple's reaction to the Christian proclamation is: "repentance and conversion." The Greek word *metanoia*, which is usually translated as "repentance," literally means "a change of mind." But in the New Testament it almost always connotes a religious turning from sin, a new beginning in moral conduct, a "response." Closely related to such repentance is "conversion," that is, a turning of the human being to God. Both repentance and conversion, two sides of the same coin, are complementary to faith for Luke, and they are God-given (Acts 18:27). But repentance and forgiveness of sins are linked in the commission by the risen Christ to the eleven who are to go forth and bear testimony to him and preach in his name (Luke 24:47). Thus repentance and conversion sum up a further reaction of the disciples to the proclamation of forgiveness.

Baptism

Faith, repentance, and conversion lead to the baptism of the disciple. As in the case of Paul before him, for Luke baptism initiates the new believer and convert into the Christian community. Such a one had not only to believe in Jesus Christ and his role in the Father's plan of salvation, but also had to be baptized in his name. This ritual washing is never described by Luke; it is simply taken for granted as known. It is never said, moreover, to stem from an action performed by Jesus himself; nor does it play a role in the great commission given by the risen Christ to the eleven in Luke 24. However, Luke takes pains to distinguish Christian baptism from that administered by John the Baptist, for he knows of the former as Spirit related, whereas the latter is not: "Repent, and be baptized every one of you in the name of Jesus Christ so that your sins may be forgiven; and you will receive the gift of the Holy Spirit." So Peter concludes his proclamation on Pentecost to the Jews assembled in Jerusalem (Acts 2:38).

For Luke, these three things, faith, repentance and conversion, and baptism, make up the fundamental response of a disciple to Christ.

The Demands of Christian Living

To the foregoing three fundamentals Luke adds further demands that should guide the Christian disciple's life and conduct. He basically refers to four: the following of Jesus, testimony, prayer, and the right use of material possessions.

The Following of Jesus

Even though "following" is merely another way of saying "discipleship," there is a special nuance given to the former in the Lucan writings. These two volumes (the gospel and Acts) are dominated by a geographical perspective with Jerusalem as its central focus. In the gospel itself, Luke depicts Jesus en route, moving without distraction from Galilee, where his ministry begins, to Jerusalem, his city of destiny. In the city, Jesus' exodus, his transit to the Father through the passion, death, burial, and resurrection takes place. In Acts of the Apostles, Jerusalem becomes the place from which the word of the Lord must be carried forth by his witnesses to all Judea, Samaria, and even "to the ends of the earth" (1:8).

In Luke's view, the Christian disciple must be a follower on the road that Jesus treads. Thus, even though Luke has taken over from his Markan source the challenge "Follow me!" as disciples are called, that call and challenge are now colored by the Lucan geographical perspective. The disciples must not only walk behind Jesus, but in his very footsteps. As the distinctively Lucan travel account begins (Luke 9:51), three would-be followers offer to come along and they are further challenged by Jesus (9:57–62); all of this takes place "as they moved along the road."

For Luke, Christian discipleship is not merely the acceptance of the Master's teaching, but an identification of the person with the Master's very way of life and destiny, a following that involves intimacy and imitation. The conditions of such following are made clear. Immediately after the first announcement of the passion (9:22), the Lucan Jesus proclaims, "If any want to become my followers, let them deny themselves and take up their cross daily and follow me"

(9:23). Though Luke has derived this saying from Mark (8:34), he has significantly modified it by adding "daily" to his form of the proclamation. He calls for daily self-denial, daily carrying of one's cross, and daily following in the footsteps of the Master.

Testimony

The Christian disciple is also to live so as to bear witness to the risen Christ and his teaching (see Acts of the Apostles 10:39–42). Such testimony plays an important role at the beginning of Acts, when Matthias is chosen by lot to take the place of Judas in the band of twelve; it had to be reconstituted for the initial proclamation of the word of testimony to the Jews assembled in Jerusalem on Pentecost; the one chosen had to be a witness to the risen Christ (1:22). Even Paul, who was not one of the Twelve and had not been with Jesus during his earthly ministry, is cast by Luke as a witness to the same Christ (Acts 22:15, 26:16). Testimony to the risen Lord becomes the lifestyle of every Christian disciple in every generation.

Prayer

Another important aspect of Christian discipleship in Luke's view is one's ongoing communion with God. It has always been noted how preoccupied this evangelist is with prayer in both his gospel and Acts. The chord is struck in the infancy narrative itself, where in the very first episode, Zechariah enters the sanctuary to offer incense while the people stand outside in prayer (1:10); in the sanctuary, Zechariah learns that his prayer has been answered (1:13). Major episodes in Jesus' ministry are linked with his own prayer (3:21; 6:12; 9:18, 28; 22:32, 41; 23:46). The Lucan Jesus not only prays himself but teaches his disciples to pray (11:2–4), and inculcates "their need to pray always and not to lose heart" (18:1). When the seventy(-two) are sent out, they are not only to preach and heal but also to "pray" for "the Lord of the harvest to send out laborers into his harvest" (10:2).

The parable of the persistent friend (11:5–8), which has prayer as its central theme, is followed by sayings on the efficacy of prayer (11:9–13). In Acts of the Apostles, a nucleus community awaiting the promise of the Father is portrayed in prayer (1:14). Peter and John go up to the Temple to pray at the ninth hour (3:1), and when the seven are appointed deacons, it is to allow the Twelve to engage in "prayer and to serving the word" (6:4). Two features of Jewish piety are taken over by Christian disciples, prayer and alms-giving. And Luke interprets them as rising before God as a memorial (Acts 4:24–30), when the community supplicates God, the sovereign Lord, on behalf of Peter and John, who have been arrested and forbidden to speak again in Jesus' name. It is a petition for courage and boldness that these disciples may carry out the roles expected of them. This prayer becomes the context of their being filled with the Holy Spirit (Acts 4:31). In all of this, one notes Luke's concern to join to the disciples' ministering activity the need for ongoing communion with God himself. Prayer has to be the source of vitality in the activity of the disciples.

The Right Use of Material Possessions

No other New Testament writer speaks out so forthrightly as Luke about the use of material possessions by Christian disciples. More than the other evangelists, Luke either preserves sayings of Jesus about this topic or puts on his lips statements that concern wealth, money, and material goods in general.

So Luke portrays Jesus speaking about this matter both in sayings that he has taken over from Mark and also a number of sayings that he has composed himself. For instance, in Mark, Jesus tells the rich young man to sell what he possesses, give the proceeds to the poor, and come, follow him (10:21), whereas in Luke, Jesus tells the man: "Sell *all* that you own" (18:22). Again in Mark, the first disciples called leave their nets to follow Jesus (1:18, 20), but in Luke they leave *"everything"* to do so (5:11).

The contrast between the rich and the poor surfaces often in the Lucan story. For example, in Mary's Magnificat (1:53), in the instruction of John the Baptist to the people (3:11, 14), in Jesus' interpretation of Isaiah 61:1–2 in the Nazareth synagogue (4:18), the first beatitude and woe (6:20, 24), in the story of the rich man and Lazarus (16:19–31), and in Jesus' advice to "invite the poor" to dinner instead of rich neighbors who might reciprocate (14:13).

In a special way, Luke is trying to teach that material possessions are liable to stand in the way of the proper response of a disciple and Luke is concerned that they do not. In a sense, he asks every disciple at every time in the history of Christianity to examine himself or herself on whether or not material possessions are a stumbling block to the practice of discipleship.

The Community Aspects of Christian Life

Finally, we turn to the community (ecclesial) dimension of Christian discipleship. It is best summed up in the first of Luke's major summaries in Acts of the Apostles.

> [42]*They devoted themselves to the apostles' teaching and fellowship, to the breaking of bread and the prayers.*
>
> [43]*Awe came upon everyone, because many wonders and signs were being done by the apostles.* [44]*All who believed were together and had all things in common;* [45]*they would sell their possessions and goods and distribute the proceeds to all, as any had need.* [46]*Day by day, as they spent much time together in the temple, they broke bread at home and ate their food with glad and generous hearts,* [47]*praising God and having the goodwill of all the people. And day by day the Lord added to their number those who were being saved* (Acts 2:42–47).

No one knows how long the idyllic common life described in Acts persisted. Nonetheless, the practice of discipleship is done within a community known in Greek as *ekklesia*, translated into English as "the church." Etymologically, the Greek word means "those having been called out." The idea is that the disciples are those called, and they are called into the assembly and practice their discipleship in the assembled community of faith. Luke does not present disciples as "Lone Rangers" but rather as members of the community witnessing in faith.

132

Luke is concerned to teach the disciples of his generation and every generation that the risen Jesus is truly present in the community, truly present in the word proclaimed, and truly present in the celebration of the Eucharist. For Luke, after Jesus rises, his continued presence on earth is preserved in the church, the assembly of those disciples who practice their faith seriously.

Discipleship in John

The fourth gospel, attributed to John, pictures Jesus as a vine and his disciples as branches that are attached to him, constantly receiving life, life in abundance (John 15:1–11). Disciples, "the branches," are joined together in growth, all of which comes from the life source, Christ. Nowhere in John's gospel are disciples told to take up the cross. Disciples are warned that if the Master has suffered surely the disciples shall too. However, the suffering will be like that of a woman giving birth; pain always leads to new life.

In all four gospels, discipleship entails following Christ. More than the other gospels, however, the fourth gospel concentrates on the root meaning of discipleship: "learning." Etymologically, a disciple is one who learns. Often, the best way to learn is to look for a model from whom to learn. The gospel of John provides such a model in a person known as the Beloved Disciple.

Only in the fourth gospel do we find a man called a disciple whom Jesus loved (John 13:23; 19:26). In John's community, this beloved disciple acts as a model. He is the learner par excellence. Introduced at the Last Supper, he leans against Jesus' chest (bosom) (13:23). This intimate action parallels the evangelist's only other use of the term *chest* (bosom.) In the gospel's prologue (John 1:18), we learned that "It is God the only Son, who is close to the Father's heart, who has made him known." In other words, Jesus explains and interprets the Father to us, and his explanation is of God's inner life.

Jesus' explanation of the Father does not come from academic study. Rather, what Jesus reveals of God is learned in a profound personal relationship which includes but transcends the intellectual.

Jesus learns from the very heart of the Father. Resting on the chest (bosom) of Jesus, the Beloved Disciple shares this same mission. As Jesus explains the Father, the Beloved Disciple explains Jesus, tells about him, draws out the meaning of his life and death, makes him known to the Johannine community and to us.

What the Beloved Disciple has learned from the heart of Jesus encourages him to stay close to Jesus in persecution (18:15), even to stand at the cross (19:26). Having learned so deeply, he can understand the meaning of the empty tomb (20:2–10).

The parallels for our own discipleship are obvious. Learning not only from theologians, books, and sermons, but from the very heart of Jesus casts us as disciples in the Johannine mold. As the Beloved Disciple learned from his relationship with Jesus, symbolized at the Last Supper in an intimate gesture, we listen as the heart of Jesus speaks in Scripture, in persons, in sacrament, in historical events, in family celebrations, in joy and in pain. John would have us develop a contemplative attitude toward all of life as an opportunity for Jesus to reveal and an opportunity for us to learn. This lifelong learning leads us to intimacy with Christ (13:23), courage in suffering and death (18:15, 19:26) and wisdom to perceive the possibilities of resurrection everywhere (20:2–10).

Notice that the Beloved Disciple does not stand as an individual in any of his scenes. At the Last Supper, he is in dialogue with Peter (13:24). At the high priest's, this disciple takes Peter into the courtyard (18:16). At Calvary, he stands with Mary and receives her as his own (19:26–27). At the tomb, he responds to Magdalene and runs with Peter (20:3–10). This model disciple calls us to relationship with others at the Last Supper, at the cross, at the tomb. In John's community, as exemplified by the Beloved Disciple, discipleship involves learning intimately from Christ, staying close in compassion with the suffering Jesus, witnessing to the meaning of the empty tomb. Far from trudging alone deep in pain, discipleship means to be deep in relationship, both with the Lord and with his friends.

What we believe about Jesus the Christ will influence the way in which we learn from him and follow him. The fourth evangelist and his community had a number of ways to understand and bear witness to Jesus. In the remainder of this chapter we will focus on Jesus as disciple of the Father, lover, and giver of life. Then we will view our discipleship as knowing, loving, and, through our attraction to Jesus, receiving life together.

Jesus is the disciple of God. As the Father knows Jesus (10:15), Jesus knows the Father (1:18, 17:25). He only does what he sees the Father doing. His works are the works of the Father. He only speaks what he hears the Father teaching. His word is the word of the Father. He promises us that we, too, will be taught by God (6:45), that we will know the truth (8:31), and that knowing will be life for us (17:3).

Let us illustrate this with some stories from John's gospel. The disciples of John the Baptist follow Jesus (1:37ff.). He asks them what they want. In asking that, Jesus asks all disciples through the ages, "What do you want?" When they ask where he is staying, Jesus invites them: "Come and see." "Come and see" invites not only those first disciples but us to come and see Jesus through this gospel. In coming to see, they follow him (1:37, 38, 40, 43). All of their subsequent activities as disciples flow from their coming and seeing, their following and knowing, their allowing Jesus to teach them.

Nicodemus, too, comes to Jesus as a seeker—"What do you want? What are you looking for?" is implied. Nicodemus comes at night (3:2). He resists understanding what Jesus means (3:10), but gradually his knowledge grows. Midway in Jesus' ministry, Nicodemus cautions the Sanhedrin not to prejudge Jesus (7:50). On Calvary (19:38, 39), Nicodemus makes a public affirmation of his discipleship when he cares for the dead body of Jesus. Jesus is sympathetic with the man's quest to know and to learn. Obviously, Nicodemus keeps on gradually learning. He is another model for all would-be disciples.

Jesus teaches women and reveals himself to them. He engages in theological discussion with the Samaritan woman at the well, revealing to her that he is the Messiah (4:26). To Martha, whom he loves (11:5), Jesus reveals that he is the resurrection and the life (11:25ff.). Both women hear, believe, and lead others (the towns-people in the case of the Samaritan woman, Mary in the case of Martha) to the Messiah. Jesus' promise applies to them: "If you continue in my word, you are truly my disciples; and you will know the truth, and the truth will make you free" (8:31).

Jesus is not only a disciple of God, but the Beloved Disciple of God. "As the Father has loved me . . ." (15:9) so Jesus loves us. We, in turn, are beloved disciples and more than disciples. "I have called you friends, because I have made known to you everything that I have heard from my Father" (15:15). We are friends because individually and together we hear Jesus, know Jesus, and so know the Father.

We are also his friends if we hear his command. At the Last Supper, Jesus proclaims, "Love one another" (John 13:35). He calls it a new commandment, yet the Torah had enjoined loving on the disciples of Moses in the Israelite community. What is new in the command that we are to love each other is that Jesus loves us. Jesus loves as he has been loved. We are to love as we have been loved (13:34, 15:12). This love is illustrated by Jesus in a prophetic gesture. Before he urges our love for one another, he himself takes off his outer garment, puts a towel around his waist, and kneels in front of his disciples washing their feet (13:3–17). What he will spell out in word, he first acts out in flesh. Jesus acts as servant.

To be sure, to be a disciple is to be a servant. Before Jesus asks us to demonstrate our love and service, however, he asks that we allow ourselves to be loved, to be served. Peter had difficulties. When Jesus knelt to wash Peter's feet, Peter protested. Jesus was firm with him—with us. To have companionship with Jesus we must be loved before we can love. We have to allow Jesus and our disciple-companions to kneel before us, take our feet in their hands, and care for us. Capable of mutuality, our loving can become service instead of paternalism or do-goodiness. After he explains the foot-washing, Jesus points out that the greatest love, the love that he has for us, is not just kneeling before us, but laying down his life for us.

In the Johannine community, love had to include action for justice. Jesus, who learned from his Father's heart, that real worship is "in spirit and truth" (4:23), attempts to set priorities in the right order by upsetting the established order. He overthrows the money changers' tables in his zeal for justice in the religious realm (2:14–22).

Then, in the first epistle of John, we read that if anyone has enough wealth and sees a brother or sister in need yet maintains a closed heart toward the companion-disciple, God's love cannot live in such a pseudo-disciple. "Little children, let us love, not in word or speech, but in truth and action" (1 John 3:18). We are told in the same epistle that love is God's gift, not our attainment (1 John 4:10ff.). Allowing God to love us casts all fear from our hearts, and we are freed, enabled to love (see 1 John 4:19–20).

We can test this mutual love of us for God, in the community of brothers and sisters, in sharing possessions, in open hearts, in work, and in truth (1 John 3:17–18). To be a disciple is to be loved as Jesus is loved, to love as Jesus loves.

Love one another, Jesus commands, so the world may realize that you are my disciples. And be one, he prays (17:21) so that the world may know that I am sent by God. Jesus is sent to bring life, life in abundance (10:10). As lifelong learners of the Father and of Jesus, we experience eternal life (17:3).

In John's theology, eternal life is not a future reward for the persevering disciple. Eternal life is now. "Anyone who hears my word and believes him who sent me has eternal life, and does not come under judgment, but has passed from death to life" (5:24). Living water, living bread, the living Sprit are ours right now.

Giving life, experiencing life in abundance himself, Jesus is attractive, drawing all to himself (12:32). We follow the Lord not out of duty but because he is so attractive. The whole world runs after him (12:19). Moving chapter by chapter through the Gospel of John, we see him drawing a variety of people to himself. "Come and see," he invites the first disciples, and they do. Nathaniel, once scornful, meets and immediately admires Jesus. Nicodemus is attracted enough to stake his reputation on a visit by night. The Samaritan woman is attracted by his interest in her, and her townsfolk are attracted by his message. Though that message can divide his disciples, the Twelve, through Peter, ask, "To whom can we go? You have the words of eternal life" (6:68). Martha hurries down the road to Jesus (11:20). His mother and his Beloved Disciple follow him to the cross (19:25–27). Mary Magdalene enthusiastically recognizes the risen Lord (20:16). Peter jumps from his boat to get to Jesus more quickly (21:7).

These disciples are attracted to him individually, but his activity with them is to make them one. His being lifted up on the cross draws all his disciples to himself (12:32), gathering into one family all the scattered children of God (11:52). The giver of life freely lays down his life, which leads to a deeper, richer life. At that moment on Calvary, his "hour," the mother of Jesus and the Beloved Disciple are given to each other. They represent the new family of disciples. Then Mary Magdalene is sent by the risen Lord to proclaim not only that he has ascended to the Father but that the disciples are in new relationships with each other, with him, with God. "Go to my brothers and say to them, 'I am ascending to my Father and your Father, to my God and your God'" (20:17).

The giver of life is still being lifted up high on a cross. For the fourth evangelist, Jesus' being lifted up is not only his dying but his being raised up by God. His being lifted up can also mean his exultation. At this very moment, Jesus is exalted in glory. Lifted up, he continues to attract us, draw us all to himself, gather us as his community of disciples. Our response of knowing and loving him is a lifelong process of experiencing life, now and in abundance, of continuing in his word, and so being his disciples, his friends, his new family. In so doing we become Jesus' disciples, and those who see us see Jesus who sent us.

For Discussion

1. What does Jesus mean by inviting people to come and follow him?
2. What is the cost of being a Christian disciple? What is the role of faith? Of the cross? Of prayer?
3. Do material possessions stand in the way of your being a disciple of Jesus?
4. How are both Jesus and the Beloved Disciple models of discipleship in the Gospel of John?
5. Can one be a disciple without being part of the church?

Further Reading

Fischer, George, and Martin Hasitschka. *The Call of the Disciple: The Bible on Following Christ.* New York: Paulist Press, 1999.

Kurtz, William. *Following Jesus: A Disciple's Guide to Luke-Acts.* Ann Arbor, Mich.: Servant Publications, 1984.

O'Grady, John F. *Disciples and Leaders.* Mahwah, N.J.: Paulist Press, 1991.

Sweetland, Dennis M. *Our Journey with Jesus: Discipleship According to Luke-Acts.* Collegeville, Minn.: Liturgical Press, 1990.

———. *Our Journey with Jesus: Discipleship According to Mark.* Collegeville, Minn.: Liturgical Press, 1987.

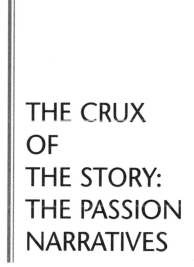

THE CRUX
OF
THE STORY:
THE PASSION
NARRATIVES

The STORIES IN THE FOUR GOSPELS THAT NARRATE the suffering and death of Jesus are known as the passion narratives. The English word *passion* is derived from a Latin verb meaning "to suffer." The stories of Jesus' agony in the garden, his trials before both Jewish and Roman authorities, as well as his death on the cross constitute what the gospel writers would call his sufferings.

Each gospel narrates Jesus' passion in a little different way, with sensitivity to issues derived from its audience as well as its own literary style. However, all four gospels agree that Jesus died by crucifixion, which, at the time, was a form of capital punishment for criminals. Before looking at the four gospel passion narratives, we will explore who was responsible for Jesus' death.

Who Was Responsible for Jesus' Death?

The question Who killed Jesus? requires a very careful answer. Throughout the centuries, some have responded that the Jews killed Jesus and, therefore, they are a "deicide" people. The word *deicide* means "to kill God." Since Jesus is divine and the Jews killed Jesus, therefore they must be a deicide people. This "ill-founded logic" sometimes gave Christians a reason and motive for killing Jews. One of the worst results of this rationale was the Nazi Holocaust *(shoah)*.

The only ancient sources that we have for who killed Jesus are the passion narratives in the four gospels: Mark, chapters 14–15; Matthew, chapters 26–27; Luke, chapters 22–23; and John, chapters 18–19. The four accounts agree on many basic points. They tell us that Jesus was arrested, underwent two hearings (trials), was sentenced to death by crucifixion, and died on the cross. Mark's account seems to have been the earliest; indeed, large blocks of it may have existed even before the gospel's composition around 70–75 C.E. Matthew follows Mark closely, though he does add some material, as, for example, the story of Judas hanging himself (Matthew 27:3–10). Luke, too, uses Mark as a source, but he includes even more material. John represents a separate tradition, while agreeing with Mark on many matters.

It is important to realize that none of the evangelists set out to write a detailed chronicle of the day Jesus died. All of them provide some reliable historical details. But their real interest lay in the theological significance of Jesus' death for us and for our sins, and how his death took place according to the Scriptures.

The best clue toward historically determining who killed Jesus is the mode of Jesus' death—by crucifixion. In Jesus' time, crucifixion was a Roman punishment inflicted mainly on slaves and revolutionaries. The usual Jewish mode of execution was stoning, as in the case of Stephen (see Acts of the Apostles 7:54–60). Crucifixion was a cruel and public way to die. Ultimately, the victim died by suffocation. As a public punishment, crucifixion was meant to shame the one being executed and to deter onlookers from doing what he had done.

The official with the power to execute Jesus by crucifixion was the Roman governor (prefect). In Jesus' time, the prefect was Pontius Pilate, who held that position between 26 and 36 C.E. Jesus was put to death "under Pontius Pilate" around 30 C.E. Although the gospels present Pilate as indecisive and somewhat concerned for justice in Jesus' case, the Alexandrian Jewish writer/philosopher Philo—a contemporary of Jesus—described him as "inflexible, merciless, and obstinate."

All four gospels recount a proceeding or hearing in which Jesus appeared before Pontius Pilate. It would be incorrect to call it a trial in the modern sense of the term. According to Mark 15:1–15 (see also Matthew 27:11–26, Luke 23:1–25), the Roman governor questioned Jesus and offered the crowd a choice between Barabbas and Jesus. The crowd, at the urging of the chief priest, called for Barabbas to be released and for Jesus to be crucified. Pilate bowed to pressure and "After flogging Jesus, he handed him over to be crucified" (Mark 15:15).

John's elaborate account of Jesus' trial before Pilate (John 18:28–19:16) ends in the same way, with Pilate handing Jesus over to be crucified (John 19:16).

The official charge of Jesus appears on the inscription placed on the cross: "The King of the Jews" (Mark 15:26, John 19:19). To Christian readers, this title ironically expresses the truth, that Jesus really was the Messiah of Jewish expectations—the anointed one who is king, priest, and prophet. To Pilate and his Jewish collaborators, however, Jesus was one in a series of Jewish political rebels bent on destroying the Roman Empire and the status quo with Jerusalem in the name of the kingdom of God. These Jewish "messiah-figures" described by the Jewish historian Josephus in his work *Jewish Antiquities* often used religious symbols and traditions to gain a popular following and to begin an uprising. The Roman governor dealt with them swiftly and brutally.

Jesus did not die alone. He was crucified along with two men described in various English translations of the Bible as "thieves," "bandits," "rebels," or "revolutionaries." The Greek word being translated in each case is *lestes*—the word applied to Barabbas, who was "in prison with the rebels who had committed murder during the insurrection" (Mark 15:7). It apparently referred not so much to petty thieves as to social bandits or revolutionaries who resisted the Roman officials and their Jewish collaborators. While the evangelists are careful to assert that Jesus was not a *lestes:* "Have you come out with swords and clubs to arrest me as though I were a bandit?" (Mark 14:48), the fact that Pilate offered a choice between Barabbas and Jesus, and then had Jesus crucified as "the King of the Jews" along with two bandit/rebels indicates that Pilate viewed Jesus as another Jewish religious/political troublemaker.

And so the mode of death—crucifixion, the legal system in force—with Pilate as having ultimate authority in capital cases, the official charge against Jesus—"the King of the Jews," and the identity of those crucified with Jesus all point in the same direction. Ultimate legal and moral responsibility for Jesus' death lay with Pontius Pilate, the Roman prefect of Judea between 26 and 36 C.E. Pontius Pilate killed Jesus.

The Role of "the Jews" in Jesus' Death

The Romans decided to take more direct control of Judea in 6 C.E. by appointing a Roman prefect (governor). The most famous of these prefects was Pontius Pilate (26–36 C.E.).

It was Roman policy to work with local people. When things got out of hand, the Roman armies would intervene with brutal force. But in normal times, the Romans relied on local officials to collect taxes and to keep the peace. And so in Judea it was natural that there would be Jews who did the Romans' bidding.

Jerusalem was a religious pilgrimage site, indeed the pilgrimage center for Jews in the land of Israel and dispersed throughout the empire. Three times a year—at Passover, Pentecost, and Tabernacles—Jews came in large numbers to worship at the Temple in the holy city. The pilgrimage trade was a major industry in

Jerusalem. The restoration and expansion of the Temple, begun as part of Herod the Great's ambitious building program, was likewise a major industry. To a great extent, all this was overseen by the chief priests and elders of the people in Jerusalem.

The pilgrimages brought many people to Jerusalem, and the themes of the great festivals—especially Passover, with its commemoration of Israel's liberation from slavery in Egypt—could incite nationalistic fervor and even rebellion. And so it was natural that the Roman prefect, whose official residence was in Caesarea Maritima, over on the Mediterranean coast, would come to Jerusalem at Passover and work with local officials, such as the chief priests and elders, to keep things under control. Pilate and the local Jewish leaders had the same goal—to keep the peace.

The four gospels (see Mark 14:53–65; Matthew 26:57–68; Luke 22:66–71; John 18:12–14, 19–24) recount a trial or hearing before the Jewish council, presided over by the high priest. The Jews who took the initiative in this proceeding were not the opponents of Jesus during his public ministry—the Pharisees—but, rather, the high priest, the chief priest and elders—those who had most at stake in the smooth running of the Temple and the peace of Jerusalem.

According to Mark 14:53–65, there were two charges made against Jesus. He threatened to destroy the Temple (14:58) and claimed to be "the Messiah, the Son of the Blessed One" (14:61). Although the first charge is denied and the second charge is given an interpretation (see Mark 14:57–59, 62), there was surely something to these charges.

Jesus' threat against the Temple fits with his symbolic prophetic action in "cleansing" the Temple (see Mark 11:15–19) and his prophecies about the Temple's destruction (see Mark 13:1–2). For the Jewish leaders, merchants, and construction workers whose livelihood depended on the smooth running of the Jerusalem Temple, the slightest—even symbolic—threat against the Temple would have been taken very seriously. Moreover, talk about Jesus as "the Messiah, Son of the Blessed One" would surely have set off alarms, not only among the Romans but also amongst the Jewish leadership. Both viewed Jesus as another religious-political messianic pretender, who had to be dealt with quickly. The kind of language being used about Jesus in some circles alerted them to the danger that he might pose to their power and to the status quo.

How effective were Jewish leaders in getting Jesus killed? The gospels suggest that Jewish leaders were the prime movers, and that the Romans only ratified their decision. There are, however, scholars who argue that no Jewish authority was involved in any way. Between these two poles there are mediating positions. One view says that the Romans were the prime movers and that the Jewish authorities reluctantly gave in to pressure from them. The other view states that even though Jewish leaders were actively involved, the main legal formalities were carried out by the Romans.

Two important points seem to emerge: Jesus was killed "under Pontius Pilate," and the Jewish authorities at Jerusalem probably played some role in getting Jesus killed. Whatever Jewish responsibility there may have been, it lay with a small group—the chief priests and elders, in a specific place—Jerusalem, and at a specific time—Passover of 30 C.E. Even the saying in Matthew 27:25, "Then the people as a whole answered, 'His blood be upon us and upon our children,' " is best taken as referring to the people (us) manipulated by the leaders and to the destruction of Jerusalem in 70 C.E. ("our children"), not to the whole Jewish people for all ages.

The official position of the Catholic Church on this matter was clearly stated in the Second Vatican Council's *Declaration on the Relation of the Church to Non-Christian Religions* (1965): "Even though the Jewish authorities and those who followed their lead pressed for the death of Christ (cf. John 19:16), neither all Jews indiscriminately at that time, nor Jews today, can be charged with the crimes committed during his passion" (4).

Christians today need to be sensitive to the manifest tendency in the gospels to emphasize the responsibility of Jewish leaders and to play down the Romans' role. One can get the impression that Jewish leaders manipulated Pilate to pass sentence on Jesus, and that he turned Jesus over to them to be executed. The impression grows as one moves from Mark to Matthew and Luke, who both used Mark as a source. Moreover, John's gospel lumps all Jesus' opponents under the title "the Jews," thus apparently extending Jewish responsibility beyond the chief priests and elders. *Such passages need to be read in their late first-century context, when Jerusalem had been destroyed and Christians were accommodating themselves to life within the Roman Empire.* When taken out of this context, these texts can contribute to anti-Judaism, and obscure the Jewishness of Jesus and the Jewish character of earliest Christianity.

The Structure of the Passion Narratives

The gospel writers present dramatizations—not videotapes—of the last events of Jesus' life in the stories of the passion. They are tragic four-act dramas that rivet the attention of the reader on the main character, Jesus. In the drama, act one presents Jesus at prayer and his arrest in Gethsemane. Act two narrates Jesus on trial before the Jewish authorities. Act three portrays Jesus before the Roman governor, Pilate. The concluding act is the way of the cross, Jesus' crucifixion and death on Golgotha.

THE DRAMATIC FORMAT OF THE GOSPEL PASSION NARRATIVES			
	Mark	Matthew	Luke	John
Act One	14:26–52	26:36–56	22:39–53	18:1–11
Act Two	14:53–15:1	26:57–68	22:54–71	18:12–28
Act Three	15:2–20	27:11–31	23:1–25	18:28–19:16a
Act Four	15:21–47	27:32–66	23:26–56	19:16b–22

Since there is a dramatic format to these accounts, it is easy for the reader to step into the shoes of the various characters in the story.

147

Often, the reader is drawn to participate in the drama and to ask just how he or she would have stood in relation to the arrest, trial, and crucifixion of Jesus.

These four-act dramas cause the modern Christian to examine his or her conscience, asking: With which character in the narrative would I most identify? Could I have been among the disciples who fled from danger, abandoning Jesus at his final hour? Could I have been like Peter? Surely in my own life there are moments when I deny Jesus. Could I be like Judas, betraying Jesus? Are there not times in my own life when I find myself like Simon of Cyrene, carrying the cross of Jesus? Or maybe even like Pontius Pilate in John's gospel, trying to avoid making a decision between good and evil, or even washing my hands of the whole affair, as he does in Matthew's gospel? Could I be sheepish about my commitment to Jesus as a disciple, like Joseph of Arimathea, who only claimed he knew Jesus under the cover of night? While these questions might seem shocking, they do help us to better embrace the profoundly dramatic character of the gospel passion stories.

Since these stories are dramatizations and not videotapes of Jesus' final days, their emphasis is theology, not biography. Each gospel tries to link Jesus' suffering and death to the Hebrew Scriptures, which was their sourcebook. Jesus is then understood as the suffering servant described in Isaiah.

Granting the gospel's shared theology, we can discern a distinctive angle of vision in each gospel passion account.

Mark's Version

Mark's narrative is rather terse and concise, but within it is a rich theological perspective of its own. Mark does not shy away from the cruelty of the passion.

Mark's passion narrative portrays the stark human abandonment of Jesus, which is reversed dramatically in the end. From the moment Jesus moves to the Mount of Olives, the behavior of the disciples is negatively portrayed. While Jesus prays, they fall asleep three times. Jesus rises from prayer, energized to face his destiny; they are debilitated by lack of prayer. Judas betrays him and Peter curses him, three times denying knowledge of him. All flee, with the last one leaving even his clothes behind in order to get away from Jesus—the exact opposite of leaving all things in order to follow Jesus. Both Jewish and Roman leaders are presented as cynical. Jesus hangs on the cross for six hours, three of which are filled with human mockery, while in the second three the land is covered with darkness. Jesus' only word from the cross is the recitation of a lament drawn from Psalm 22: "My God, my God, why have you forsaken me?" And even that plaintive cry is met with derision.

Another element in the Markan narrative is irony. All through Mark's gospel, only God and the demons have acknowledged Jesus' identity as the Messiah, Son of God (1:11, 24; 9:7). But the other characters in the story wonder in amazement at Jesus' needs without knowing his true identity. Only at the time of the crucifixion does a human character, a Roman centurion who is a Gentile, acknowledge Jesus' identity. "Truly, this man was God's son!" (Mark 15:39). It is ironic that a Gentile achieves the insight no Jew in the story achieves. Even Jesus' disciples are portrayed in Mark as rather dense, slow to catch on to Jesus' true identity (see Mark 8:17–18, 33).

Mark also emphasizes the theme of kingship. Throughout Mark, the characters are filled with expectation of a royal messiah, but they do not understand the nature of that identity. In the passion narrative, the notion of kingship comes to the fore to clarify Jesus' identity by means of his mission. Unlike earthly kings, this anointed king comes as a suffering servant. Paradoxically, only when one sees Jesus on the cross does one understand that his mission as a royal messiah is one of service and sacrifice (10:45, 14:24).

As Jesus breathes his last, God acts to confirm his Son. The trial before the Jewish Sanhedrin had concerned his threat to destroy the Temple and his claim to be the messianic Son of the Blessed One. At Jesus' death, the veil of the Temple is rent, meaning that now there is no separation between God and humans, and a Roman centurion confesses, "Truly, this man was God's Son!" After the cross it is possible, then, to see that Jesus was not a false prophet.

In sum, Mark's version of the passion maintains that despite human rejection, Jesus is vindicated in the end.

Matthew's Version

Matthew expands and edits certain parts of the passion story to create his own eloquent emphases. From the beginning of Matthew's gospel, Jesus is called Emmanuel, God-with-us (1:23). Most likely, this title serves Matthew's mixed Jewish and Gentile community well. After the destruction of the Jerusalem Temple in 70 C.E., a frequently asked question was where God could be found. Matthew responds—in Jesus! The passion brings out the theme of God-with-us in a subtle way at a crucial moment.

In Gethsemane, Jesus asks his disciples to be "with" him (26:38, 40) in his hour of need. Unfortunately, the disciples abandon Jesus at the time of his arrest (26:56). Jesus had promised to be with them in times of similar trial (10:16–20, 26–33), and even to the end of the ages (28:20), but they do not have sufficient faith to stay with him in his time of trial.

Although all passion accounts note the importance of prophecy and fulfillment in Jesus' death, only Matthew heightens it to a major motif. A series of fulfillment citations punctuates both the infancy and passion narratives (1:22–23; 2:5–6, 15, 17, 23; 26:31; 27:9–10). Moreover, during the passion Jesus himself twice observes that the Scriptures are being fulfilled (26:54, 56). For Matthew, the passion is not simply a miscarriage of justice but the divinely ordained route for Jesus to fulfill his salvific ministry (1:21). Further confirmation of the divine purpose is found in the cosmic events that occur at both the beginning and the end of Jesus' life. A heavenly star announces his arrival (2:2); an earthquake and the resurrection of the saints accompany his death (27:51–53).

For Matthew, Jesus' last cry marks a birth pang. The light of the new Israel—the church—breaks into the darkness of Calvary. As in all four gospels, the veil that shields the Holy of Holies (which only the high priest could enter, and he but once a year) from the rest of the

Temple is rent from top to bottom. Matthew adds an earthquake and shattered rock; the holy dead leave their tombs to walk in the city. The whole Roman guard proclaims Jesus as the Son of God.

Only Matthew records the fate of the betrayer Judas (27:3–10). Judas finally recognizes his terrible deed and tries to reclaim his innocence by returning the thirty pieces of silver he had taken for the betrayal. Neither he nor the Jewish leaders who plotted against Jesus can reclaim lost innocence, however, for they have shed "innocent blood." Ironically, Judas' suicide heightens Jesus' innocence, which is also confirmed by the pronouncement of Pilate's wife (27:19), who, like the Gentile magi of the infancy narrative, has a dream that reveals this to her.

Luke's Version

Luke's narration of Jesus' passion is filled with poignant and deeply moving moments. Luke intensifies the emotional impact of the passion in some of his short scenes.

One is in Gethsemane, when Jesus is at prayer. So intense is the moment that an angel comes to Jesus' aid, and Luke alone records that Jesus' sweat became "like great drops of blood" (22:44). Only Luke speaks of this moment as an "agony" (from Greek *agonia*, meaning the intensity of an athletic or gladiatorial contest).

THE BLOODY SWEAT OF JESUS IN LUKE

One striking thing about Luke's account of Jesus' passion is that Jesus does not appear to experience any deep anguish over his coming fate. This becomes clear in a comparative study of what Jesus does prior to his betrayal and arrest (Luke 22:39–46, Mark 14:32–42). In Mark's account, Jesus is said to become "distressed and agitated" (14:33). Luke's version says nothing of the sort. In Mark, Jesus tells his disciples that his soul is sorrowful unto death (14:34), words not found in Luke. In Mark, Jesus leaves his disciples and falls to his face on the ground to pray (14:35). In Luke, he simply prays on his knees. In Mark, Jesus prays fervently three times for God to "remove this cup from me" (14:36, 39, 41). In Luke, he asks only once and prefaces his prayer with "if you are willing." Thus in comparison with Mark, Jesus does not seem to appear to be in gut-wrenching distress over his coming fate. But consider the famous and uniquely Lukan verses found in the middle of the scene, Luke 22:43–44, where an angel from heaven comes to give Jesus much needed support and where his sweat is said to have become "like drops of blood falling to the ground." Don't these verses show Luke's Jesus in profound agony?

They do indeed! But the question is whether these verses were originally penned by Luke or were added by later scribes who felt somewhat uneasy over the fact that in this gospel version Jesus does not seem distraught by his coming fate. If you are using a modern translation of the Bible, like the *New Revised Standard Version,* you will notice that these verses are in double brackets. These brackets show that the translators are fairly confident that the verses did not originally form part of Luke's gospel but were added by well-meaning scribes at a later time. One reason for thinking so is the fact that these verses about Jesus' bloody sweat are absent from our oldest and many of our best manuscripts of the New Testament.

Luke makes much of the contrast between Jesus and the disciples in this garden scene. It is framed at beginning and end by a warning to pray so "that they might not come into the time of trial" (11:40b, 46b; see the final petition of the Lord's Prayer, 11:4c). Where Jesus watches and prays, the disciples, despite this warning, fall asleep because of grief (11:45). They model an inappropriate response to the time of trial, just as Jesus models what is truly right.

The scene is the climax of the many occasions when Luke has shown Jesus at prayer. Throughout the gospel of Luke, prayer has been the great vehicle and channel of Jesus' communion with the Father. Like the disciples, readers of the gospel, in good times and in bad, are invited to become Jesus' apprentices in this respect, so that in their lives God's will may be done and they may not be led into temptation.

Another scene occurs during Peter's denials. Only Luke positions the scene in such a way that Peter and Jesus can be in the same line of vision: "The Lord turned and looked at Peter" (22:61). If there is remonstrance in this look of Jesus, there is also healing—certainly not judgment or condemnation. Peter goes out and weeps bitterly (22:62), the beginning of a conversion of heart that will give him the capacity to strengthen his brothers and sisters. Such a scene as this creates enormous emotional identification with the reader.

Luke's portrait of Jesus as the one who seeks out the lost to save them is well known (see Luke, chapter 15). In the passion narrative, Luke notes that Jesus continued his healing ministry even in the midst of his own suffering. On the way to the cross, Jesus sees the women of Jerusalem who weep for him, but he selflessly directs their sorrow to themselves for their loss (23:27–29). Only Luke records the famous words of Jesus from the cross, "Father, forgive them; for they do not know what they are doing" (23:34). Jesus also reaches out to the one repentant criminal (thief) crucified with him. Jesus says to him: "Truly I tell you, today you will be with me in Paradise" (23:43). The crucifixion becomes an occasion of divine forgiveness and care, and Jesus dies tranquilly, praying: "Father, into your hands I commend my spirit" (23:46). Paradoxically, even Jesus' persecutors are reconciled; Jesus' passion brings peace and friendship between Herod and Pilate (23:12).

Finally, Luke emphasizes that Jesus dies the death of an innocent martyr. Pilate declares him innocent three successive times (23:4, 14, 22), as does Herod (23:15), one of the criminals (thieves) crucified with him (23:41), and the centurion standing guard (23:47). Jesus' martyrdom prepares for the future martyrs of the church who will be called to follow Jesus' example.

John's Version

John's passion narrative presents a sovereign Jesus who has defiantly announced, "I lay down my life in order to take it up again. No one takes it from me" (10:17–18). When Roman soldiers and Jewish police come to arrest him, they fall to the earth, powerless, as he speaks the divine phrase, "I am." In the garden he does not pray to be delivered from the hour of trial and death, as he does in the other gospels, for the hour is the whole purpose of his life (12:27). His self-assurance is an offense to the high priest (18:22); and Pilate is afraid of the Son of God, who states, "You have no power over me" (19:8–11). No Simon of Cyrene appears; the Jesus of John carries his own cross. His royalty is proclaimed in three languages and confirmed by Pilate. Unlike the portrayals in the other gospels, Jesus is not alone on Calvary; at the foot of the cross stands the Beloved Disciple and the mother of Jesus. He relates these two highly symbolic figures to each other as son and mother, thus leaving behind a family of believing disciples. He does not cry out, "My God, my God, why have you forsaken me?" (Mark 15:34) because the Father is always with him (16:32). Rather, his final words are a solemn decision, "It is finished"—only when he has decided does he hand over his spirit. Even in death, he dispenses life as water flows from within him (see 7:38–39). His burial is not unprepared, as in the other gospels; rather, he lies amidst one hundred pounds of spices, as befits a king.

The Interrogations of Jesus
in the Gospel of John (John 18:12–19:16)

By comparing the synoptics and John's account of Jesus' interrogations, a gap emerges. John does not mention the main trial of Jesus before the ruling council, the Sanhedrin. No formal charge is made and no witnesses are called (see Matthew 26:57–27:2, Mark 14:53–15:1, Luke 22:54–23:1).

Instead, only John says the arresting officers delivered Jesus to Annas, who obviously held a place of honor in Jewish society. (Annas was a high priest deposed by the Romans in 15 C.E.) After questioning Jesus, Annas transfers him to the current high priest, his son-in-law, Caiaphas (John 18:24). John does not report an interrogation by Caiaphas. Next we read that Jesus is moved to Pilate's headquarters (John 18:28).

John's sketchy version of the Jewish hearings betrays his low opinion of these hearings. At this point, a trial before the religious authorities could only be a sham. The Sanhedrin, under the guidance of Caiaphas, had already passed their sentence (John 11:45–53). Note the satirical prophetic reminder of this in John 18:14: "Caiaphas was the one who had advised the Jews that it was better to have one person die for the people."

Still, the trial is important for John. It shows the faithfulness of Jesus to his mission, even when his disciples are unfaithful. John sets a dramatic contrast between Jesus and Peter to make the point. Two investigations are happening simultaneously.

Inside, Jesus stands before his questioners with nothing to hide. Jesus declares, "I have spoken openly. . . . I have said nothing in secret" (John 18:20). Everyone who has heard him in the synagogue or Temple can report his teaching. He challenges his interrogators to find fault in anything he has said.

Simultaneously, outside, Peter furtively shadows Jesus and denies everything. Three times he is asked if he belongs with Jesus. Three times he denies the association (John 18:17, 25, 27). In spite of specific warnings (John 13:36–38) and a flawed track record (John 18:11–12), Peter has tried to follow and has failed. He now vanishes and will not reappear until after the resurrection.

The juxtaposition of the disciple and his Lord is profound. Jesus is the only one who can complete God's saving work. His disciples cannot follow him to the cross and on to the Father—yet. Jesus must first go alone; then he will enable and call believers to follow.

Moving on to the Roman trial, most of this narrative concerns Pilate's interaction with Jesus and his accusers (John 18:28–19:16). Again the narrative creates dramatic contrast by shifting from inside to outside. Seven scenes alternate to take the reader from Pilate's introduction of the case to his sanctioning of the crucifixion (see below). Pontius Pilate shrinks in stature from the impartial Roman governor of Judea to an intimidated subject of mob rule. All the while, he stands in the shadow of the true King of the Jews.

Kingship is the issue in the trial of Jesus before Pilate. Some of his own people accuse Jesus of claiming to be King of the Jews, a trea- sonous crime punishable by crucifixion under Roman law. More than stoning, crucifixion would signify in a Jewish context that God had cursed Jesus (Deuteronomy 21:23). John, by contrast, sees the insistence on crucifixion as another fulfillment of Jesus' words (John 18:32).

THE SEVEN SCENES OF THE TRIAL BEFORE PILATE IN THE GOSPEL OF JOHN

"Then they took Jesus from Caiaphas to Pilate's headquarters" (John 18:28).

Inside	Outside
	Scene 1: Pilate went out and asked: "What accusation do you bring against this man?" (John 18:29–32)
Scene 2: Pilate enters and asks Jesus, "Are you the King of the Jews?" Jesus acknowledges his kingship (John 18:33–38).	
	Scene 3: Pilate tells the Jews, "I find no case against him." He offers to release Jesus according to the Passover custom. The crowd refuses (John 18:38–40).
Scene 4: Pilate has Jesus flogged. The soldiers mock him, saying, "Hail, King of the Jews!" (John 19:1–3)	
	Scene 5: Pilate repeats, "I find no case against him." He brings Jesus out and says, "Here is the man!" The crowd demands, "Crucify him!" (John 19:4–7).
Scene 6: Pilate becomes afraid at the report of Jesus' claim to be the Son of God. He asks Jesus, "Where are you from?" He tries to release Jesus but instead bows to political pressure (John 19:8–12).	
	Scene 7: Pilate brings Jesus out and pronounces his judgment: "Here is your King!" The chief priests say, "We have no king but the emperor." Pilate hands Jesus over to be crucified (John 19:13–16).

Pilate asks his prisoner if he is King of the Jews. In response, Jesus admits he is a king, but his kingdom is not of this world. Pilate does not perceive the truth of Jesus' claims, but neither does he perceive Jesus to be a threat. He derisively proclaims him, "King of the Jews" (John 18:39; 19:13, 19, 22), yet declares three times, "I find no case against him" (John 18:38; 19:4, 6).

With corresponding blind ridicule, the soldiers use thorns to crown Jesus "King of the Jews" and then hit him. Presenting the pathetic figure before the people, Pilate heaps the scorn higher: "Here is the man!" (John 19:5). Pilate sees nothing more than a humiliated, harmless mortal. Jesus' accusers insist he must be put to death "because he has claimed to be the Son of God" (John 19:7).

The mention of the Son of God stops Pilate short; he "was more afraid than ever" (John 19:8). The way John describes it, Jesus' transcendent demeanor through the whole ordeal of the trial has piqued Pilate's suspicions of Jesus' divine origin. Pilate asks Jesus, "Where are you from?" (John 19:9). He has asked the most pertinent question one could ask the Johannine Son of God.

Pilate had not earlier heard the truth (John 18:37–38) and so Jesus does not answer now. Pilate's threats do not shake Jesus. The Son of God replies, "You would have no power over me unless it had been given you from above" (John 19:11). After this response, Pilate decides to release Jesus.

By now, though, Pilate has been trapped by his own maneuvering. He cannot release Jesus and still maintain control over his province. As with all who meet Jesus, Pilate must ultimately decide for or against Jesus. He makes his choice and brings Jesus out to the mob.

Out above the crowd, Pilate takes his place on the judge's bench (John 19:15). "Shall I crucify your King?" he asks. Provoked, the crowd blasphemes, "We have no king but the emperor" (John 19:15). Like Pilate, they have been caught in their manipulations. By rejecting Jesus, they have traded all messianic hope in exchange for a Gentile oppressor. They have rushed into the arms of another king rather than accept God's anointed one.

The verdict comes down; Pilate hands Jesus over to Jewish authorities for crucifixion (John 19:16).

Most important for John is to understand that Jesus is not a victim. Rather he voluntarily lays down his life, just as the "good shepherd" does for his sheep (10:17–18). Nothing happens to Jesus in the passion that he is not aware of ahead of time. No one, not even Pilate, holds power over him (19:8–11). He is in charge of his own destiny because he is the Word made flesh, God come to dwell in our midst (1:14). He even carries his own cross without assistance. Such is his willful obedience unto death (19:30).

Further, John's version of the passion sees it as part of a cosmic conflict between the power of darkness and the power of light. Jesus was light that came into the darkened world (1:1–9, 3:19–21). Jesus is the world's light (8:12), but the sad reality is that many people prefer to walk in darkness rather than in light. Judas accomplishes his betrayal by cover of night (13:30), and when Jesus' enemies come to arrest him in the garden it is at night. Though they are in the presence of the "light of the world" (8:12), they rely on torches and involuntarily bend down for a moment in his presence (18:3–6). In short, the passion of John brings to a climax the cosmic drama between light and darkness, between truth and falsehood, between life and death.

In sum, in John's gospel Jesus reigns, even from the cross. He is totally in control, right up to the very end. He remains sovereign over the final moments of his life.

In the gospel passion stories, we really have four versions. Seeing the four accounts of Jesus' passion in the context of their respective gospels helps us appreciate both their unity and their diversity. All four are faithful in recording the story of Jesus' final days. Yet each evangelist does it with an eye toward what speaks most powerfully to his individual community. Whether Spartan, eloquent, poignant, or majestic, they all seek to present faithfully the tradition they have inherited.

It is important that we avoid the tendency to blend the passion stories into one seamless story and ask instead what we learn anew from each retelling and from each individual evangelist. Like a common picture painted by four different artists, we have been given a multifaceted account of Jesus' suffering and death. This fourfold version gives us multiple ways to reflect on how Jesus' suffering brought new light into the world and how we ourselves can face the suffering that comes into our lives.

For Discussion

1. In the passion narratives, Jesus is strengthened by prayer to face his cross. Are you?
2. Have you ever denied Jesus, as Peter did? Have you ever betrayed Jesus, as Judas did?
3. Have you ever forgiven your enemies or those who do you wrong, as Jesus did?
4. Like Jesus, do you ever feel that God has abandoned you?
5. Are you willing to carry your own cross behind Jesus, as did Simon of Cyrene?

For Further Reading

Binz, Stephen J. *The Passion and Resurrection Narratives of Jesus: A Commentary.* Collegeville, Minn.: Liturgical Press, 1989.

Brown, Raymond E. *The Death of the Messiah* (2 vols.). New York: Doubleday, 1994.

Heil, J. P. *The Death and Resurrection of Jesus.* Minneapolis: Augsburg/Fortress, 1991.

Matera, F. J. *Passion Narratives and Gospel Theologies.* New York: Paulist Press, 1986.

Senior, Donald. *The Passion Series* (4 vols.). Collegeville, Minn.: Liturgical Press, 1984–91.

7

"HE HAS BEEN RAISED; HE IS NOT HERE"

(MARK 16:6)

Without THE RESURRECTION OF JESUS FROM THE dead, there would be no Christianity. In fact, had Jesus not been understood to have been raised from the dead, we would probably know nothing at all about him, for nobody would have been moved to write the New Testament. Belief in the resurrection is the cornerstone of Christian faith and the heart of the New Testament.

The importance of the resurrection of Jesus for the faith of Christianity cannot be underestimated. It is a bedrock teaching. The resurrection of Jesus is referred to explicitly and with emphasis in seventeen of the twenty-seven books of the New Testament. Paul proclaims the resurrection in all his letters. Many of these passages indicate very clearly the centrality of the resurrection:

> If there is no resurrection of the dead, then Christ has not been raised; and if Christ has not been raised, then our proclamation has been in vain and your faith has been in vain (1 Corinthians 15:13–14).

> Blessed be the God and Father of our Lord Jesus Christ! By his great mercy he has given us a new birth into a living hope through the resurrection of Jesus Christ from the dead (1 Peter 1:3).

> Jesus said to her [Martha], "I am the resurrection and the life. Those who believe in me, even though they die, will live, and everyone who lives and believes in me will never die" (John 11:25–26).

What these passages and the many others found in the New Testament about the resurrection indicate is that for believing Christians, this earthly life is not the be all and end all. For believing Christians, death—for all of its seeming finality—does not speak the last word. On the other hand, for a multitude of modern men and women to whom death is the end, the claim that Jesus was raised from the dead is nonsense.

Yet, the truth of the resurrection comes ultimately from the Holy Spirit and the faith of the believer. The resurrection is not so much a proof for Jesus' divinity as it is a challenge for our entire faith life. Resurrection is a faith tenant, something that defies empirical proof. Such a faith believes that Jesus the Christ was raised from the dead, and that his faithful followers will also rise, but it does not know how this will occur. Such a position of faith further believes that the risen Jesus is present right now in the individual believer and the community of believers, but it does not know how he is present. Finally, Christian faith in the resurrection believes that Christians someday, like the risen Jesus, will be joined with God in heaven and embrace eternal life. How this will happen it does not know.

Succinctly put, Christians do not have certitude about the resurrection, but rather faith in it.

Without the resurrection, Jesus was a good man, like many others before him, who attempted to bring about a conversion of hearts and failed. He died and only his inspiration continues in the lives of his followers. But if Jesus is the risen Lord, he then communicates his spirit and makes it possible for all to hope not only for a future personal resurrection but for the experience of the saving presence of God in human life. With the resurrection, Christianity as a credible religious tradition becomes possible.

Gospel Texts on the Resurrection

The four gospels provide two kinds (types) of stories that deal with the resurrection of Jesus. There is a group of narratives referred to as the empty tomb narratives. These appear in Mark 16:1–8, and with some variation in Matthew 28:1–8, Luke 24:1–12, and John 20:1–10. The other type of narratives are referred to as the postresurrection appearances. In these the risen Jesus appears to different followers and disciples in a variety of contexts. The appearance stories are found in Mark 16:9–20, Matthew 27:9–10 and 27:16–20, Luke 25:13–53, and John 20:11–29 and 21:1–23. It is not clear which type of story may have been composed first, even though the empty tomb becomes the important link between the crucifixion and the resurrection. What is clear is that all four gospels contain both types of stories.

The gospel accounts agree on the following points: (1) the Jesus who was crucified truly was raised from the dead; (2) he appeared to some women and to some of his other disciples; (3) he sent his disciples to bring the Good News to others.

The Resurrection Stories in the Gospel of Mark

In the gospel of Mark, chapter 16 deals with the resurrection. It is made up of two units. The first is the women discovering the empty tomb (Mark 16:1–8); the second is a series of three postresurrection appearances of Jesus (Mark 16:9–20).

The Women at the Tomb (Mark 16:1–8)

The *women* are the central characters of the whole story, and Mark tells the story entirely from their point of view. They provide a connection not only with Jesus' burial but also with his entire public life, leading up to his death. The women have followed him, ministered to him, accompanied him from Galilee to Jerusalem, and have witnessed his last moments (see 15:40–41). Unlike the male disciples who deserted Jesus (see 14:50), the women have stayed with him to the end. The mention of their intention to anoint Jesus recalls their previous service toward Jesus and emphasizes their continuing attachment to Jesus, as opposed to the male disciples' defections. The women's proposal to perform these belated funeral rites also shows a conviction that Jesus is dead. They do not expect or hope for anything extraordinary to happen at their visit. As far as they are concerned, Jesus is dead, his story has ended.

What is astounding about this usage of the women is the fact that Jewish tradition at the time of Jesus was characterized by an extreme patriarchal bias in favor of men. This bias led the Jewish scribes to teach that women were not reliable witnesses and could not testify at a trial. However, what might be a human standard for the appropriateness of women as witnesses is not a divine standard. Namely, now that Jesus has been raised, God can choose whom God wills to choose to witness to the resurrected Jesus.

The earliness of the women's visit expresses their keenness to accomplish their service, while the reference to "the sun had risen" (verse 2) anticipates a possible objection that the women go to the wrong tomb precisely because it is so early. Although it is early, the sun had risen and, therefore, the women can see where they are going. It is also possible that the allusions to the "first day of the week" and "the sun had risen" have a symbolic value, "the first day of the week" suggesting that the women are about to become involved in a new creation and the phrase "the sun had risen" that the resurrection of Jesus dispels the darkness of death.

The concern of the women about how to move the large stone from the door of the tomb creates dramatic tension and prepares us for the discovery of the stone's "mysterious removal." The storyteller wants us to know that God is involved here.

When the surprised women enter the tomb, they are astonished by a revelatory encounter with an "interpreting young man," who announces that the tomb is empty because Jesus has been raised (Mark 16:5–6). At this point, Mark augments the young man's message to the women: "But go, tell his disciples and Peter that he is going ahead of you to Galilee; there you will see him, just as he told you" (Mark 16:7). The young man thus commissions the women to share in proclaiming that Jesus is not dead but alive.

We know that Mark 16:7 explicitly refers to the prediction that Mark had already placed on Jesus' lips in 14:28: "But after I am raised up, I will go before you to Galilee." Mark wished to conclude his gospel with a declaration previewing the appearances of the risen Jesus to Peter and the other disciples in Galilee.

Let us now look at the character of the *young man* in the story. To begin with, he is in the tomb and he is seated at the right. In the vocabulary of the Bible, to be seated at the right is to be seated at the place of honor. A reaffirmation of this point is the Apostles' Creed, where it says that Jesus is seated at the right hand of God—the place of honor.

In the Book of Daniel, apocalyptic or end time mysteries concerning the end of the world are repeatedly revealed to Daniel through an interpreting angel. When Daniel receives these awe-inspiring revelations, he is consistently overwhelmed with fear and trembling and rendered speechless (Daniel 7:15, 27; 8:17–18, 27; 10:7–11). Mark 16:8 describes the three women as acting in precisely this manner after the interpreting young man reveals Jesus' resurrection. "So they went out and fled from the tomb, for terror and amazement had seized them; and they said nothing to anyone, for they were afraid" (Mark 16:8).

The revelation of the empty tomb's meaning by an interpreting young man—possibly an angel—is an apocalyptic sign that the "end time" has arrived and its mysteries are beginning to unfold. The women's terrified response, therefore, is entirely appropriate and expected by the gospel writer of Mark.

At the time of Jesus, most religious Jews in Palestine had embraced some form of the eschatological (end time) hope introduced by the Book of Daniel. Many Jews who had embraced this hope believed that when the Messiah came he would preside over the end of history and usher in the new creation promised by apocalyptic writers. Some Jews also believed that a gloriously messianic reign on earth would come as a temporal preamble to eternal life and the new creation.

It is understandable, therefore, that some Jews objected that Jesus could not be the promised Messiah because the new creation had not yet arrived. The early Jewish Christians replied that the new creation had mysteriously begun with the resurrection of Jesus. The risen Jesus, they declared, is God's guarantee that everlasting life in the new creation will soon arrive in its eschatological (end time) fullness because it has already been inaugurated in Jesus. The church understands, therefore, the risen Jesus as the foundation stone of the new creation (Romans 9:32–33). The new creation began on Easter Sunday and will be completed when Jesus returns in glory to preside over the conclusion of history.

To validate their conviction that the risen Jesus is the beginning of the new creation, the Jewish-Christians searched the Old Testament for proof texts. They assumed that everything that God intends to accomplish in history is mysteriously foreshadowed in the Scriptures.

Christian teachers in search of proof texts remembered that in Genesis the old creation was called into being during a period of seven days, beginning with "the first day of the week" when God called "light" out of "darkness" (Genesis 1:3–5). They then concluded that God had raised Jesus as the "light" of the world on Easter Sunday, "the first day of the week," to signify that the new creation had begun and is hastening toward its completion when the cosmic Sabbath will begin.

Because of the importance of new creation theology in the earliest church, all four gospels announce that the empty tomb was discovered on "the first day of the week" at or near the time of sunrise (Mark 16:1; Matthew 27:1; Luke 24:1; John 20:1, 21:4). This announcement is tantamount to proclaiming that the new creation promised in the Book of Daniel has begun with the resurrection of Jesus. The earliest church includes an allusion to "the first day" of creation (Genesis 1:3–5) in her recital of the empty tomb story to remind Christians of the proof text needed to defend their faith in the disputed messiahship of Jesus.

Let us turn our attention to the character of the narrator (storyteller). The narrator tells the story to show that death is not the final outcome for Jesus. His primary concern is to convey a new status for Jesus, one that goes beyond the finality of death and tomb.

The cause of the women's flight is that they are seized with terror and amazement (Mark 16:8b). These emotions are reactions to the experience of the supernatural or the divine (6:51). By allowing themselves to be so overcome by these emotions, the women have failed to obey the order of the young man, "Do not be alarmed" (16:6). This disobedience precedes their noncompliance with the same divine envoy's command to tell the good news to the disciples. The young man ordered the women explicitly to tell the disciples about the raised Jesus' journey into Galilee. Mark states explicitly that the women "said nothing to anyone" (16:8). The contrast or opposition between what the young man commands the women to do and what they actually do could not be more stark.

This fear experienced by the women is the human reaction to the experience of the divine. The overall impression given to the reader by Mark 16:8 is that the women's experience of this young man, his message concerning Jesus' destiny, and his commission to them to relay this message overwhelms and dumbfounds them. Mark uses this strategy for dramatic effect so that he can also overwhelm the audience with the resurrection experience. The Markan church is awestruck by the awesomeness of the resurrection. And this is the way the gospel ends.

Postresurrection Appearance Narrative (Mark 16:9–20)

This section of the gospel was added at a later point. It is sometimes referred to as the "long ending." It begins in Mark 16:9–11 with an appearance by Jesus to Mary Magdalene. This appearance gives her the courage to do the very thing the young man had previously commanded: she goes to tell those who had been with him who were mourning and weeping. In describing the reaction of these disciples to Magdalene's message, the author shows that he shares the pessimistic view of Jesus' followers that characterizes Mark. He reports (16:11) that when these disciples heard that Jesus was alive and had been seen by Magdalene, they were unbelieving.

But disbelief does not defeat the risen Lord. Afterward he appears "in another form" to two disciples as they are going into the country-side (16:12–13). In this text, the reference to "another form" tells us how Christians came to explain why the postresurrected Jesus could not be easily recognized. Evidently, however, such a different appearance is enough to overcome previous disbelief, for the two return to the city of Jerusalem to tell the rest of the disciples. Just as they had not believed Magdalene, the others do not believe these two. Thus, the long ending of Mark presents us with a remarkable sequence where ultimately only an encounter with the risen Jesus himself overcomes previous failure to believe.

In Mark 16:14–18 one discovers that there are quite a few usages of the term *believe*. The harshness of Jesus' rebuke to "the rest" of the disciples for their disbelief and hardness of heart is intelligible considering the reason offered: "they had not believed those who had seen him after he had been raised." They did not believe the witness. The community that is reading or hearing Mark consists of people who have to believe those who saw the risen Jesus, since the community had not seen him.

When Jesus makes himself visible to the eleven, they are at table—possibly an implied eucharistic celebration. Nevertheless, the meaning of the long ending's account of this third appearance of Jesus centers on another feature characteristic of the gospel resurrection appearance stories, namely, the commissioning of those who now become apostles. In Mark 16:15, it is both startling and encouraging that those who have just been challenged for lack of faith and hardness of heart are now entrusted with preaching the Gospel to the whole world. What better way to show that God's grace and not human merit is a primary element in the good news proclaimed by Jesus.

In this text, Jesus makes the promise that "signs will accompany those who believe." Mark 16:17 is again trying to show the wonders performed by Jesus' followers. These signs show the power and the life the risen Jesus gives to those who believe in his name. Yet, since the proclamation of these disciples is "to the whole creation," the manifestation of that power is wider than during Jesus' earthly ministry.

The long ending of Mark has developed this third appearance—to the eleven—at greater length than the first two appearances because the community derives their faith from the proclamation by the disciples to whom Jesus appeared. The commissioning of these disciples is the concluding action of "the Lord Jesus" on earth; accordingly, in Mark 16:19, he is now taken up to heaven and seated at the right hand of God. The doubts that the disciples once had (16:13–14) are totally overcome, and they obey by going forth and preaching everywhere (16:20).

Matthew's Narrative of the Empty Tomb and Postresurrection Appearance

The gospel of Matthew differs from Mark and Luke in its structure of the resurrection stories. Matthew frames his story in five episodes. The first episode deals with the burial of Jesus by Joseph of Arimathea (27:57–61). The second reflects on the placing of guards at the tomb by the chief priests and Pharisees (27:62–66). Next there is an episode in which the women come to the tomb. The angel frightens the guards, revealing to the women that Jesus is risen and they are to tell the disciples that Jesus is going to Galilee, followed by Jesus' appearance to the women (28:1–10). This experience is followed by an episode in which the chief priests and assembled elders bribe the guards to lie and say that Jesus' disciples stole the body (28:11–15). Finally, there is the appearance of Jesus to the eleven disciples and his commissioning them to go to all the nations (28:16–20).

Interestingly, within this structure there are two groups: one favorable to Jesus and the other hostile to Jesus. Matthew's unique framing of the resurrection in light of favorable and hostile persons toward Jesus' ministry and resurrection requires the reader to examine his or her own position in relationship to the risen Jesus.

Burial of Jesus by Joseph of Arimathea (Matthew 27:57–61)

In the first episode, the burial of Jesus by Joseph of Arimathea, we are presented with a compassionate action by a previously unknown disciple with the women followers of Jesus sitting in attendance opposite the tomb. This passage serves as a transition piece in Matthew from the crucifixion and death of Jesus to the resurrection stories. It sets the stage for what will follow.

Now Matthew turns to the hostility paid to the tomb. While other gospels end with the crucifixion and the hostility by the chief priests and Jewish rulers toward Jesus, Matthew carries the theme of hostility over to the resurrection. He uses it to fill the Sabbath between Jesus' death and burial and the opening of the tomb. At the end of the Gospel of Matthew, the chief priests and the Pharisees or elders (27:62, 28:12) work with the secular ruler (Pilate) to prevent the survival of Jesus' ministry. God will frustrate the armed might of these authorities; and at the end of the resurrection story Jesus emerges triumphant, a lesson of encouragement to Matthew's readers and also to us.

Placing of the Guards (Matthew 27:62–66)

The posting of a guard is unique to Matthew and, like much popular narrative, ignores certain implausibilities. Three times in Matthew's gospel Jesus predicted to his disciples his suffering, violent death, and resurrection on the third day (see 16:21, 17:22–23, 20:17–19). The disciples never gave evidence of having understood what he meant.

Here, however, the chief priests know that Jesus predicted "After three days I will rise again" and they understand perfectly what he meant. Consequently, the authorities want the tomb made secure until the third day to frustrate Jesus' prophecy. In the Sanhedrin trial of Jesus, the issues were his ability to destroy the Temple and whether he was the Messiah, the Son of God. Now the interest has shifted to the truthfulness of the resurrection claim. Jesus' accusers call him an "impostor," a description that will become common in later Jewish polemic against him.

The skepticism of the authorities, and their allegations that his disciples will steal the body (repeated in Matthew 28:13), suggests that we may have here an issue that Matthew's church was facing when writing their gospel. The Pharisees are noticeably absent during the passion narrative in Matthew. They played little direct role in the death of Jesus. They have reappeared here because in the experience of Matthew's church they were the chief opponents to the Jesus movement and undoubtedly were skeptics about the resurrection of Jesus.

The message here is the inability of human power to frustrate God's plan. In their attempt to prevent the resurrection by posting guards, the chief authorities of the Jews enlist the help of the governing power, addressing their requests to Pilate. Thus, the governing and religious authorities conspired together against the resurrection of Jesus, according to Matthew's interpretation. Despite the use of armed force, neither group of earthly powers proved successful. Sealing the stone and setting the guard will be useless precautions against the power that God is about to release.

The Women at the Tomb (Matthew 28:1–10)

When the Sabbath is over and the first day of the week is beginning, Mary Magdalene and the other Mary set out to see the tomb. What they see is a stunning series of events narrated in no other gospel. First, there is an earthquake: "The earth shook, and the rocks were split. The tombs also were opened, and many bodies of the saints who had fallen asleep were raised" (27:51b–53). Matthew seeks to convey the wider importance of what God has done for Jesus. When Jesus died with the charge written on the cross over his head, "The King of the Jews," the earth quaked, pouring the dead out of their tombs, something seen by the Gentile centurion and the solders with him. Now, to herald Jesus' resurrection, the earth quakes again. The main focus of the passion narrative in Matthew has been on the role of Jesus and the salvation history of Israel. But Matthew wishes to signal that Jesus' role from birth through death to the resurrection is of "cosmic importance," shaking the foundations of the world and raising even those long dead.

In addition to the earthquake at the tomb, an angel of the Lord descends from heaven and rolls back the stone—again a detail unique to Matthew. The appearance of the angel fits the apocalyptic context: he is "like lightning," even as the great angel who came to reveal to Daniel the last times had a face "like lightning" (Daniel 10:6). His garment is "white as snow," even as Daniel's Ancient of Days who judges the nations had a garment white as snow (Daniel 7:9). The power of God has intervened definitively at the tomb of Jesus, and before it the human powers who had conspired to frustrate the resurrection are as nothing. In fear, the guards are shaken even as the earth was, and they become "like dead men" (28:4). This is truly ironical: Jesus lives and those set to prevent that are "as if dead."

The next task of Matthew's "angel of the Lord" is to interpret the emptiness of the tomb. This angel interpreter reminds us that the "angel of the Lord" served as a revealer and interpreter in the infancy narrative, as well in Matthew's gospel. So also here the "angel of the Lord" gives the women instruction to go quickly and tell the disciples that Jesus has been raised. Those male disciples of Jesus forsook him and fled when the authorities arrested him (26:56). Peter, the one exception who hesitantly tried to continue with Jesus by following at a distance (26:58), denied him three times and cursed him (26:69–75, especially 26:74). Yet, these men are still in God's plan and are to receive the revelation about the resurrection from the women. These women, although present at Golgotha, previously had only a passive role of looking on the death of Jesus from afar (27:55), and sitting opposite the tomb when he was buried (27:61). Now the women are rewarded for their initiative in coming to see the tomb by being made the first human proclaimers of the resurrection in Matthew and the intermediaries through whom the faith of the male disciples is rekindled. Matthew is surely presenting the women as role models for his Christian readers to imitate in receiving and sharing the news of the risen Lord; they are being invited to go quickly, with reverential fear and great joy to tell others.

In a further affirmation of the faithful women, Jesus himself appears to them. The reaction of the women to the risen Jesus is interesting. They "come up" awe struck and worship him. That reaction serves as a model for how Christians should respect the presence of the risen Lord. Furthermore, the women clutch his feet. This tactile expression shows human affection for Jesus by the women and that Jesus is not a ghost.

The storyteller is now explaining that a new status will emerge for those who hear and believe in the resurrection. They will be intimate with the risen one, able to cuddle the Lord. They become God's children and thus brothers and sisters of Jesus. Whereas women may not have exercised power before the resurrection, the Matthean community (church) sees them as fully empowered after the resurrection. Women's empowerment is mind-boggling when one considers the fact that members of the Matthean community are converts from Judaism. In the Judaism of the time, women played no important religious leadership role at all.

The Bribing of the Guards (Matthew 28:11–15)

In the fourth episode (28:11–15), Matthew returns to the story of the guard. Although the chief priests hear all that had taken place, they do not cease their opposition; they do not repent and come to believe. Earlier in the gospel, the chief priests and the elders gathered and took counsel on how to arrest Jesus secretly and kill him. They paid Judas silver pieces to hand Jesus over. They also sought false testimony to convict Jesus (26:59). A similar process of paying silver pieces (money) and using falsehood is followed here: "You must say, 'His disciples came by night and stole him away' " (28:13).

This picture of plotting, a bribe, deliberate falsehood, and a promise to placate is surely a reflection of popular prejudice among Matthean Christians. They attribute ill will to those Jews who oppose them. While in individual instances of anti-Christian opposition, there may have been ill will, Matthew's use of "the Jews" is a generalization that goes beyond historical accuracy. It reflects wide antagonism and rumors in circulation among ordinary folk—Jesus' followers and Jews—at the time of the composition of the gospel. In the more sensitive interreligious relations of our own times, such a broad portrayal of the Jewish authorities as scheming liars and the generalization of the lie as one circulated among "the Jews" should make Christians uneasy. In other words, this statement is not for all time. Rather, it is historically conditioned by the Matthean community that experienced hostility from a particular Jewish community at a particular point in time and in history. We should not use this statement to support anti-Semitism or to accuse the Jews of deicide.

One aspect of Matthew's story remains an important lesson. He is impugning the nasty position—Jesus' disciples stole the body—that has developed in some Jewish circles of his day against the resurrection of Jesus. Christians must learn that hostile defensiveness on either side is futile and does little to further the religious cause that one deems right.

Postresurrection Appearance of Jesus and the Commissioning of the Disciples (Matthew 28:16–20)

In the fifth episode (28:16–20), the final scene shifts from Jerusalem to Galilee. Matthew 4:15 describes the land where Jesus began his ministry and the first call to his disciples (4:18–22) as the "Galilee of the Gentiles." In Matthew, Jesus proclaimed at the beginning of the passion that although the disciples would be scattered, he would go before them to Galilee after he was raised (26:32). At the tomb, both the angel of the Lord and the risen Jesus (28:7–10) reiterate the Galilee directive with the added promise that it was there the disciples would see him.

Now at "the mountain," Jesus fulfills the promise. Matthew does not think of a specific geographical mountain, but the mountain where Jesus sat when he taught the disciples the Sermon on the Mount (5:1), and where he was transfigured before Peter, James, and John (17:1). Just as Moses encountered God and received from him the Law on Mount Sinai, so on a mountain during the earthly ministry, the disciples had seen the glory of God in the transfigured Jesus. They will now come to this mountain again to see the risen Jesus. It is not surprising then that, despite the dismal history of failure by the male disciples in the Passion, they worshiped the risen Jesus when they saw him (28:17). At the beginning of the gospel of Matthew, the Gentile magi came and fell down and worshiped him; at the end, his followers (females and male disciples) rendered the same worship.

The motif of doubt recurs frequently in appearances of Jesus as recounted in the various gospels. This is true in Matthew—some disciples doubt. These are members of the Twelve; they heard Jesus' threefold prediction of the resurrection during his ministry; they heard his promise to go before them to Galilee; they heard that promise reiterated by the women—yet some doubt. This doubt has a very human dimension, showing that even the disciples were not anxious to believe and were incredulous. More important, the doubt would remind the readers that even after the resurrection, faith is not

175

a facile response. It also encouraged them, showing that Jesus is not repelled by doubt, for he now comes close to the disciples to speak. Doubting or not, they have worshiped him, and Jesus responds to them.

If appearance stories point back by insisting that the Risen One is truly the Jesus who was crucified and buried, some of them also point forward to the mission of sharing with others what God has done. These are commissioning experiences. In Matthew, Luke, and John, there is such an appearance to members of the Twelve that makes them apostles, that is, those sent to proclaim the resurrection. The sending shows that as Jesus carried on God's work, the apostles carry on Jesus' work. Matthew 28:18–19 has Jesus articulate this relationship: "All authority in heaven and on earth has been given to me. Go therefore and make disciples of all nations." Such wording echoes Daniel 7:14, where authority is given in heaven by the Ancient of Days to a Son of Man so that "peoples, all nations, and languages should serve him."

Thus the eschatological and apocalyptic atmosphere established by the earthquake and the appearance of the angel of the Lord at the tomb continues on the mountain in Galilee. The authority of the church is delegated from Jesus, who has been elevated by God and has authority in heaven and on earth; the mission that flows from it will touch all nations. It is entrusted to the eleven, even though some doubted. We are left to discover whether the word of Jesus solves the doubt, or by proclaiming to others their faith was strengthened.

The wording of the mission given to the eleven is significant: "Go therefore make disciples of all nations." Jesus already had authority during his public ministry. But when he sent the twelve out, he instructed them: "Go nowhere among the Gentiles, and enter no town of the Samaritans, but go rather to the lost sheep of the house of Israel" (Matthew 10:5–6). Now the risen Jesus, with full eschatological power ("all authority"), sends them out to all the nations (Gentiles). Israel is not excluded (see 23:34), but the progression in these two commands, one in the ministry and one after the resurrection, embodies the experience of Matthean community.

Jesus himself spoke only to Jews in Matthew (15:24). At first so did those who had been with him in the public ministry as they went out after the resurrection to proclaim the kingdom. Yet in the first two decades of church development they discovered that the plan of God was wider. At the beginning of the gospel, Matthew signaled the wide extension of God's plan by writing of Gentile magi who came to Jerusalem. Now, however, clearly the apostles cannot simply wait for the Gentiles to come; they must go out to them.

The solemn last words of Jesus in Matthew (28:20), "I am with you always, to the end of the age," echo the first words ever spoken about him in the beginning of the gospel (1:23): " 'Look, the virgin shall conceive and bear a son, and they shall name him Emmanuel,' which means, 'God is with us'." For Matthew, the resurrection is evidence not only that God was with Jesus, who conquered death, but also that in Jesus God's abiding presence is with all those who are baptized and who observe all that Jesus has commanded, as taught by the disciples. In Isaiah 41:10, God promised his people Israel: "[D]o not fear, for I am with you." Here, Matthew conveys the promise to an enlarged people, including Gentiles, who have come to know him in Jesus Christ. Earthly powers represented by the secular ruler, the chief priests, and the scribes/elders tried to prevent the plan of God, both at the conception/birth of Jesus and at his crucifixion/resurrection. They were unsuccessful then, and they will be equally unsuccessful in preventing it till the end of time.

The Resurrection in the Gospel of Luke

In Luke's version of the resurrection, everything happens in one day, and it all happens around Jerusalem. Just as Luke had his gospel start in Jerusalem, it also ends there.

Empty Tomb (Luke 24:1–12)

While Luke follows Mark 16:1–8, he does modify it by adding a variety of clarifications: In verse 3, when the women went in they did not find the body; a dramatic question in verse 5: "Why do you look

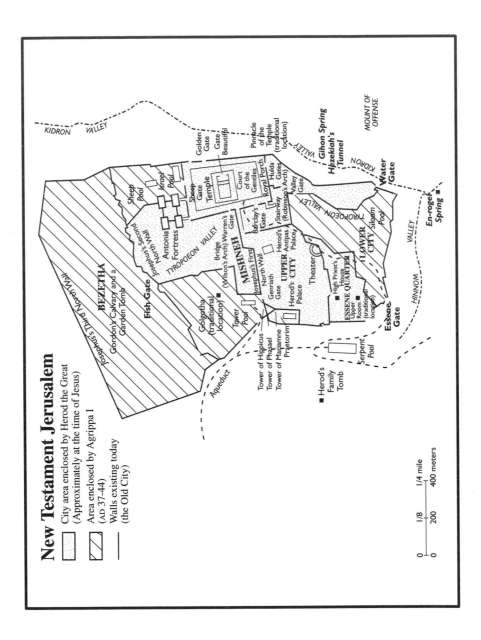

New Testament Jerusalem

City area enclosed by Herod the Great (Approximately at the time of Jesus)

Area enclosed by Agrippa I (AD 37-44)

Walls existing today (the Old City)

for the living among the dead?" In addition, Luke makes some interesting adaptations to Mark. For example, the women are not told Jesus will appear in Galilee but, instead, are asked to remember that he said that. The women did not stay silent, but told all this to all the rest. Interestingly, only Luke reports that, although the women were not believed, Peter ran to the tomb, saw only the burial wrappings, and went home wondering. It is quite close to what is narrated in John 20:3–10—without the disciple whom Jesus loved. In sum, Luke's empty tomb story is quite similar to the other synoptic gospels. Where his gospel differs a great deal is in the appearance stories.

Appearance on the Road to Emmaus (Luke 24:13–35)

This dramatic and very long appearance account is found only in Luke. It is filled with good storytelling techniques: the disappointed hope of the disciples that Jesus might have been the deliverer, Jesus asking the disciples questions about what has happened in Jerusalem, Jesus pretending to want to go on farther. Yet there are curious and intriguing elements in the story: for example, a town named Emmaus seven miles (sixty stadia) from Jerusalem is not easily located; we know nothing of Cleopas or his unnamed companion.

In typically Lucan fashion the first account of an appearance of the risen Jesus occurs on a journey, just as Jesus' birth occurred on the long journey to Bethlehem. Jesus gives important revelations to his disciples. He appeals to the whole of Scripture in order to explain what he has done as the suffering Messiah. In the Book of Acts of the Apostles, the apostolic preachers will do this. Luke wants to root their use of Scripture in revelation given by Jesus. Yet even though the disciples' hearts glowed when Jesus opened to them the meaning of the Scriptures, they recognized him only when he broke bread. This is obviously a reference to the Eucharist as being the place where the risen Jesus is present.

The episode in Luke 24:13–35 would have supplied important instruction for Luke's community. These readers might have reflected to themselves nostalgically that half a century before in a nearby land there were people fortunate enough to have seen the risen Jesus with their eyes: "Would that we had been there." Luke is reporting that those who were in that enviable situation and saw Jesus could not truly know Jesus until the Scriptures were expounded and they recognized him in the eucharistic meal. The Christians of Luke's time had the Scriptures and the breaking of bread—those same means of knowing and recognizing the risen Lord. So have the Christians ever since, for the Scriptures and the Eucharist are the essential components of our Sunday worship. In the matter of encountering the risen Jesus with faith, a past generation is not more privileged than the present one.

Appearance in Jerusalem and Ascension to Heaven (Luke 24:36–53)

Like the gospel of John, the first appearance to the assembled disciples in Luke (24:36–49) is set in Jerusalem on the evening of the resurrection day. In both Luke and John, these features are found: Jesus stands in their midst and says, "Peace be with you"; there is reference to Jesus' wounds (hands and feet in Luke; hands and side in John); and the mission given by Jesus involves forgiveness of sins and the role of the Spirit, which is explicit in the Gospel of John and symbolically designated as "what my Father promised" in Luke. Luke is particularly insistent on the reality of Jesus' appearance, for Jesus eats food and affirms that he is flesh and blood and bones and not a ghost. Jesus explains the Scriptures to these disciples too—a sign that this is fundamental to any understanding of what God has done in him. Here the revelation consists of a mission to all the nations beginning from Jerusalem. Jesus commissions his disciples to be witnesses of these things that have happened to him in fulfillment of Scripture.

The appearance ends with the ascension scene (Luke 24:50–53), when Jesus goes to Bethany, blesses his disciples, and is carried up into heaven. Then the disciples return with joy to Jerusalem and the

Temple, praising God. The gospel began in the Temple when an angel came down from heaven to Zechariah; it ends in the Temple, as Jesus has gone to heaven.

The Resurrection in the Gospel of John

John's gospel approaches the resurrection in a somewhat different fashion than the synoptics. As do the synoptics, John verifies the evidences of the empty tomb and the abandoned grave clothes with the witness of Mary Magdalene and Peter. Then John proceeds with a series of distinctive cameo vignettes in which Jesus encounters individuals, meeting them at their level so that each may respond in faith (see below).

RESURRECTION APPEARANCES IN THE GOSPEL OF JOHN

Mary Magdalene in Her Mourning (John 20:11–18)

Outside the tomb, Jesus meets Mary. She mistakes him for the gardener until he calls her by name. Jesus sends her with the news of the resurrection to the disciples.

The Disciples and Their Fear (John 20:19–23)

The disciples are meeting together behind closed doors in an upper room, when Jesus appears in their midst. He says, "Peace be with you," commissions them, and gives them the Holy Spirit.

Thomas and His Doubt (John 20:24–29)

This scene is unique to the gospel of John. Again in a locked room, Jesus comes to the disciples. This time, Thomas is present. Jesus again greets them with, "Peace be with you," and Jesus shows Thomas his crucifixion wounds. Thomas proclaims, "My Lord and my God!" Jesus pronounces a beatitude: "Blessed are those who have not seen and yet have come to believe" (John 20:29).

The Disciples in Galilee (John 21:1–23)

Peter and six other disciples, including the Beloved Disciple, have gone fishing. Jesus appears on the shore and enables a miraculous catch of fish. The Beloved Disciple realizes who is on the shore and, when he tells Peter, Peter jumps overboard and swims to meet Jesus. Jesus restores Peter after his denials and gives him a pastoral commission.

The writer of the gospel of John asks every generation: "Have you believed because you have seen me? Blessed are those who have not seen and yet have come to believe" (John 20:29). The challenge of the resurrection stories in John is a call for the reader to respond, as did the Beloved Disciple, in faith without seeing. He, unlike the others, comes to resurrection faith based on the evidence of the empty tomb, not an appearance of Jesus.

The Foundations of Faith (John 20:1–8)

All four gospels name Mary Magdalene as the first to find the empty tomb, although other women were present (Matthew 28:1, Mark 16:1, Luke 24:10). In Matthew, Luke, and John, the women report their discovery to the disciples. Only Luke and John describe a subsequent visit to the tomb by any disciples other than the women (Luke 24:12, 24; John 20:3–10). Faith in the resurrection was not part of the traditions of the empty tomb as they originally circulated. The women left afraid that the body was stolen; Peter departed from the tomb wondering what had happened. However, the gospel of John develops the empty tomb into an occasion for faith.

Sunday morning, while it was still dark, Mary Magdalene came to the tomb to discover it was open. Because the synoptics tell us that Mary came at sunrise (Matthew 28:1, Mark 16:2, Luke 24:1), we should interpret the mention of darkness as another of John's many symbolic comments. Mary was in mourning; as yet, none of the disciples believed that Christ was resurrected. All were still walking in spiritual darkness.

Upon discovering the open tomb, Mary ran to report the news to Peter and the beloved disciple: "They have taken the Lord out of the tomb, and we do not know where they have laid him" (John 20:2; see 20:13). Her words suggest that others were with her. More important, however, they imply that she thought the body of Jesus was stolen. She may not have been accusing specific enemies of Jesus bent on discrediting him and his disciples; tomb robbery was a frequent crime in the region.

Peter and the Beloved Disciple start running to the tomb together, but both verse 4 and 8 say that the Beloved Disciple reaches the site first. Oddly, he stops short, outside the tomb. Peter arrives and enters the tomb immediately. John is carefully ordering the arrivals and entrances to build suspense as he leads to a climax.

Before the Beloved Disciple enters the tomb, the gospel details Peter's discovery (John 20:6–7): "He saw the linen wrappings lying there, and the cloth that had been on Jesus' head, not lying with the linen wrappings but rolled up in a place by itself." Clearly, the body of Jesus was not stolen. What hurried grave robber would undress the corpse and neatly fold the clothes?

Different Responses of Faith (John 20:8–29)

The remainder of John 20 narrates in four scenes how various disciples came to faith in the resurrected Jesus. The hero and disciple par excellence of the Johannine community—the one whom Jesus loved—is the first to do so.

The Beloved Disciple (John 20:8–10)

The beloved disciple came to the proper conclusion, based on the evidence of the empty tomb; he believed (20:8). What is more, he had not seen his resurrected Lord. The gospel writer has constructed his narrative to bring his readers to the same point of faith. They, too, have not seen Christ, but are still asked to emulate the beloved disciple's response to the evidence of the resurrection.

John intends no contrast between the beloved disciple's faith and Peter's apparent lack of it. Rather, the two disciples play complementary roles in a unified summons to faith. One is a witness, the other a believer. Peter *not* the beloved disciple, verifies the conditions of the empty tomb. The beloved disciple, *not* Peter, trusts those conditions to be a sign from God. The scene ends as the disciples walk off to their homes (20:10). The first call of faith is now complete.

Mary Magdalene (John 20:11–18)

Next, Mary Magdalene embraces the resurrection faith. Driven by her mourning of the loss of Jesus, she looks into the tomb. Two angels were sitting where Jesus had lain. Their position in the tomb signifies God, not robbers, touched the body of Jesus. Mary, however, is slow to realize this. The angels ask her a question: "Woman, why are you weeping?" Mary's response reveals that she still does not understand that God emptied the tomb: "They have taken away my Lord, and I do not know where they have laid him" (20:13). This interchange is virtually repeated after Mary turns around. She sees, but does not recognize, Jesus. He, too, says, "Woman, why are you weeping?" By now, the simple question carries the force of a gentle admonition: there is no reason for weeping; Jesus is standing before her.

Probably because Jesus was buried in a garden, Mary assumes she is speaking with the gardener. More to the point, though, is Mary's failure to recognize her Lord. Jesus has changed. People can no longer relate to him in the same way as they did before his death and resurrection. His physical presence means less and his spiritual presence means more.

When Jesus calls her by name, the truth breaks through her grief. Jesus is alive! She uses her familiar name for him, "Rabbounī," which John translates for his readers as "Teacher" (20:16).

The exchange of names signifies the renewal of their previous relationship. Yet, it is not simply renewed; it is deepened. Evidently, Mary has reached out to Jesus in her joy, for he responds: "Do not hold on to me, because I have not yet ascended to the Father. But go to my brothers and say to them, 'I am ascending to my Father and your Father, to my God and your God'" (20:17). Jesus' enigmatic words raise several questions: What does ascension have to do with holding on to Jesus? How do we relate Jesus' caution to Mary with his invitation to Thomas to touch him (20:27)? When does Jesus ascend to the Father?

No answer can remove all the mystery surrounding these questions. Still, the apparent tension between the experiences of Mary and Thomas lies in the motivation for touching Jesus. The tense of the Greek verb used here implies that Mary is presently holding on to Jesus and he is asking her to stop clutching his feet in adoration. By contrast, Jesus is inviting Thomas to touch his wounds so that Thomas may be convinced of the resurrection.

In other words, Mary must stop clinging to her physical relationship with the earthly Jesus. Thomas must believe that the figure before him stands in continuity with the earthly person. Jesus calls both to move into a deeper spiritual relationship with him, the resurrected Lord. During the interim period between the resurrection and Jesus' complete return to heavenly glory, his disciples must come to accept this new eternal and spiritual basis for their relationship with Jesus.

To facilitate the transition, Jesus sends Mary to his "brothers" with a message from him: "I am ascending to my Father and your Father, to my God and your God" (20:17). Jesus uses the language of the new family of God, a family he inaugurated on the cross (19:25–27). Mary carries his announcement to the disciples, saying, "I have seen the Lord" (20:18).

The place of Mary Magdalene in the resurrection narratives shows something of John's attitude toward women. A woman was the first to enter an empty tomb, the first to see the risen Lord, and the first commissioned to proclaim the Good News. In other words, John does not restrict the role of a disciple according to gender.

The Disciples (John 20:19–23)

Fear crippled the disciples after Jesus' death (20:19). Afraid of continued persecution by the Jewish authorities, they met behind locked doors. At least one of the Twelve, Thomas, was absent.

Jesus miraculously joins them in the locked room, giving the traditional Jewish salutation, "Peace be with you" (20:19). Physical constraints do not impede Jesus' ability to be with his disciples. This illustrates both Jesus' initiative in meeting their need and his bodily transformation.

Jesus' body is not new; it is changed. The wounds on his hands and side show the continuity between the crucified Jesus and the risen Lord. Although John's account of the crucifixion does not mention it, three references here confirm that the soldiers nailed his hands to the cross (20:20, 25, 27). The reference to his side recalls the spear thrust (19:34). Once the disciples saw the wounds, they realized what it meant and "rejoiced when they saw the Lord" (20:20).

Jesus' immediate repetition of the phrase "Peace be with you" (20:21) elevates the common greeting to a sign that he has conquered the world. He had promised to give them peace that the world could not give them (14:27, 16:33). Now, victorious through the cross, he can bless believers with the peace of God in all its fullness.

The gift of peace is for witness and mission in the world. Jesus says to his followers, "As the Father has sent me, so I send you" (20:21). After commissioning his disciples, Jesus breathed on them and said to them, "Receive the Holy Spirit" (20:22). The gospel writer is probably alluding to Genesis 2:7, where God formed the human and "breathed into his nostrils the breath of life; and the [human] became a living being." Christ creates new life through his death and resurrection and bestowal of the spirit. That new life is the life of baptism. Through it Christians are filled with the breath of God.

The disciples have seen the risen Lord. Their fear has given way to joy that comes with Christ's peace. They have received both their commission and the spirit that empowers its fulfillment. It seems that Jesus' earthly ministry has drawn to a close. Yet there will be another resurrection appearance before this chapter of John ends.

Thomas the Doubter (John 20:24–29)

Doubt has engulfed Thomas, who was absent from the disciples' previous Sunday gathering. The others have seen the Lord, but he insists, "Unless I see the mark of the nails in his hands, and put my finger in the mark of the nails and my hand in his side, I will not believe" (20:25). Thomas's stance does not represent the voice of reason over naiveté. Rather, it typifies faith based on the wondrous character of miracles that Jesus criticizes in John 4:48: "Unless you see signs and wonders you will not believe."

Aware of Thomas's skepticism, Jesus meets his terms. He invites Thomas to touch his wounds and challenges him with the words, "Do not doubt but believe" (20:27). John's description leads the reader to conclude that Thomas moves from doubt to faith without touching Jesus' hands and side, for he immediately utters the paramount faith confession of the gospel: "My Lord and my God!"

As lofty as the title "Lord" is in a creedal context, it is here overshadowed by the unequivocal use of "God" as a title for Christ. With this the fourth gospel ends as it began, declaring that Jesus is God (1:1). This is both the ultimate and foundational tenet of Christian faith.

It would be easy to overlook the profoundly important pronouns in Thomas's statement. In saying *My* Lord and *my* God," he makes a personal profession of faith/belief. The author of John has arranged this entire chapter as a call to belief for his readers, who have not seen the resurrected Jesus.

While Jesus affirms Thomas' faith based on eyewitness experience, he pronounces a special blessing on "those who have not seen and yet have come to believe" (20:29). Like the Beloved Disciple, who came to resurrection faith without seeing the resurrected Lord, those who hear the proclaimed word and believe are no less favored by God. The resurrected Lord meets each individual at his or her point of insight and kindles faith that transforms adversity into blessing.

For Discussion

1. Which one of the gospel resurrection stories is your favorite? Why?
2. Why do you think women play important roles in the gospel resurrection stories?
3. Is there a difference between immortality and resurrection?

4. How do you recognize the risen Christ in your life? In the life of others? Explain.

5. Do you ever question your faith? How is this questioning similar to or different from Thomas doubting Jesus' resurrection? What kind of role has questioning played in your religious upbringing?

For Further Reading

Binz, Stephen J. *The Passion and Resurrection Narratives of Jesus: A Commentary.* Collegeville, Minn.: Liturgical Press, 1989.

Brown, Raymond E. *A Risen Christ in Easter Time: Essays on the Gospel Narratives of the Resurrection.* Collegeville, Minn.: Liturgical Press, 1991.

O'Collins, Gerald. *Jesus Risen: An Historical, Fundamental and Systematic Examination of Christ's Resurrection.* New York: Paulist Press, 1987.

Perry, John Michael. *Explaining the Resurrection of Jesus.* Kansas City, Mo.: Sheed and Ward, 1993.

Swain, Lionel. *Reading the Easter Gospels.* Collegeville, Minn.: Liturgical Press, 1993.

ACTS
OF THE
APOSTLES

The SEQUEL TO LUKE'S GOSPEL, HIS SECOND OR companion volume, is known as Acts of the Apostles. It adopts a literary form common to the first century of the common era, relating the deeds of outstanding men. Two such volumes that would have made the top ten of the list were known as the *Acts of Augustus* and the *Acts of Julius Caesar.*

The word *apostle* means "one who is sent." Luke's second volume relates the deeds of two great men who were sent to take the good news of Jesus to the world. Peter was sent to the Jewish world, Paul to the Gentiles dwelling in the Greco-Roman world. But the book does not simply describe the work of these two men. Rather, Acts describes how the postresurrection church, through the light and power of the Holy Spirit, grew in numbers, in understanding its own life, and in recognition that the good news of Jesus was meant for the whole world. Further, Acts surveys the development of the church after Jesus' resurrection.

The purpose of the Book of Acts is described by the risen Jesus who says to his apostles: "But you will receive power when the Holy Spirit has come upon you; and you will be my witnesses in Jerusalem, in all Judea and Samaria, and to the ends of the earth" (Acts 1:8). This statement of the risen Jesus provides an easy outline for Acts of the Apostles.

OUTLINE OF ACTS OF THE APOSTLES

I.   Prologue (1:1–11)

II. The church bears witness to Jesus in Jerusalem (1:12–5:42)

III. The church bears witness to Jesus in Judea and Samaria (6:1–12:25)

IV. The church bears witness to Jesus to the ends of the earth (13:1–28:31)

Further, in the verse quoted above, the risen Jesus speaks of the Holy Spirit. In truth, almost every verse of Acts tells how the Holy Spirit is enlightening, guiding, and empowering the church. In Acts, the Spirit is mentioned about seventy times.

For instance, when Peter calls upon the community to choose someone in the place of Judas (1:15–26), he credits the decision to the Holy Spirit speaking through the Scriptures. It is also the Holy Spirit who comes at Pentecost (chapter 2) and gives the apostles the necessary energy to both announce the resurrection of Jesus and be his representatives all over the world.

Chapter 2 gives a dramatic description of the pouring out of the Spirit on Pentecost:

²And suddenly from heaven there came a sound like the rush of a violent wind, and it filled the entire house where they were sitting. ³Divided tongues, as of fire, appeared among them, and a tongue rested on each of them. ⁴All of them were filled with the Holy Spirit

*and began to speak in other languages, as the Spirit gave them
ability* (Acts 2:2–4).

The disciples are able to speak to people from all over the world
and be understood. This is a new Sinai with a new covenant. The
conversion of Babel is reversed. The Holy Spirit will now bring a new
unity to the human race. The Spirit's coming is no longer restricted to
a few holy people. Young and old, men and women, alike will be able
to prophesy.

Again, in chapter 15, it is the Holy Spirit who helps the
community see that Gentiles can be baptized without submitting to
the Jewish Law.

In the rest of Acts, we see the Holy Spirit active in all the developments of the church. The Spirit inspires Peter and Paul in their
preaching, Paul and Barnabas on their missionary journeys. The
Spirit both leads Paul through Asia Minor to Greece and warns Paul
of the sufferings that lie ahead for him.

The Structure of Luke's Second Volume

Any careful reading of the Gospel of Luke alongside Acts of the
Apostles will reveal that Luke followed the same basic outline for both
volumes. We can view this best by arranging the material in parallel
columns:

Luke's Gospel	Acts
Preface to Theophilus (1:1–4)	Preface to Theophilus (1:1–5)
Spirit descends on Jesus as he prays (3:32–22)	Spirit comes to apostles as they pray (2:1–13)
Sermon declares prophecy fulfilled (4:16–30)	Sermon declares prophecy fulfilled (2:14–40)
Jesus heals a lame man (5:17–26)	Peter heals lame man (3:1–10)
Religious leaders attack Jesus (5:29–6:11)	Religious leaders attack apostles (4:1–8:3)
Centurion invites Jesus to his house (7:1–10)	Centurion invites Peter to his house (10:1–23)

Jesus raises widow's son from death (7:11–17)	Peter raises widow from death (9:36–43)
Missionary journeys to Gentiles (10:1–12)	Missionary journeys to Gentiles (13:1–19:20)
Jesus travels to Jerusalem (9:51–19:28)	Paul travels to Jerusalem (19:21–21:17)
Jesus is received favorably (19:37)	Paul is received favorably (21:17–20)
Jesus is devoted to the Temple (19:45–48)	Paul is devoted to the Temple (21:26)
Sadducees oppose Jesus, but scribes support him (20:27–39)	Sadducees oppose Paul, but Pharisees support him (23:6–9)
Jesus breaks bread and gives thanks (22:19)	Paul breaks bread and gives thanks (27:35)
Jesus is seized by an angry mob (22:54)	Paul is seized by an angry mob (21:30)
Jesus is slapped by high priest's aides (22:63–64)	Paul is slapped at high priest's command (23:2)
Jesus is tried four times and declared innocent three times (22:66–23:13)	Paul is tried four times and declared innocent three times (23:1–26:32)
Jesus is rejected by the Jews (23:18)	Paul is rejected by the Jews (21:36)
Jesus is regarded favorably by centurion (23:47)	Paul is regarded favorably by centurion (27:43)
Final confirmation that Scriptures have been fulfilled (24:45–47)	Final confirmation that Scriptures have been fulfilled (28:23–28)

You will note in the above chart, in the second half of Acts, Luke seems to be especially conscious of the parallels between Jesus and Paul. In this way, Luke suggests that Jesus' life is a pattern or model not only for Paul but also for all Christians, and that Paul (and every Christian) cannot be understood apart from Christ.

Both Jesus and Paul are prophesied to have special significance for the Gentiles and to be destined to suffer (Luke 2:29–35, Acts 9:15–16). Both Jesus and Paul begin their ministries with a speech in a synagogue, which stresses the fulfillment of the Scriptures in Christ and indicates that the mission to the Gentiles is in accord with the Old Testament (Luke 4:16–30, Acts 13:14–52). Both Jesus and Paul are determined to go to Jerusalem where they will be arrested (Luke 9:51, Acts 19:21). Both Jesus and Paul predict their sufferings in some detail (Luke 9:22, 44–45; Acts 20:22–24, 21:10–14). Both Jesus and Paul give a farewell speech that emphasizes the need for humility in Christian service and warns against apostasy (Luke 22:21–38, Acts 20:18–35). Both Jesus and Paul heroically accept their martyrdom as being in accord with God's will (Luke 22:39–46; Acts 20:36–38, 2:5–6, 13–14). And both Jesus and Paul undergo a series of investigations, the effect of which is to establish their innocence with regard to the charge that they are political agitators (Luke 22:47–23:25; Acts 21:27–26:32).

In these many ways, Luke establishes the point that Jesus the faithful witness (*martyr* is the Greek word for "witness") provides the good example and sets the pattern for Christian life not only in Paul's case but also in the case of every Christian.

In addition to parallel outlines between Luke and Acts, both volumes seem to teach or purvey theology by geography. This is best seen by looking at how the two volumes handle their use of the city of Jerusalem.

In the infancy account of the Gospel of Luke, the gospel has Jesus going from Galilee to Jerusalem, both at his birth and as a boy of twelve. This same pattern is followed in Jesus' public life. The gospel insists that Jesus must go to Jerusalem to realize God's plan of salvation. In the Gospel of Luke, Jerusalem is the place where God's promises are fulfilled; it is the place of Jesus' destiny.

In Acts, the church begins in Jerusalem but then moves toward Rome, the symbolic center of the known world. In the final chapter of the book, Paul arrives in Rome and seems established there. The last sentence of Acts (28:31) forcefully indicates that the work of the Spirit will continue and the preaching of the kingdom will go on without bounds. Luke is telling the reader that the saving action of God is meant for the whole world.

In both volumes, Luke helps the reader to see that the gospel life is a journey. Christians are to travel from one phase of life to the next, witnessing—in good times and bad—to the good news of God's merciful action. Let us now compare the church's journey with that of Jesus.

Jesus begins his journey in Luke 9:51. From that point on, "he set his face to go to Jerusalem." The Gospel of Luke repeats this theme over and over, until Jesus finally arrives at Jerusalem, suffers, dies, and enters into his glory (24:46).

In Acts, the church begins its journey in Jerusalem, but quickly makes its way to the ends of the earth (Acts 1:8). But, as with Jesus, the way is fraught with rejection and persecution (Acts 5:17–42). Paul's journeys are particularly illustrative (Acts, chapters 13–28).

Among other things, the church of today learns from Acts of the Apostles that gospel life and witnessing are both glorious and painful. The journey of the Christian—like the journeys of Paul, Stephen, and Peter in Acts—will encounter opposition, hatred, persecution. Attacks may be subtle or blatant. But the same Spirit that was present to Jesus and the apostles continues to lead and empower the church today.

The Speeches in Acts

A literary element *not* found in the gospel of Luke, but quite conspicuous in Acts, is the use of speeches. Many of these are "missionary speeches," delivered to both Jewish and Gentile audiences. These would include such important speeches as those delivered by Peter at Pentecost (2:14–20) and Paul at Pisidian Antioch (13:16–41). Other speeches also have important roles in the narrative. These include Stephen's "defense" or "witness" speech to the Jerusalem council prior to his martyrdom (7:2–53), Paul's farewell addresses to the Ephesian elders (20:18–35), Paul's powerful addresses before Roman officials (e.g., 24:10–21, 26:2–23), addresses by both Peter and James at the Jerusalem council (15:7–11, 13–21), and so on. Almost one-third of the thousand verses in Acts are found in minor and major speeches. The function of these speeches was to summarize the faith, bear witness to Jesus, and to exhort others to embrace the faith through baptism. They can be described as performative utterances that require the audience of Acts and the audience of every generation to ponder their meaning for the practice of Christian faith.

The Situation Behind the Text of Acts of the Apostles

Having described the structure and some of the themes and content of Acts, we will now turn our attention to the situation behind the story. As the book begins, we learn how the early church—the one the apostles left behind—was configured. Christians lived together as a community, celebrated Eucharist in homes or what might be called house churches, preached that Jesus was the risen Lord, had baptism as a rite of initiation into the community, and worshiped in the Temple in Jerusalem. These people were all Jewish.

There were two distinct types of Jews at the time of Acts. Palestinian Jews, who lived in Palestine, and Hellenistic (Greek) Jews, who lived in various parts of the Roman Empire. This latter group was sometimes called *diaspora* (dispersed) Jews. Hellenistic Jews practiced their religion in the synagogues, observed the Mosaic Law to the extent that it could be observed while living among non-Jews, and hoped to visit Jerusalem at least once in a lifetime. These Jews spoke Greek as a first language.

Early in the story of Acts we learn that several Hellenistic Jews were in Jerusalem—possibly they had come for the feast of Pentecost—and had joined the followers of Jesus. The first martyr, Stephen, was a Hellenistic Jew. He was put to death by stoning, the common form of execution in those times (6:8–8:1).

The dominant figure in the early chapters of Acts is Peter. Peter was a Palestinian Jew, very observant and steeped in the traditions of his ancestors. But Luke carefully shows us how Peter was forced out of his set ethnocentric ways and made to accept new ideas.

This is marvelously narrated by Luke when he describes that at Caesarea Peter converted the Roman centurion Cornelius and entered his house (10:1–48). Cornelius, of courses, was a Gentile; a Jew

195

entering his house would, according to Jewish law, be rendered ritually unclean.

Peter then had a vision while praying on the roof of Cornelius' house, in which he was told that all food was clean and that it was permissible to eat anything. Jews had strict dietary *(kosher)* laws and many foods were forbidden. Peter was so appalled at this that three times he refused to believe it (see Acts 10:1–48).

Luke carefully constructed these events in his narrative to show the reader that there was a definite move away from Judaism. As a matter of fact, we see an early manifestation of this shift when Luke introduced Saul at the stoning of Stephen. Saul (*Paul* is the Greek form of the name) held the coats of those who put Stephen to death.

Saul was a young man, trained in the Jewish law by the best teachers of the day. He was a student of the renown Gamaliel (22:3). Saul was so conscientious about observing the law that he was willing to round up all those suspected of not following the law and haul them to Jerusalem to answer to the authorities. But on the Damascus road, Saul had an experience of Jesus that changed him utterly (9:1–22). Like Peter, he was forced to reconsider all the convictions that he had held dear.

Saul was blinded by the experience and thrown into a state of confusion. Christians were understandably frightened of him, and it took a vision from the Lord for Ananias, a devout follower of Jesus living in Damascus, to welcome Saul into his home. Saul seems to have disappeared for a while, perhaps to allow both himself and the Christian community time to adjust to his change of heart.

Barnabas, a Hellenistic Jew from Cyprus, realized Saul's worth, value, and sincerity, and invited him to live with the community in Antioch in Syria. It was in Antioch that the disciples of Jesus were first called "Christians" (11:26).

Luke tells us that many Christians fled to Antioch—a move away from Judaism's holy city of Jerusalem—following the death of Stephen, and that they preached to the Jewish community living there. Then they started to spread the Good News to the Greeks. Many

Gentiles were converted, though not necessarily circumcised according to Jewish law.

The problem of circumcision became a real issue among Gentile converts. Jews underwent circumcision, a sign of their covenant with God, at eight days old. But the Gentile converts were grown men, and for them the operation could be life threatening due to a greater chance of infection. Paul, always a practical minister, allowed them to become Christians without circumcision. He required only baptism. This caused serious concern among some of his Jewish followers, most especially those dwelling in Palestine, in the city of Jerusalem.

Paul made a big issue of circumcision. For him it was not needed to become a follower of Jesus, but baptism was. So he and Barnabas went to Jerusalem, where a special council was called (see Acts 15) to determine whether new converts—especially those who were adult Gentiles—needed to observe the whole Mosaic Law and undergo the traditional initiation rites. The council, led by Peter and James, determined that circumcision was no longer required of the Gentiles for admission into the church.

This decision, however, did not put an end to the question. There were groups who could not imagine a "Jewish-Christian" religion without circumcision, and it continued to be a volatile issue in the church for some time.

What these stories in Acts can teach us is not to be surprised or demoralized, because argument and debate exist within today's church. This is by no means a new experience in the Christian community. In his letter to the Galatians (3:11), for example, Paul tells how he had rebuked Peter himself for refusing to eat with Gentiles. Luke's account in Acts of the early church prompts us to listen carefully to what others have to say.

Women and Witness in Acts of the Apostles

Acts, like the gospel of Luke, has special concern for women, who play a significant role in the early church community. Acts of the Apostles names twelve women: Mary the mother of Jesus (1:14); Sapphira

(5:1); Candace, the Queen of Ethiopia (8:27); Tabitha, whose name in Greek is Dorcas (9:36); Mary, the mother of John Mark, and apparently leader of a household church (12:12); Rhoda, a servant (slave) girl (12:13); Lydia, a businesswoman and leader of a house-church (16:14); Damaris, an Athenian convert (17:34); Priscilla, the wife in a missionary couple (chapter 18); Artemis, the patron goddess of Ephesus (19:24); Drusilla, wife of Felix (24:24); Bernice, wife of Agrippa (25:13, 23, 30).

In addition, Acts mentions the widows in the church in Jerusalem (6:1–6), Jewish women of high standing in Pisidian Antioch (13:50), Timothy's Jewish mother (16:1), a slave girl with a spirit of divination (16:16–18), and four daughters of Philip of Caesarea who were prophets (21:9). Taken together, these women, with the exception of the goddess Artemis, represent an outstanding number of human categories including married, single, professional, "homemaker," Jew, Greek, Roman, sister, mother, mother-in-law, prophet, missionary, teacher, queen, and slave. This shows how egalitarian and inclusive the early church of Acts was, and provides a model for the church of today.

According to Acts, common to both women and men who were Christians was the need to witness to the faith. Some form of the noun *witness* or the verb *to witness* is used more than fifteen times in Acts to describe the task of the disciples of Jesus. They are to stand before the world as before a court of law and, by their words and their lives, testify to the truth about Jesus.

The only use of the word *witness* in the Gospel of Luke is in 24:48. Luke is already speaking of the task that the disciples will have when the Holy Spirit comes upon them. The word is a connecting link between the gospel and Acts. It continues to be a connecting link between the gospel and Acts on the one hand and the church today on the other. The followers of Christ have the never-ending task of witnessing to the world today. For the risen Jesus still asks us to "be my witness in Jerusalem, in all Judea and Samaria, and to the ends of the earth" (Acts 1:8).

For Discussion

1. The Holy Spirit plays an active role in the lives of the apostles and the church in Acts of the Apostles. How do you see the Holy Spirit active in you, and in your church community?
2. Acts of the Apostles describes the faith life as a journey. What has been your journey of faith?
3. Read Acts 2:14–42, 3:12–26, 4:24–30, 5:30–32, 7:1–53, 10:34–43, 13:16–41. These passages are all speeches by various apostles. How do they refer to Jesus? Explain.
4. Is the parallelism between Jesus and Paul in Acts a realistic model for Christian life?
5. How are Christians of every era called to be witnesses to the faith?

For Further Reading

Barrett, C. K. *Acts of the Apostles* (2 vols.). Edinburgh: Clark, 1994, 1998.

Brown, Raymond E. *The Church the Apostles Left Behind*. Mahwah, N.J.: Paulist Press, 1984.

Fitzmyer, Joseph A. *The Acts of the Apostles* (Anchor Bible 31). Garden City, N.Y.: Doubleday, 1998.

Johnson, Luke T. *The Acts of the Apostles*. Collegeville, Minn.: Liturgical Press, 1992.

Marshall, I. Howard, and David Peterson, eds. *Witness to the Gospel: The Theology of Acts*. Grand Rapids, Mich.: Eerdmans, 1998.

Winter, Bruce W., ed. *The Book of Acts in Its First Century Setting* (5 vols.). Grand Rapids, MI: Eerdmans, 1994–96.

9

PAUL, HIS LETTERS, AND OTHER NEW TESTAMENT LETTERS

It IS FAIR TO SAY THAT, AFTER JESUS, THE APOSTLE PAUL IS the next most important character in the New Testament. Paul was the one who carried the Gospel out beyond the Jews in Jerusalem to the Gentiles in the Roman world. We know more about Paul than any other figure in early Christianity. Of the twenty-seven books of the New Testament almost half are attributed to Paul or his followers. Paul's life is easily divided into three stages: his life as a Pharisee prior to faith in Christ, his conversion experience itself, and his activities as an apostle afterward.

Paul the Pharisee

We can say very little for certain about Paul prior to his conversion. He does tell us that he was a Jew, born to Jewish parents, and that he was zealous for the Law, adhering strictly to the traditions endorsed by the Pharisees (Galatians 1:13–14, Philippians 3:4–6). He does not tell us when he was born, where he was raised, or how he was educated. The Book of Acts of the Apostles, however, does provide some information along these lines. In Acts, Paul is said to be from the Greek city of Tarsus (21:3–39) in Cilicia, in the southeastern part of Asia Minor (the southeast of present-day Turkey), and to have been educated in Jerusalem under the renowned rabbi Gamaliel (22:3). Tarsus was the location of a famous school of Greek rhetoric, that is, a school of higher learning reserved for the social and intellectual elite, something like an Ivy League university. Jerusalem, of course, was the center of all Jewish life, and Gamaliel was one of its most revered teachers.

Paul's own letters give little indication of the extent of his formal education. Simply his ability to read and write shows that he was better educated than most people of his day; 85 to 90 percent of the population in the Roman Empire could do neither. Moreover, Paul writes on a fairly sophisticated level, showing that he must have had at least some formal training in rhetoric, the main focus of higher education at the time. Paul's native tongue was almost without question Greek, and he gives no indication at all of knowing Aramaic, the language more widely used in Palestine.

Paul did study the Jewish Scriptures extensively. He appears to be able to quote the Scriptures from memory and to have meditated and reflected on their meaning at a deep level. He knows these Scriptures in their Greek translation, the Septuagint. Since his letters are all addressed to Greek-speaking Christians, it is difficult to know whether he quoted the text in this way in order to accommodate his readers or whether this was the only form of the text he knew. In other words, it is hard to know whether or not he could also read the Jewish Scriptures in their original Hebrew.

What is certain is that prior to becoming a believer in Jesus, Paul was an avid Pharisee (Philippians 3:5). In fact, Paul's letters are the only writings to survive from the pen of a Pharisee prior to the destruction of the Jerusalem Temple in 70 C.E. Paul claims that he rigorously followed the "traditions of my ancestors" (Galatians 1:14). These are usually understood to be the Pharisaic "oral laws" that were in circulation in Paul's youth. We get the picture, then, of a devout and intelligent Jewish young man totally committed to understanding and practicing his religion according to the strict standards available.

As a Pharisee, Paul's religion would have centered around the Law of God, the Torah of Moses, the greatest gift of God to Israel, the exact and thorough adherence to which was the ultimate goal of devotion. Looking back on his early life, Paul could later claim that he had been "blameless" with respect to the righteousness that the law demands (Philippians 3:6). Further, as a Pharisee, Paul would have shared a belief in a future resurrection of the dead at the end of the age, which would be imminent. God would send a deliverer for his people, who would set up God's kingdom on earth; the dead would rise and all would face judgment.

What else can we say about the life of this upright Jewish Pharisee? The one aspect of his former life that Paul himself chooses to emphasize in his autobiographical statements in Galatians 1 and Philippians 3 is that it was precisely as a law-abiding, zealous Jew that he persecuted the followers of Jesus. At first, far from adhering to the Gospel, he violently opposed it, setting himself on destroying the church, and he interpreted this opposition as part of his devotion to the one true God.

Why was Paul so opposed to Jesus' followers, and how exactly did he go about persecuting them? One of the main reasons, if not *the* reason for Paul, was the Christian proclamation of Jesus as the Messiah. Such a claim would have struck most Jews as ludicrous. Various Jews had different expectations of what the Messiah would be like. He might be a warrior-king who would establish Israel as a sovereign state, an inspired priest who would rule God's people through his authoritative interpretation of God's Law, or a cosmic judge who would come to destroy the forces of evil. Each of these expectations involved a messiah who would be glorious and powerful. Jesus, on the other hand, was commonly viewed as nothing more than an itinerant Galilean preacher with a small following who was opposed by the Jewish leaders and executed by the Romans for sedition against the state. For most faithful Jews, to call him God's Messiah was an affront to God.

For Paul, there seems to have been an additional problem, relating to the precise manner of Jesus' execution. Jesus was crucified; that is, he was killed by being attached to a stake of wood. Paul, well versed in the Jewish Scriptures, recognized what this meant for Jesus' standing before God, for the Torah states, ". . . for anyone hung on a tree is under God's curse" (Deuteronomy 21:23, see Galatians 3:13). For Paul, far from being the Christ of God, the one who enjoyed divine favor, Jesus was the cursed of God, the one who incurred divine wrath. For Paul the Pharisee, to call Jesus the Messiah was probably blasphemous.

This problem would have given Paul sufficient grounds for persecuting the church. According to the Book of Acts, he received authorization from the high priest in Jerusalem to capture and imprison Christians. His functioning as a Jewish persecutor of Christians apparently gained him some notoriety. He later acknowledges his reputation among the Christian churches as a sworn enemy (Galatians 1:13, 23).

All this changed, of course, when the great persecutor of the church became its greatest proponent. The turning point in Paul's life came with his encounter with the risen Jesus. Both Acts of the Apostles and Paul's letters intimate that this happened when Paul was a relatively young man.

Paul's Conversion

It is difficult to know what actually happened to make Paul "turn around," the literal meaning of convert. Both Acts and Paul's writings attribute his conversion to the direct intervention of God. The Book of Acts provides three detailed accounts of the event that occurred on the road to Damascus. The event itself is narrated in Acts 9:1–19; Paul later recounts it to a hostile Jewish crowd after his arrest in 22:6–16 and then again to King Agrippa in 26:12–18.

The first thing to observe about Paul's conversion is that he traces it back to an encounter with the resurrected Jesus. In 1 Corinthians 15:8–11, he names himself as the last person to have seen Jesus raised from the dead and marks this as the beginning of his change from persecutor to apostle. He seems to be referring to the same event in Galatians 1:16, where he indicates that at a predetermined point in time God "was pleased to reveal his Son to me." When Paul experienced this revelation from God, he became convinced then and there, according to his later perspective, that he was to preach the good news of Christ to the Gentiles.

Paul interpreted his experience on the road to Damascus as an actual appearance of Jesus himself. We don't know how long this was after Jesus' death, or how Paul knew it to be Jesus, but there is no doubt that he believed that he saw Jesus' real but glorified body raised from the dead. Later in his letters Paul will tell Christians that they would eventually experience a bodily resurrection from the dead because he knew that Jesus did. For him, Jesus was the "first fruits" of those who would be raised (1 Corinthians 15:20). For Paul, Jesus has already returned to life, which means that God has begun to defeat the power of death.

As a result of his conversion, Paul set out to spread the message of Jesus with great vigor. He saw himself as an apostle.

Paul the Apostle

After his conversion, Paul spent several years in Arabia and Damascus (Galatians 1:17). After a brief trip to Jerusalem, he then went on to Syria and Cilicia, and eventually became involved in the church at Antioch. It is not altogether clear when he began his missionary activities further west in Asia Minor, Macedonia, and

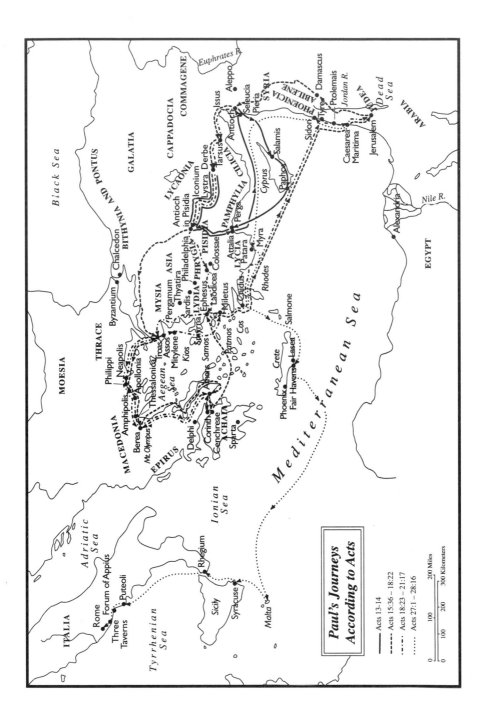

Paul's Journeys According to Acts

Achaia, but according to Romans 15:19 he was actively involved in spreading the Gospel all the way from Jerusalem to Illyricum, north of modern-day Greece. It is estimated that Paul covered about ten thousand miles in his ministry on both land and sea.

Throughout his career as a preacher of the Gospel, Paul saw himself as the "apostle to the Gentiles." By this he meant he had been appointed by God to bring the good news of salvation through faith in Christ to those who were not Jews. Paul's normal practice appears to have been to establish a Christian community in cities that had been primarily untouched by a Christian presence. After staying with the new church for some time and providing it with some basic instruction, he would move on to another city and start from scratch. He did this right up to his imprisonment and execution.

LIFE OF PAUL	
Circa 10 C.E.	Born and raised in Tarsus (father a Roman citizen and a leather worker).
Circa 31–33 C.E.	Becomes a zealous member of the Pharisees. Is actively engaged in persecuting members of a new Jewish sect centered in Jerusalem that claimed Jesus as Messiah.
Circa 33–35 C.E.	The conversion or vocation of Paul.
Circa 35–38 C.E.	Missionary activity in Arabia and Damascus.
Circa 38 C.E.	First visit to Jerusalem; meets Cephas (Peter) (Galatians 1:18–22).
Circa 38–49 C.E.	Missionary activity in the region of Syria and Cilicia.
Circa 49 C.E.	Second visit to Jerusalem with Barnabas and Titus; meets Cephas (Peter).
Circa 49–53 C.E.	Mission to Galatia, Philippi, Thessalonica, Corinth; writes 1 Thessalonians.
Circa 54–58 C.E.	Mission to Galatia, Ephesus, Corinth; writes 1 Corinthians, 2 Corinthians, Romans, and Galatians.
Circa 58 C.E.	Trip to Jerusalem and arrest.
Circa 58–60 C.E.	Imprisonment in Caesarea for two years.
Circa 61 C.E.	Sea journey to Rome.
Circa 62–67 C.E.	Executed after imprisonment in Rome.

Paul and His Letters

Paul stayed in touch with the churches he established by means of letters. Thirteen letters of the New Testament are attributed to Paul by name. They are Romans, 1 and 2 Corinthians, Galatians, Philippians, 1 and 2 Thessalonians, Colossians, Ephesians, Philemon, 1 and 2 Timothy, and Titus. Scholars are in almost unanimous agreement that 1 Thessalonians, Galatians, Philippians, 1 and 2 Corinthians, Romans, and Philemon are authentic letters of Paul. Due to differences in writing style and thought patterns, doubt has been raised concerning Paul's authorship of 2 Thessalonians, Colossians, and Ephesians. Therefore, these letters are referred to as "Deutero-Pauline" letters because they probably arose in the Pauline churches, were written by a disciple(s) of Paul, and ascribed to him. Such literary ascription was very popular in the ancient world. The remaining letters, 1 and 2 Timothy and Titus, are considered by most scholars as not from the hand of Paul. Since they *claim* to be written by Paul, scholars have referred to them as "pseudo Pauline" letters. They present a picture of the church which is vastly different from the picture presented in the authentic Pauline letters. They seem to come from a period toward the end of the first century.

Due to the constraints of space, we will now provide a brief description of each of these letters. For a more detailed analysis, the reader is encouraged to consult the bibliography at the end of the chapter.

Authentically Pauline Letters

1 Thessalonians

This letter has the distinction of being the first one written by Paul. Paul founded the community at Thessalonica in northern Greece on his second missionary journey in the year 50. This event aroused severe Jewish hostility (according to Acts 17:1–10), so much so that Paul and Silas left town by night. Concerned about the well-being of the Thessalonians, Paul sent Timothy to give the community support and encouragement (3:2–3). Timothy reported to Paul that the

Thessalonians were remaining faithful and progressing well. This was the occasion for Paul's letter to them.

Writing this letter, Paul follows the general format of Jewish Hellenistic letters in the opening. He starts with an identification of himself, the writer, an identification of the readers, a greeting ("grace and peace . . ."), and a prayer. In the body of the letter we find two sections. Paul first establishes his personal connection with the church by recalling his own experiences after departing. He then answers the questions of the Thessalonians.

Paul deals with two specific questions. What will happen to those who have died? When will the end be? He answers: The dead will rise, and we should not even try to calculate the end times.

Galatians

The dating of this letter runs the span of five years, fluctuating between 50 and 55 C.E. Galatia is a region in Asia Minor where Paul founded a Christian community in the early 50s on his second missionary journey. In this letter we meet an angry apostle who is exasperated with the Galatian community. It has welcomed Jewish-Christian teachers from Jerusalem who are demanding that the Gentile converts observe the Mosaic Law. These "Judaizers" are draining all the meaning from the saving works of Christ as preached by Paul.

Paul starts the letter *not* with a prayer for blessing or thanksgiving but, rather, with his own authority. He identifies himself as: "an apostle—sent neither by human commission nor from human authorities, but through Jesus Christ and God the Father" (1:1). He addresses the issue immediately. He is amazed at the Galatians' susceptibility to error after which Paul returns to the issue of his authority, providing us with a first-hand account of his call by Christ (1:11–17). Paul reports the decision of the Council of Jerusalem (see Acts 15)—namely that Gentile converts did not have to follow the Mosaic Law—but is very concerned to show his independence from other leaders as a chosen apostle (2:1–14).

In chapter 3, Paul presents his basic argument of justification by faith, and the inclusivity of all in the church, in Christ: "There is no longer Jew or Greek, there is no longer slave or free, there is no longer male and female; for all of you are one in Christ Jesus" (Galatians 3:28).

Though Paul is angry and harsh in this letter, his love for the Galatians shines through. The vigor and intensity of his language is meant to impress upon the readers his serious concern for their happiness and salvation. The best way to fulfill the true law, the Law of Christ, is to "[b]ear one another's burdens" (6:2). Paul tries to lift a false burden from their shoulders and is willing to receive their displeasure or even the scorn of their teachers if only he may bring them back to peace, mercy, and the grace of Jesus (6:14–18).

Philippians

This letter was composed around 55 or 56 C.E. It was most likely written by Paul from prison. According to Acts 16, Paul founded the Christian community at Philippi, his first on European soil, during his second missionary journey. The congregation at Philippi greatly respected Paul, and he shows evident affection for them.

Paul's letter to the Philippians is basically a letter of thanks. It is his warmest letter. Paul's gratitude for the Philippians' help in prison leads him to describe his situation. Paul appears to have no worries about misconduct in the Philippian church.

This letter is known for one of the most beautiful Christian hymns about Christ:

> *5Let the same mind be in you that was in Christ Jesus, 6who, though he was in the form of God, did not regard equality with God as something to be exploited, 7but emptied himself, taking the form of a slave, being born in human likeness. And being found in human form, 8he humbled himself and became obedient to the point of death—even death on a cross. 9Therefore God also highly exalted him and gave him the name that is above every name, 10so that at the name of Jesus, every knee should bend, in heaven and on earth and under the earth, 11and every tongue*

should confess that Jesus Christ is Lord, to the glory of God the Father (Philippians 2:5–11).

In 2:6–11, the hymn describes Jesus in three stages: as preexisting, as a human being, and as exalted after his death. Paul offers this hymn as the very foundation of his faith in Christ. Paul says: "I want to know Christ and the power of his resurrection and the sharing of his sufferings by becoming like him in his death, if somehow I may attain the resurrection from the dead" (3:10–11). He encourages the Philippian community to have the same faith and concludes with a thank-you note for the aid the community sent him when he was in need in Thessalonica (4:10–23).

1 Corinthians

Paul composed this letter toward the end of his stay in Ephesus, around the year 57 c.e. He had founded the Christian community in Corinth around 50 or 51 and tried to stay in touch with developments there. This letter was a response to a number of pastoral/theological questions brought to him by representatives from Corinth. The city serving as a seaport was notorious for its moral depravity.

The apostle to the Gentiles begins immediately to attack the divisions that have emerged in the Corinthian community (chapters 1–4). The believers claim various leaders as the founders of their factions: some actually claim a superior wisdom which would put them on a higher spiritual level. Paul states that the only true wisdom is the folly of the cross, and that the very leaders that they are proclaiming as their patrons are "fools for the sake of Christ" (4:10).

Before dealing with the questions addressed to him, Paul discusses other problems of which he is aware. He addresses cases of incest and other sexual immorality and strongly chides members of the community for taking their private quarrels into the arena of public law (chapters 5–6). The responses to particular questions beginning in chapter 7 have greatly influenced the history of Christianity and are a veritable gold mind for understanding a wide variety of theological topics: marriage and virginity (chapter 7), charity and religious observance (chapters 8–9), the Eucharist and other assemblies of worship (chapters 10–11), spiritual gifts (chapters 12–14), the resurrection of the body (chapter 15). In speaking of the gifts of the Spirit, Paul uses the analogy of the body for the first time in describing the church (12:12–31) and pens the famous hymn to love (charity) in chapter 13.

While the aforementioned chapter is often heard read at weddings, the most theologically profound chapter of 1 Corinthians is chapter 15, which deals with the resurrection. It merits a very careful reading for: "If there is no resurrection of the dead, then Christ has not been raised; and if Christ has not been raised, then our proclamation has been in vain and your faith has been in vain. . . . But in fact Christ has been raised from the dead, the first fruits of those who have died" (1 Corinthians 15:13–14, 20).

2 Corinthians

Paul wrote this letter from Ephesus, probably a few months after he wrote 1 Corinthians. The letter seems to have two parts to it. In the early chapters, Paul expresses personal affection for the readers and his deep love of the Gospel. In the closing pages he makes a sharp defense of his apostleship. The marked differences among the sections of this letter, particularly between chapters 1–9 and 10–13, have prompted a variety of theories of composition. The majority opinion among scholars today is that the letter is from Paul, but that it did not originally exist as one unified document. Granting this, then, chapters 1–9 could be subtitled "the letter of reconciliation," while chapters 10–13 could be called "the angry letter."

Sometime after Paul wrote 1 Corinthians, he heard that he was being criticized at Corinth and that his apostleship had been called into question. The Corinthians' attitude hurt Paul deeply. In this second letter, the apostle describes his trials for the Gospel and tries to convince the Corinthians of his sincerity. Paul describes his work as a "ministry of reconciliation" (5:18), in which the Gospel is carried to the world like a treasure contained in earthen vessels (4:7). In chapters 8 and 9, Paul encourages generosity in a collection for the community in Jerusalem.

Paul's defense of his ministry becomes much more vitriolic and aggressive in chapter 10:13. He is scornful of adversaries who "commend themselves" (10:12) and those who are "false apostles" (11:13). Paul paints a vibrant and vivid history of his own labors and sufferings for the Gospel (chapters 11–12); he reproaches himself for letting himself be driven to such foolishness by the criticism of those he has served. He closes the letter by issuing a final challenge to his opponents.

Romans

Romans is Paul's longest and most theologically developed and reflective letter. Written in 57–58 C.E. from Corinth to God's beloved in Rome, where Paul—at the time of the writing of this letter—had never been but had friends. Romans is clearly distinct from Paul's other letters: it has the structure of a letter, conveys the warmth of personal correspondence, addresses real concerns of the Roman church, and deals with uncertainties about the apostle's imminent visit.

Considering that the letter consists of sixteen chapters, only a brief summary of its content will be presented here.

Into the unusually short, stereotyped greeting (1:1–7), Paul crams the tradition undergirding his gospel and supporting his apostleship. Appealing to tradition, the apostle authenticates his apostleship and legitimates his gospel, thus countering the charge of being a dangerous innovator.

The thanksgiving (1:8–15) underscores Paul's commission to the Gentiles. He intends to visit the Roman church to reap some harvest there as among "the rest of the Gentiles" (1:13). He announces his obligation to "Greeks and to barbarians" (1:14). The summary of his gospel (1:16–17) speaks of God's power to "everyone," Jew and now Greek.

From Romans 1:18 and forward, Paul explains his Gentile gospel and defends it against challengers. He argues that Jews and Gentiles have historically failed to honor the Creator or do his will and thus need God's grace (3:23). Nevertheless, Paul's gospel of grace appears to some as a pernicious provocation. If it erases every distinction between Jews and Gentiles, why be a Jew (3:1)? If human sin elicits divine favor, why not sin with abandon to multiply God's grace (3:8)? Before dealing with these objections (6:1–11:36), Paul treats related concerns. Recalling how God counted Abraham righteous on account of his faith (Genesis 15:6) rather than by circumcision (Genesis 17:10), Paul argues that Gentiles may now become children of Abraham by faith. Through faith in Christ they are counted righteous (chapter 4) and receive access to and reconciliation with God (5:1–11).

For those who question how Jesus' act of obedience can benefit others, Paul recalls a familiar example (5:12–19). Because of his disobedience, Adam was exiled from Eden to a life marked by toil and want, fratricide and fear, pain and death. Ever since, through repeated acts of disobedience (not by biological inheritance!), humankind has shared in his frustration and futility. The first Adam and the last (i.e., Jesus) correspond in the way the action of each influences the destiny of all. They differ in the result they effect. Through the first Adam "many were made sinners" (5:19); through the last Adam came acquittal for all. Paul contends that those understanding humankind's solidarity with the first Adam should comprehend how Christ can unite all peoples.

In Romans 6:1–7:6, Paul answers the charges (see 3:8) that his gospel of grace encourages sinning. The behavior of believers in Corinth, where some took salvation to mean all things were lawful (1 Corinthians 10:23; see Romans 14:14), gave the charge substance. Drawing on three examples—baptism, slavery, and marriage—Paul refutes the charge. In baptism, the believer symbolically dies to sin and becomes alive to God. How, Paul wonders, can one making his transition continue living in sin's bondage (6:1–14)? In Romans 6:15–23, Paul asks how those redeemed from slavery to sin for service in Christ can still behave like slaves of the old master. In Romans 7:1–6, he notes how the death of a husband frees his wife to remarry. Similarly, believers who have died to the law belong to Christ. How, therefore, can they act as if they were still in the prior marriage?

Through these examples, Paul means to correct the mistaken impression that his gospel encourages libertarianism.

While Paul's last example solved one problem, it raised another. Any pious Jew would bristle at Paul's suggestion that the Law, God's gift to Israel, inflicted bondage. If the Law is evil, then questions arise: Is God so sinister as to give malevolent gifts? Is the Law indeed evil? Paul immediately retorts, "Absolutely not" (see Romans 7:7). Later, Paul adds, "The law is holy, and the commandment is holy and just and good" (7:12). The defect is not in the law but in the human heart. Corrupted by sin, the heart twists the law, a good thing, into an ugly distortion. While the law forbids one to "covet" (7:7), all persons crave most what is explicitly forbidden. The flaw is not in the law or its giver, but in the person.

The language of Romans 7:7–25 is all first person singular, sometimes referred to as Paul's "I" autobiography. Paul speaks here not as a guilt-ridden Pharisee, anxious over his failure to keep the law. Instead he tells the universal story of the corruption of the good law by the power of sin.

In Romans, chapter 8, the new age breaks into view. The Law of the Spirit, Paul affirms, sets believers free from "the [principle] law of sin and of death" (see 8:2). Paul knows God's words to Jeremiah, "I will put my law within them, and I will write it on their hearts" (Jeremiah 31:33). Through Christ the law of the Spirit has been inscribed on the heart, eliminating resistance to God. Thus, Paul argues, the charge that his gospel repudiates the law is false. In the light of God's final day, Paul does not reject the law but revalues it.

Romans chapters 9–11 answers urgent questions raised by Jewish objections to Paul's Gentile mission: God promised to be Israel's God and to make Israel his people. In offering the Gospel to the Gentiles, has God rescinded this promise? Paul's reply—that God has always chosen to bless some over others, and is, therefore, free to turn away from Israel to the Gentiles—raises another objection: Is God fair to choose the rejected (Gentiles) and reject the chosen (9:14)? If God chooses Gentiles, how can Jews be condemned for rejecting the Gospel

(9:19)? If Gentiles who do not pursue righteousness now achieve it by faith, and Jews who seek righteousness are denied salvation, can God be just? Paul's reply is that God is free to turn to Gentiles but has not forsaken Israel. In the future, God will join Jews with Gentiles in one community (11:25–32). Fearing Gentile arrogance over their salvation, Paul warns, "For if God did not spare the natural branches [Jews], perhaps he will not spare you [Gentiles]" (11:21; cf. 11:13–24).

Sensitive to the charge that his gospel encourages immorality, Paul earlier argued that moral license and Christian freedom are incompatible (6:1–7:6). Chapters 12 through 15 give instances of the work of the Gospel in everyday life. First, concerning insiders, Paul exhorts all with charismatic gifts—prophecy, teaching, administration, and benevolence—to use the charisms for the church's nurture (12:3–13). Toward outsiders, Paul encourages love (12:14–21). Christian love also dictates respect for "governing authorities" and payment of Roman taxes (13:1–7). The state serves God, Paul argues, when it preserves order (13:3–4) and provides an arena for witness until the end (13:12). Moreover, God's care for and claim on the world allows no Christian to abandon it. While Paul offers no advice for occasions when loyalty to God conflicts with loyalty to the state, it is, nevertheless, mistaken to base a blind allegiance to the state on Romans 13. Why? Because Paul's opening argument against idolatry (1:21–22) would preclude such deification of the state.

In Romans 14:1–15:13, Paul encourages church factions to "[w]elcome one another . . . as Christ has welcomed you" (15:7). The identity of the quarreling parties is strongly disputed. Whatever the issues in dispute may have been, Paul gently pushes both factions toward reconciliation.

In the closing of the letter, Paul shares his travel plans. His eastern mission complete (15:19, 23), he intends to deliver the offering to Jerusalem (15:25–28), then travel via Rome to Spain. Questions flood his mind: Will the Roman church endorse his gospel? Will it support his mission to Spain, as did the Macedonian church his work in Greece (see 2 Corinthians 11:9)? Will the "unbelievers in Judea" frustrate his plans (15:31)? Will his offering "be acceptable to the saints" (15:31)?

The Acts of the Apostles (21:17–28:31) gives substance to Paul's premonition of failure. While Paul tells us nothing more in the epistle to the Romans, Acts of the Apostles reports that once in Jerusalem, Paul was arrested and charged with speaking against the Temple, the law, and Judaism. His appeal to Caesar eventually took him to Rome and there, tradition holds, he died a martyr's death.

Philemon

The epistle to Philemon might better be described as a note which Paul wrote about the year 62 to a wealthy young Colossian named Philemon. This letter represents Paul's personal plea—which becomes more like a command as the letter progresses—for Philemon to accept back in a spirit of Christian love his runaway slave, Onesimus.

Onesimus had somehow made his way to Rome, where Paul met him and converted him to Christianity. Perhaps Onesimus was serving a jail sentence for some petty crime in the same Roman prison where Paul was confined. At any rate, Paul returned Onesimus to Philemon "confident" that Philemon would welcome his slave back as he would welcome Paul himself (see verse 17).

Nothing could more vividly dramatize the life-changing effect of a person's conversion to Christianity than for a master to take back under his roof a runaway slave—and not just to take him back, but to accept him as a "beloved brother" (see verse 16). Philemon was challenged by Paul to demonstrate his desire for deeper intimacy with Jesus in a very practical and painful way.

Paul gave Philemon a challenge every Christian must face—to show that the Gospel is indeed real in his or her life. Paul constantly affirms that Christianity is much more than an assent to a doctrine; it is a response to a personal call from the resurrected Lord to "[l]ove your neighbor as yourself" (see Romans 13:9b).

Deutero-Pauline Letters

2 Thessalonians

While it is universally accepted that Paul did not write 2 Thessalonians, the letter itself seems to have been sent not long after the first letter. In it, the author admonishes the assembled church about the second coming of Christ, in that the church had not heeded what he had said in the first letter. The imminent coming of the Lord still agitated some of the community. The author of 2 Thessalonians was especially concerned about those who stopped working because the end was near. They gave the community a bad reputation just at the time that persecution intensified.

Because of the more impersonal style of this letter and the different treatment of some issues dealt with throughout the letter, scholars believe that 2 Thessalonians was written by a later disciple in Paul's name. The letter's introduction addresses words of comfort to the community in distress from persecution (1:3–10). The author then confronts the issue of the *parousia* (second coming of Jesus), which had probably become more acute because of suffering. The author reassures his readers, reminding them of his earlier teaching that certain events must precede the coming of Jesus (2:1–12).

The author refers to the mysterious "lawless one" who will do Satan's work but be overcome by the Lord. This figure and the reference to "what is restraining" eludes practically every scholar's understanding today. The author emphasizes that the important thing is to remain firm without fear, holding fast to the traditional truths (2:13–17). The final chapter evokes Paul's own example of work as a contrast to the Thessalonians who are sitting idle. The author asks the community to pray for him but reminds them that he, and not the troublesome teachers, speaks with God's authority.

Colossians

The Christian community at Colossae, in Asia Minor, was founded by Epaphras, a Gentile Christian, probably one of Paul's converts. Epaphras visited Paul in prison and brought news of some problems in the Colossian church caused by superstitious teachings. One doctrine seems to have come from Greek sources: the idea that human affairs are controlled by angelic beings who must be appeased; the other was the familiar Judaizing emphasis on observance of the Mosaic Law. Some of the false teachers advertised a secret knowledge beyond the Gospel, to which the author of Colossians responded that perfect knowledge is found in Christ (2:3).

Further, in reply to such teachings, the author of Colossians emphasizes the unique and all-powerful role of Christ and the present, saved existence of the Christian community. Christ, the "image" of God (1:15), in whom "the whole fullness of the deity dwells bodily" (2:9), creates (1:16), gives coherence to (1:17), and has absolute power over (1:18–20) all beings, whether earthly or heavenly. Indeed, the cosmic principalities and powers have no independent authority but are mere captives in Christ's triumphal procession (2:15). The community does not need some new form of protection or deliverance; it already has been "rescued" and "transferred" to the kingdom of the Son (1:13), even resurrected with Christ (2:12). The author stresses that "forgiveness of sins" (1:14, see also 2:13, 3:13) is a present reality; perhaps some had viewed the rigorous new teaching as a solution for moral imperfection. Men and women, insists Colossians, need not retreat from the world in order to live upright lives; they have power here and now from Christ, through baptism, to act morally. Indeed, for Colossians, the family household is a privileged locus for healthy, ethical activity (3:18–4:1).

Ephesians

There are very good scholarly grounds for doubting whether Paul was the author of Ephesians. Much of it is written in an elevated and liturgical style, and, though Paul writes brief passages in this manner, he never sustains it for long. In addition, the sentences are longer and more complex than those that Paul normally writes. Because of these and other reasons, it is universally accepted that a disciple of Paul probably wrote the letter about 80–90 C.E., wishing to continue his master's teaching and apply it to changing circumstances. He directed it to the churches in Asia Minor, most of whose members were Gentiles. The letter itself affords no clue as to why it was written.

The author meditates on a number of interrelated themes centering on the church and its relation to Christ and on Christian behavior. A divine plan, in God's mind since before the creation of the world (1:4), has now been revealed to the apostles and prophets (3:5) and is being accomplished through the death, resurrection, and ascension of Christ. He is Lord not only of humanity but also of all supernatural powers, both good and evil (1:20–23), and in him all things will finally be united (1:10). Thus God redeems the whole universe as well as humanity.

Prior to Jesus, Jews alone were central to God's plan. Now Gentiles are also included, for both have been delivered from sin and reconciled to one another through Christ's death (2:13–18). Jewish and Gentile Christians form a third group, the church, which is neither Jewish nor Gentile but Christian. Like a building, the church has a chief corner-stone, Christ, and the foundation the apostles and prophets (2:20). As a body with various members (4:7–11), its head is Christ, by whom it is continuously nourished (4:15–16). As a bride, the church's groom is Christ, who died for it (5:22–33). It brings God's salvation to the super-natural powers (3:9–10) as well as to all humanity. Paul himself has a special place in this in relation to the Gentiles (3:2, 3, 8).

The church is involved in the full accomplishment of God's plan. Christians must therefore stand firm in love (3:17) and display love in daily living (chapters 4 through 6). Since the readers of the letter are ex-Gentiles, detailed guidance is given in respect of behavior. Christian behavior reflects in its turn the cosmic dimension, since it is a struggle against supernatural powers (6:10–18).

Pseudo-Pauline Letters

1 Timothy

Three epistles—1 and 2 Timothy and Titus—are grouped together for two reasons. They are a part of what is usually called the pseudo

Pauline literature, meaning that they were not really written by Paul. Further, they are grouped together as "pastoral letters." They reflect a church order of the late first century and are generally acknowledged to have been written by a disciple(s) after Paul's death. These letters provide a window or lens to the next stage of development after Acts of the Apostles. The communities founded by roving missionaries had special needs for continuing stability. Thus, the pastoral letters stress sound doctrine and rules for choosing leaders.

Acts of the Apostles describes Timothy as the son of a Hebrew mother and a Greek father (Acts 16:1). He was the companion of Paul on some of his journeys. In this epistle, he is stationed in Ephesus as the leader of the local Christian community (1 Timothy 1:3). The letters contain advice for exercising this role. 1 Timothy begins with an attack on the teachers of false doctrines (see chapter 1). Then the author reviews rules for correct conduct and liturgical assemblies (chapter 2), and the list of qualifications for various ministries in the community (chapter 3). The letter returns to the issue of false doctrine, this time concerned with misguided asceticism (see 4:1–5). The final two chapters give practical advice for guiding widows, presbyters (elders with some leadership responsibilities), slaves, and their masters.

2 Timothy

This letter is more of a personal message from Paul to Timothy than the first one. In 1 Timothy, advice was given for problems in leading a community; here the author speaks of his own situation, confessing a feeling of loneliness and abandonment, and gives personal encouragement to Timothy, "my beloved child" (1:2). But the tone of this letter is more severe in some ways. Some followers have defected from the faith. Timothy must hold to his sacred charge and rely on the just judgment of God to vindicate and reward him after his difficult labors are over.

The personal tone is set immediately with a description of the last meeting of Paul and Timothy and references to the latter's family

(1:4–5). The apostle confesses to feeling the pains of desertions (1:15); he tells Timothy what he considers essential for a good Christian leader in these difficult times (chapter 2). Paul offers himself as a model for the young Timothy (3:10–17) and repeats the commission of a sacred charge (4:1–5). With "I have fought the good fight" (4:7), and his instructions about his cloak, papyrus rolls, and parchments (4:13), Paul sounds like an old warrior signing off at the end of this letter.

Titus

The man Titus is known to us from the letters of Paul as a Greek convert (see Galatians 2:1–3), who fulfills several important missions for the apostle (2 Corinthians 7:6–7, 8:16–18). Paul called him "my partner and coworker in your service" (2 Corinthians 8:23). The letter to Titus indicates that Titus was left on the island of Crete to finish Paul's work there. Paul is sending more detailed instruction for this work.

This letter is closer in theme to 1 Timothy than to 2 Timothy. The fluid state of church order is reflected, however, in the fact that in 1 Timothy the offices of bishop and presbyter were distinct; in Titus they are equated. Chapter one gives the qualifications for a Christian leader, with the familiar warnings about false teachers; chapter two gives practical counsel for family relations; chapter three expands this to the responsibilities in the broader society.

Hebrews

This New Testament document is almost certainly neither a letter nor written by Paul. The original composer(s) and audience do appear to be Christians with deep connections to Judaism, particularly to the temple liturgy and the Jewish Scriptures. Hence, there is some accuracy in the title stemming most likely from the second century, "to the Hebrews." Apart from this identification, we know very little of where this letter comes from, who wrote it, or why it was written.

The epistle to the Hebrews might best be seen as a sermon. It is noted for its balanced emphasis on the divinity and humanity of Jesus. This is evident right from the beginning. Jesus is God's ultimate word, higher than the angels (chapter 1), but he abased himself to become human and die for us (chapter 2). Because he is one of us, Jesus can understand us when we approach his throne (2:18, 4:15–16). Jesus is the fulfillment of Jewish hopes. He brings the rest that the people of God have been looking for (chapters 3–4). Jesus is also fully divine, and the letter to the Hebrews describes this four times by referring to Jesus as seated at the right hand of God (see 1:3, 8:1, 10:12, 12:2).

The central section of the book (chapters 5–10) presents Jesus as the eternal high priest whose sacrifice overcomes sin once and for all and establishes a new covenant with God. The theology of Christ the priest "according to the order of Melchizedek" is unique to this New Testament book (see chapter 7). The author centers his message on the saving death of Jesus as a means by which a new access to God has been opened up, and a new covenant from God purveyed.

The third major section (chapters 11–12) turns to the practical living out of the Christian salvation described earlier. The author presents models of faith from Judaism leading to the supreme model, Jesus. Here the author urges members of the Christian church to forge ahead in faith and hope on pilgrimage to the heavenly Jerusalem (12:22). The sermon closes with exhortations for daily Christian living (chapter 13), including the warning about false teaching, which is practically standard in the Christian literature of the time.

The Catholic Epistles

The next seven letters in the New Testament have been known traditionally as the "Catholic epistles" because the ancient interpreters considered them addressed to the universal church—the basic meaning of *catholic*—rather than individuals or individual communities.

James

The letter from James is addressed to "the twelve tribes in the dispersion," a Jewish designation probably meant as a symbol for the Christian church gathered throughout the Roman Empire. The author is either James, a leader of the Jerusalem church (see Acts of

223

the Apostles 12:17) who died in the early 60s, or—as is more likely because of Helenistic language, polished Greek, and the developed state of the church—an anonymous disciple from the 80s or 90s.

The book is written in the spirit of the Old Testament, with some literature that bears comparison with Proverbs and Sirach for its themes—such as wisdom, humility, use of the tongue ("no one can tame the tongue," 3:8), public behavior—and for its loose organization. Though the author shows familiarity with earlier New Testament writings, Jesus is mentioned only twice (1:1, 2:1) and reference to concepts specifically Christian is rare. One of these references is to the controversy over faith and works (2:14–26).

Chapters 1 and 4 contain various rules for conduct. Chapter 3 is well known for its graphic imagery on the use of the tongue. Chapter 5 contains one of the few passages that have been officially interpreted by the Catholic church. The Council of Trent declared that James 5:14–15 refers to the sacrament of anointing of the sick.

1 Peter

The addressees of this letter, like those of James, are dispersed throughout the world, "the exiles of the Dispersion," but in this instance the world is located as Asia Minor (1:1). Later in the letter we find out that the readers live with the danger of persecution. This is what makes them "sojourners"; they are aliens in the pagan world. This letter is dated, therefore, to the 90s, quite likely the work of a Christian pastor writing in the name of Peter. Unlike James, 1 Peter's moral exhortations are closely related to Christian salvation themes. The beautiful baptismal exposition has given rise to the suggestion that some of the materials originated in early baptismal liturgy.

1 Peter highlights conversion as "a new birth." By numerous contrasts, the author stresses that a radical change has taken place in the lives of converts by joining God's covenant. They have moved from no hope to true hope (1:21), impurity to purity (1:18; 4:3), slavery to freedom (1:18), perishability to imperishability (1:4, 23), ignorance to knowledge (1:14), flesh to spirit (4:6), death to life (1:3), disobedience to obedience (1:2, 22), "not a people" to "God's people"

224

(2:10), no mercy received to mercy received (2:10). This is one of the most detailed explanations of conversion in the entire New Testament. It is what is considered as the true foundation for admittance to baptism.

The rest of the epistle of 1 Peter is an instruction on the response to this rich inheritance and living the Gospel. Though Christians are treated as strangers and exiles, they should live as good citizens (2:11–17). An example of early Christian application to the Old Testament is the reflection of Jesus as the suffering servant of Isaiah in 2:21–25. 1 Peter provides particular admonitions for married couples (see chapter 3), for church leaders, and for young men (see chapter 5). Recurring themes for all the believers are mutual charity and fidelity in the midst of suffering.

2 Peter

2 Peter reflects a church structure similar to that of the pastorals of Paul and incorporates much of the letter of Jude, which dates to the last part of the first century. 2 Peter refers to a collection of Paul's letters (3:15–16); such a collection was not made until the 90s. The author, like the author of 1 Peter, writes in the name of the great apostle to address needs of the church in a later time: in this case, to discuss the difficulty caused by the delay of the second coming of Jesus (the *parousia*). 2 Peter is generally dated by scholars early in the second century.

The letter is addressed in a general way to all Christians of the time, a mixture of converts from Judaism and paganism. The author is concerned about the challenge of two orthodox teachings, particularly the denial of the Lord's coming and the consequent disregard for proper Christian conduct. Chapter 1 claims the authority of Peter, with reference to his unique privilege as a witness to the transfiguration of Jesus (1:16–18). This punishment of evildoers is proof from past history (see chapter 2). False teachers are warned and true teaching about the coming of the Lord is taught by one who is qualified to interpret the Scriptures (see chapter 3).

1 John

By now, the reader should be familiar with the practice of attributing late New Testament writings to great apostles. The Johannine epistles are another important example of this. The Gospel of John reflected the situation (around 90 C.E.) of the community, which had taken its inspiration from the "Beloved Disciple." This group of Christians probably centered around Ephesus in Asia Minor. The gospel of John showed the followers of Jesus in bitter struggle with the Jews. 1, 2, and 3 John point to a situation in the Johannine community about a decade later, therefore at the turn of the century. Here groups of Christians argue over the correct interpretation of John's gospel. The author of the Johannine letters, probably not the same as the author of the gospel, writes against the people he considers false teachers, "antichrist," who "went out from" (2:18–19). These false teachers have distorted the teaching about Jesus and the Christian life presented in the Gospel of John.

The principal error or mistake of the adversaries was the minimizing of Jesus' humanity. 1 John begins with a dramatic and graphic description of the "word of life" as something heard, seen, and touched. This theme appears again in 2:18–23 and in 4:1–6. A destructive moral teaching flowed from disregard for the human reality of Jesus: the human actions of his followers are not important either. Therefore, the admonition to "keep my commandments" (John 15:10) is undermined. Those who deny sinfulness, the "liars," are mentioned in 1:6–10 and 4:20–21. The author is especially concerned about disregard for the commandment to love one another and has penned some of the most memorable lines on love in the New Testament. They are:

For this is the message you have heard from the beginning, that we should love one another (1 John 3:11).

And this is his commandment, that we should believe in the name of his Son Jesus Christ and love one another, just as he commanded us (1 John 3:23).

Beloved, let us love one another, because love is from God; everyone who loves is born of God and knows God (1 John 4:7).

2 John

In 2 and 3 John, the author introduces himself as "the elder," probably a title indicating his prestige and authority as a disciple of the first followers of Jesus. He wrote to "the elect lady and her children," members of a Christian community, to encourage them and warn them against dangers that may be coming. The dangers were those mentioned in 1 John, particularly the overly aggressive view about Jesus (see verse 9), which disregards his humanity, his "coming in the flesh" (see verse 7).

3 John

The Johannine author had mentioned an intention to visit the community addressed in 2 John (2 John 12). In 3 John, he writes to a different group to encourage the acceptance of the missionaries he will send (verses 5–8). The local leader, a certain Diotrephes, was unfriendly to those traveling preachers (see verses 9–10). The author intends to visit soon to straighten out the problem. The letter reveals friction between two orders of leadership in the early church.

Jude

The author identifies himself not as the apostle Jude, but as the "brother of James," the leader of the Jerusalem community (Acts of the Apostles 15:13). Jude's letter seems to date from late in the century because of its references to "the apostles of our Lord Jesus Christ" (verse 17) as a group from the past. Jude warns about false teachers who are "intruders" (verse 4) in the church. Their error is more in their sinful practice than in some particular doctrine. Most of this letter was later used in 2 Peter. Of note is the use of two Jewish works which were not accepted into the biblical canon—1 Enoch (see verses 14–15) and the Assumption of Moses (see verse 9).

In conclusion, we have attempted in a succinct summary fashion throughout this chapter to explore both the life of Paul and his letters as well as the remaining letters of the New Testament. By means of an overview, and with large brush strokes, we have painted a functional picture. Of course, more could have been included, but since this book is geared toward beginners, the objective was to inform not overwhelm the reader.

For Discussion

1. How important do you think Paul's conversion was to his ministry as an apostle to the Gentiles?
2. In one of Paul's letters, he says we are justified by faith. What does that mean to you?
3. In another one of his letters, Paul refers to the church as the body of Christ. What does this metaphor for the church mean to you? Explain.
4. Read chapter 11 of the epistle to the Hebrews. How do you react to its description of "faith"?
5. In the first epistle of John, there are extensive descriptions of love of God and love of fellow human beings. Look these up and react and reflect on each.

For Further Reading

Fitzmyer, Joseph. Pauline *Theology: A Brief Sketch* (Second Edition). Englewood Cliffs, N.J.: Prentice Hall, 1989.

Murphy, O'Connor, Jerome. *Paul: A Critical Life.* New York: Oxford University Press, 1998.

———. *Paul the Letter Writer: His World, His Options, His Skills.* Collegeville, Minn.: Michael Glazier, 1995.

Puskas, Charles B. *The Letters of Paul: An Introduction.* Collegeville, Minn.: Liturgical Press, 1993.

Roetzel, Calvin. *The Letters of Paul: Conversations in Context* (Third Edition). Atlanta: John Knox Press, 1991.

Sanders, E. P. *Paul and Palestinian Judaism.* Philadelphia: Fortress Press, 1977.

10

THE
BOOK OF
REVELATION:
BREAKING
THE CODE

Are PEOPLE AFRAID OF THE BOOK OF REVELATION? Do our minds become confused when we hear all those sevens and twelves, and all those strange titles applied to Jesus—the Alpha and Omega and the bright morning star? Indeed, some might feel Revelation's symbols and metaphors are so confusing that they avoid this book of the Bible.

Yet avoidance is no remedy for confusion. The Book of Revelation is part of the church's Scriptures. We owe it to ourselves as God's people to become familiar with this part of our religious heritage.

The Book of Revelation reveals how God's salvation has entered the world in the birth, life, death, and resurrection of Jesus. As Catholics, we reject the approach of those who use this book to guess wildly about the future or to create fear and mistrust among Christians or to support their own political agendas. The last book of the Bible was not intended for any of these purposes, but rather to be "the revelation of Jesus Christ" (Revelation 1:1) and a "call for the endurance and faith of the saints" (Revelation 13:10). In this sense, it is like the gospels. But the manner of revealing is unlike the gospels.

The Book of Revelation is a piece of *apocalyptic* literature, a style very popular between 200 B.C.E. and 200 C.E., during a great crisis in Israel. The Greek word *apocalypse* (in English, "revelation") literally means "to draw back the veil." Apocalyptic literature attempts to give assurance that however bad things may be, one need only draw back the veil and see things in the perspective of the great battle against evil. God's victorious power is always at work among us.

Watered-down Faith?

The Book of Revelation was written sometime in the early 90s of the first century by an author who perceived that some Christians were compromising their faith—giving in to the surrounding culture to avoid persecution. The events leading up to this persecution merit a closer look.

When the early Christian community split with Judaism, they found themselves without the protection of the Roman Empire. It was Roman law that any secret society or religious group that originated after the foundation of the empire was considered a superstition. Such groups could not practice in the empire. Since Judaism had been founded long before the empire, Jews were free to practice their beliefs. As long as Christianity was under the aegis of Judaism, the Christians were also considered legal. Now that Christianity had split from Judaism, the Christian belief was considered a superstition, a violation of Roman law.

Toward the end of the reign of Emperor Nero, unrest began to mount in the empire. Nero was assassinated, as were three of his successors, during the next three years. Finally, Vespasian, a general, was called back from Judea, where he was trying to put an end to the Zealot revolt that ultimately escalated into the Jewish War.

Vespasian's son, Titus, continued the war in Judea. Vespasian became emperor. During his reign some stability returned to the empire. Titus succeeded his father as emperor and continued the policy of stabilization. Titus's son, Domitian, succeeded Titus.

Vespasian and Titus had brought some stability to Rome after the chaos of the late 60s. Still, there was urgent need for some principle of unity that would bring the empire together. That unity was secured by the army (legions) who protected the vast regions of the empire by force.

Domitian realized that military might could never bring lasting unity to his empire. He needed the loyalty of his subjects, a loyalty that arose from moral or religious conviction. As a result, he had himself proclaimed a god (*Dominus et Deus Noster*—"Our lord and god"). He commanded that all loyal Romans not exempted by law should burn incense before his statue. The penalty for refusing to acknowledge the divinity of the emperor was a prohibition from carrying on commerce or business within the empire.

Most people in the empire did not find this a hardship. There were, however, a few groups who found it unacceptable, particularly the Jews and the Christians. When they protested the requirement, the Jews were exempted because of their position as a legal religion within the empire. The Christians, on the other hand, whose religion the Romans considered superstitious, were not exempted.

Domitian wanted the Christians to conform to this command since he didn't trust them. Christians in the empire found themselves faced with a dilemma. They wanted to obey the civil mandate. Yet, obedience to it meant violating the covenant they had entered through belief in Jesus as Lord.

Some within the church took the road of compromise. They thought this would be the greater good. They felt that placing incense before the emperor's statue was a civil act with no bearing on one's commitment to Christ. Thus, it would be legitimate to perform this new simple civil act in order to continue spreading the Gospel. The Nicolaitans, mentioned in chapter 2 of Revelation, are a group who held this view.

Others in the Christian community saw compromise as totally incompatible with belief in Jesus. The author of Revelation was one of them. He believed there was a necessity for the Christian community to take a stand. Those who believe in Jesus must remain strong in their faith. That would be a sign that the church is alive and active in the empire. Christians must refuse to follow the command to burn incense before the emperor's statue. Rather, the author of the Book of Revelation felt that they must speak forcibly the words, "The emperor is not god. The emperor is not Lord. Jesus is Lord." The author of Revelation writes to encourage those who might compromise their faith.

The Book of Revelation is a drama. *Who* are its principal players? *Where* does the drama unfold? and *What* happens? We can outline the drama's cast, setting, and plot as follows.

Cast of Characters

Producer/Director: God the Father, "the Alpha and the Omega . . . who is and who was and who is to come, the Almighty" (Revelation 1:8).

Leading Actor: The Lamb, "I, Jesus . . . the descendant of David, the bright morning star" (22:16); "the Alpha and the Omega" (22:13). Note that the leading man shares titles with the producer/director.

Leading Actress: "[W]oman clothed with the sun" (12:1), bride of the Lamb who is Christ (see 19:7), the church (21:9).

Principal Supporting Actress: Whore of Babylon—"a woman sitting on a scarlet beast that was full of blasphemous names" (17:3); Rome.

Principal Supporting Actor: Devil or Satan (20:2), a huge dragon, flaming red (12:3), the power behind the two beasts.

Additional Characters: Michael the Angel (12:7); twenty-four elders (4:4, 10; 5:8; 11:16; 19:4); seven spirits before the throne—that is,

God's Spirit manifesting itself in fullness (1:4, 3:1, 4:5, 5:6); four horsemen (6:1–8); first beast—ten horns and seven heads, the Whore of Babylon under another guise (13:1); second beast—servants of the first beast, the imperial priesthood (13:11); four "living creatures" (4:6b); numerous angels.

Chorus: "[O]ne hundred forty-four thousand, sealed out of every tribe of the people of Israel" (7:4); "a great multitude" (7:9); those who "have washed their robes and made them white in the blood of the Lamb" (7:14); the elect.

Various Settings

Throne Room in Heaven: Throne encircled by rainbow (suggesting God's mercy—Genesis 9:12) and situated on a crystal clear glass floor. Twenty-four smaller thrones surrounding God's throne. Twenty-four elders clothed in white garments with gold crowns on their heads. Thunder and lightening. Seven torches burning before the throne. Four living creatures praising God day and night without pause. Abode of the Lamb.

Earth: The location of the seven (i.e., "all") churches (1:4–3:19). The time of the present. The Christian's day-to-day involvement in the cosmic struggle going on all around the earthly church. Habitation of the two beasts (i.e., all earthly power opposed to God).

The Heavens: Place where the plot unfolds. The battleground for the spiritual warfare in which God ultimately defeats Satan and all the powers of evil.

The Plot in a Nutshell

Imagine you are seated in a huge amphitheater waiting for the drama to begin. A person walks on stage and says, "The revelation of Jesus Christ, which God gave him to show his servants what must soon take place" (Revelation 1:1). This stirs your sense of suspense and you pay closer attention.

"I wonder if the outcome of the drama will be good or bad," you ask yourself. The narrator gives you a clue: "[B]lessed are those who hear and who keep what is written in it" (Revelation 1:3).

"Aha! A 'message'!" you think. "I'd better pay close attention. There's going to be a moral in this story."

Message to the Seven Churches

The drama begins on earth. The author wants to situate his audience firmly within the confines of the cosmic struggle about to be described. Yet he wants the audience to understand that this struggle takes place on earth also, and that it affects the Christian in his or her day-to-day life in the church. Thus he gives an introductory view of seven churches, by which he means the church as a whole, intending to illustrate how the church must attend daily to its role in the cosmic struggle.

John reads advice to the seven churches revealed to him by God. The seven churches are local churches in the vicinity of John's head-quarters. John's words of praise and admonition are to be read as general advice to the church of his day and today about spiritual concerns.

Having heard the messages to their local churches, the audience is prepared to enter into the ensuing conflict; it now knows that what is to follow affects its own daily existence. "Let anyone who has an ear listen to what the Spirit is saying to the churches" (3:22), the author says, as he now turns the audience's attention from earth to heaven.

The Seven Seals

In a scene reminiscent of Ezekiel 1 and 10, John brings the audience into God's heavenly court. The cosmic struggle which is about to be unleashed has its origin in the breaking open of a scroll sealed by "seven seals" (Revelation 5:1)—that is, a scroll absolutely locked to humanity's comprehension. To center stage comes a lamb with "seven horns and seven eyes" (5:6)—that is, Christ possessed of absolute power and knowledge. To him has been given the authority to open the scroll—to initiate the last era of history, the coming of God's final judgment and his victory for the elect.

The drama now begins in earnest. The Lamb begins to open the seven seals one by one. With the breaking of the first four seals, four horsemen ride forth distributing persecution, war, famine, and sickness. This is the human condition prior to God's judgment and is meant to represent all of human history. The message is that God permits suffering until his victory can be completed. Suffering is part of God's salvific plan.

With the breaking of the first seal, God introduces martyrdom into human history (history seen here as all ages of the past, even before the time of Jesus). God's martyrs (from the Greek *martyria* or "witness") are those who have been called in a special way—by laying down their lives—to witness to God's holiness in the face of evil. The martyrs are told to be patient and exercise endurance.

With the opening of the sixth seal, we reach the last moment of earthly history. Before God comes in glory, John says, nature itself will give testimony to the evil it has harbored all these many centuries. The great day of God's vengeance upon this evil has now come (Revelation 6:17), and thus we are ready for the opening of the seventh seal.

To set the stage for the events that follow the opening of the seventh seal, the author pauses to inject into the drama the theme of victory. All of saved humanity (the 144,000 of Revelation 7:4) are brought on stage into the heavenly court. The Lamb breaks open the seventh seal and, like a lull before a storm, "there was silence in heaven for about half an hour" (8:1). Then begins the period of cataclysms attendant to the ushering in of God's final judgment.

John parallels these cataclysms to the great plagues of the Exodus, once again illustrating the theme of the continuity of salvation history. Just as God punished Pharaoh for holding the Israelites in captivity, so now the new Pharaoh (the world typified in the Roman Empire) must be punished for keeping the church, the new Israel, imprisoned in a climate of oppression, persecution, and evil.

Satan and the Church

The final act of the drama finds Satan desperately trying to destroy the church (Revelation 12). War breaks out "in heaven" (12:7) between the spiritual forces of good—championed by Michael—and the evil forces—led by Satan and the fallen angels. Michael drives Satan out of heaven and onto the earth, where he attacks the "woman" (the church).

For an indefinite period of time (12:14), the church is preserved from harm, even though it must undergo the "desert" of persecution brought upon it by Satan's chief lieutenants on earth. These lieutenants are the two beasts: Rome (the beast with ten horns and seven heads—13:1), and the imperial priesthood (the beast with "two horns like a lamb"—13:11, which speaks "like a dragon," that is, in the name of Satan).

The two beasts represent worldly power and false religion, the two powers most opposed to God's rule on earth. The second beast "exercises all the authority of the first beast on its behalf, and it makes the earth and its inhabitants worship the first beast" (13:12). Further, the second beast performed "great signs" (13:13) to impress humanity with its spiritual prowess. Just so the reader understands who the symbols of the beast represent, John pauses to give his audience a clue. The "number" of the beast stands for a certain "person; its number is six hundred sixty-six" (13:18).

Who does John intend by six hundred sixty-six? In Hebrew, the name for Nero Caesar (the most dreaded of Roman emperors for early Christians) was spelled NRWN QSR. Applying a numerical/alphabetical table, prevalent in John's time, the letters add up to 666. This conclusion would obviously be in keeping with John's condemnation of Rome's wickedness.

John's purpose in choosing the number is clear. The opponents of God exist in a state of absolute imperfection, symbolized by 666, the number which falls short of the symbol for absolute perfection—seven and its combinations.

God's Ultimate Victory

After introducing the two beasts, John quickly leads us to the moment of their demise. Another angel comes forward and announces, "Fear God and give him glory, for the hour of his judgment has come" (14:7). In the person of the resurrected Christ—the one like a Son of Man of Daniel 7:13—judgment begins (Revelation 14:4). Prolonging the suspense perhaps a bit too long, John repeats in Revelation 15–16, essentially the same prejudgment cataclysms of Revelation 8–9. (We could just as well have passed right to Revelation 17 without this redundant interlude.) Finally, after telling us who the beast is (17:8—it is obviously Rome), and having the choir come back on stage to sing the final chorus of victory (18:2–19:8), the slaughter of the wicked is accomplished.

Having promised his audience victory and happiness in his opening chapters, John now delivers. The world is created anew; the church likewise shines forth in heavenly glory. The "new Jerusalem" (21:2)—the abode of Christ victorious—replaces the old Jerusalem, the church on earth—the abode of Christ suffering. Everything in John's heavenly city suggests fullness and completion.

To complete this act of re-creation, God proclaims: "See, I am making all things new" (21:5). History, having begun with God's creation in Genesis, now concludes with his re-creation in Revelation. Revelation is thus the Christian theology of history; it explains the purpose of existence and of time in terms of the endpoint of existence and time—God's final victory for God's people and God's re-creation of all things.

The drama having concluded, the "narrator" returns to the stage (22:8–21). Lest anyone in the audience doubt the veracity of this amazing production, the playwright himself now appears to put his personal seal of authenticity on the script: "I warn everyone who hears the words of prophecy of this book" (22:18). To still any remaining doubts, the Lord himself authenticates John's transcription of the revelation; the one who testifies to these things says, "Surely I am coming soon" (22:20). The audience responds, "Amen. Come, Lord Jesus!"

Sevens and More Sevens

The overall structure of the Book of Revelation reveals its literary artistry. The author loves the number *seven*. He first sends seven letters to the churches of western Asia (1:4–3:22) in which he both praises and blames the individual communities. Then, after a glorious vision of God's heavenly throne and Christ the Lamb (4:1–5:14), the Lamb opens the seven seals (6:1–8:1), and the angels blow on seven trumpets (8:7–11:19) and pour out the seven bowls of wrath (16:1–21). These three *septets* (sets of seven) constitute punishments for rebelliousness against God and warnings to repent.

The septets are introduced by scenes of the heavenly court (4:1–5:14, 8:2–6, 15:1–8) and punctuated with reports on the faithful and their struggles against the unholy trinity of Satan, the beast and their prophet (13:1–18). The book reaches its climax with God's triumph over Babylon (Rome) in chapters 17 and 18, and the appearance of the new Jerusalem in chapters 21 and 22.

It is possible to see the new Jerusalem as the seventh event in another septet: the *parousia* of the word of God (19:11–16), the last battle (19:17–21), the binding of Satan (20:1–3), the millennium (20:4–6), the defeat of Satan (20:7–10), the last judgment (20:11–15), and the new Jerusalem (21:1–22:5). And at seven points in the text we have the beatitude form, "Blessed is the one who . . ." (1:3; see also 14:13; 16:15; 19:9; 20:6; 22:7, 14). Seven letters, seven seals, seven trumpets, seven bowls, seven eschatological (end-time) events, and seven beatitudes—the basic structure of the book is clear and impressive.

TRANSCULTURAL MEANING OF THE NUMBER SEVEN

We have often heard that bad things come in threes, but perfection, at least according to some sources, comes in the number seven. The Pythagorean society of philosophers of ancient Greece believed that the number seven represented divine order.

The number seven knows no cultural bounds. The importance of seven is found in the Phoenician civilization, the Persian civilization, in Egypt, China, and other cultures as well.

In Hebrew, the word for seven derives from the concept of fullness or sufficiency, which may explain why, according to the Old Testament, God rested on the seventh day. One scholar found the Hebrew word for the number seven 287 times in the Hebrew Scriptures alone. But the importance of the number seven transcends the creation story of the biblical Book of Genesis. It continues through to the end, to the seven seals, trumpets, signs, and bowls of the Book of Revelation, the Apocalypse.

The importance of seven in Christian tradition is legion:

- The seven gifts of the Holy Spirit

- The seven times Christ spoke on the cross

- The seven deadly sins (pride, envy, sloth, gluttony, covetousness, anger, lust) and the seven virtues (faith, hope, charity, prudence, chastity, fortitude, temperance)

- The seven sacraments

- The seven sorrows and seven joys of Mary

- The seven names of God (*El, Elohim, Adonai, Yhwh, Elyey-Asher-Wehyey, Shaddai, and Sabbaoth*)

Originally, the idea of seven goes back to ancient civilizations. They didn't know about the outer planets in the solar system. To them, the sky consisted of two kinds of objects: those that were fixed and those that were changing each night, the planets. So the ancients looked up and saw seven planetary spheres in the heavens. They believed that when we were born, the soul descended down through seven planetary spheres to earth, where we were trapped in the physical world. The idea was to ascend back through seven planetary spheres.

And so the idea of the seven celestial bodies sort of governed the ancient's religion, their philosophy, just about everything. This is most likely why we have seven days in the week, seven days of creation, seven notes in a musical octave, seven branches of the golden candlestick (menorah), seven wonders of the world, seven colors in the rainbow spectrum, seven pillars of wisdom, seven original arts and sciences, and even a very recent, popular self-help book titled *The Seven Habits of Highly Effective People* by Steven Covey.

In the English speaking traditions, its most articulate bard, Shakespeare, ascribed seven stages of man in *As You Like It*. And significant sevens are also found in American Indian cultures. The Cherokee Nation is symbolized by a seven point star, representing seven original clans and the seven characters of the Sequoyah's syllabary, meaning "Cherokee nation."

Famous Sevens

- Seven hills of Rome (Aventine, Capitoline, Caelian, Esquiline, Quirinal, Palatine, and Viminal).
- Seven wise men of Greece (Thales, Bias, Periander, Cleobolus, Pitacus, Solon, and Chilo) who all lived in the sixth century B.C.E.
- Seven champions of Christendom (Saint George of England, Saint Andrew of Scotland, Saint Patrick of Ireland, Saint David of Wales, Saint Dennis of France, Saint James of Spain, and Saint Anthony of Italy).
- Seven churches of Asia (Ephesus, Smyrna, Pergamum, Thyatira, Sardis, Philadelphia, and Laodicia).
- Seven deadly sins (anger, pride, lust, sloth, gluttony, envy, and covetousness).
- Seven virtues (faith, hope, charity, prudence, temperance, chastity, and fortitude).
- Seven seas (Arctic Ocean, Antarctic Ocean, North Atlantic Ocean, South Atlantic Ocean, North Pacific Ocean, South Pacific Ocean, and Indian Ocean).

A World of Symbolic Images

Apocalyptic writers, like the author of Revelation, drew from a stockpile of apocalyptic images that helped one cope with the immediate crisis. Among the standard images were angels, demons, beasts, stars falling from the sky, the sun and moon darkened, lightning, thunder, dragons, creatures with many eyes, four horsemen, trumpet blasts, water turning to blood, plagues.

To understand the Book of Revelation we need to understand the meaning of its images and symbols. This is not as difficult as it might seem, for there were many books like Revelation written, especially by Jews in the ancient world. These books used many of the same symbols. In several cases the author of Revelation has engaged in wholesale borrowing of earlier symbols, such as in his description of Jesus in chapter 1. The symbols used there are drawn largely from Daniel (7:9–13) and Ezekiel (1:7). By studying such books we can work out the significance of many of Revelation's symbols.

240

One obvious set of symbols involves numbers. Numbers in the book are symbols, not meant to be taken literally or arithmetically. A thousand years simply means a long time, and a certain number of months means a short time. They are not quantities; they represent qualities, with each number possessing its own qualitative significance.

THE SEVEN BEATITUDES (BLESSINGS) IN THE BOOK OF REVELATION

Note: *Seven times the reader of the last book of the Bible encounters a blessing for reading the book. Since the number seven, as used in Revelation, means completeness or totality or wholeness, the implication is that the reader will receive a complete blessing by reading the Book of Revelation and taking its meaning to heart. While the beatitudes listed below are different from those presented in the gospels (see Matthew 5:1–12), they are nonetheless still part of Jesus' teachings.*

Revelation 1:3	"*Blessed* is the one who reads aloud the words of the prophecy, and blessed are those who hear and who keep what is written in it; for the time is near."
Revelation 14:13	"And I heard a voice from heaven saying, 'Write this: *Blessed* are the dead who from now on die in the Lord.'"
Revelation 16:15	"See, I am coming like a thief! *Blessed* is the one who stays awake and is clothed, not going about naked and exposed to shame."
Revelation 19:9	"And the angel said to me, 'Write this: *Blessed* are those who are invited to the marriage supper of the Lamb.'"
Revelation 20:6	"*Blessed* and holy are those who share in the first resurrection."
Revelation 22:7	"See I am coming soon! *Blessed* is the one who keeps the words of the prophecy of this book."
Revelation 22:14	"*Blessed* are those who wash their robes, so that they will have the right to the tree of life and may enter the city by the gates."

The number seven represents wholeness, totality, perfection or universality, not a literal quantity. Seven is the sum of three (which represents heaven) and four (which represents earth). When the author writes letters to seven churches, this is a synonym for writing to the church universal. When the author says there are "seven spirits before the throne" (see 4:5), we must understand that he refers to the Holy spirit who, along with Jesus and "him who is," gives grace and peace to the church.

Other numbers in Jewish apocalyptic writings have qualitative values; for example, the product of three and four, twelve, stands for God's people. Ten and all the multiples of ten represent totality. Multiples and squares of numbers simply intensify their basic meaning. The number six means incompleteness and meaninglessness.

When 144,000 are marked with a seal (7:4) to protect them from the destruction of the four horsemen, we should understand that it is twelve times twelve (144), times ten (1,440), times ten (14,400) times ten (144,000)—meaning *all* God's people. When the period of tribulation is said to last for three-and-one-half years (see 11:3; 12:6, 14), we should interpret this as symbolic of a half-seven, a broken seven, for evil can never be complete. Evil is always a perversion of good. When the beast is referred to as having the number 666, it simply means total incompleteness, meaninglessness, or complete inadequacy (13:18).

THE MEANING AND SYMBOLISM OF NUMBERS AS USED IN THE BOOK OF REVELATION

Number	Meaning
One, first	Exclusiveness, primacy, excellence. (The adjective *first* in Greek *protos,* occurs eighteen times in the Book of Revelation as compared with a total of ninety-two times for the New Testament. This total usage (eighteen) is the highest for an individual book.)

Three	Represents heaven. (The adjective *third* or *a third* in Greek *tritos,* is used twenty-three times in the book of Revelation out of a total of forty-eight times for the entire New Testament—practically half.)
Three-and-one-half	Limited time, restricted period. Three-and-one-half is symbolic of a half-seven, a broken seven, and is often applied to evil which can never be complete (see 11:3, 12:6, 14).
Four	Universality (the whole of the inhabited world): four winds, four corners of the earth. (The number *four* in Greek *tessares,* appears twenty-nine times in the Book of Revelation out of a total of forty-one times for the entire New Testament.)
Six	Imperfection, incompleteness, meaninglessness: 666 (13:18).
Seven	Completeness, fullness, totality, wholeness, perfection. Seven is the sum of three (which represents heaven) and four (which represents earth). Seven churches of Asia (chapters 2 and 3), seven spirits (4:4), seven golden lampstands (1:12), seven stars (1:16), seven burning lamps (4:5), seven seals (5:1), etc. (The number *seven* in Greek *hepta,* is the favorite number of the author of Revelation. He uses it fifty-four times out of the eighty-seven times that it appears in the whole New Testament. The Book of Revelation has more than 60 percent of the uses of this number.)
Ten	Ten and all the multiples of ten represent totality.
Twelve	Twelve is the product of three and four. It often represents the twelve tribes of ancient Israel and the twelve apostles. There are twelve stars crowning the woman's head (12:1), twelve tribes, twelve gates, twelve angels, twelve seated figures, twelve names, twelve apostles (21:12, 14, 20, 21). When 144,000 are marked with a seal (7:4) to protect them from the destruction of the four horsemen, we should understand that it is twelve times twelve (144), times ten (1,440), times ten (14,400), times ten (144,000) . . . meaning all God's people. (The number *twelve* in Greek *dodeka,* is already found in the Gospels: thirteen times in Matthew, fifteen times in

	Mark, and twelve times in Luke; however, the Book of Revelation has the highest total: twenty-three times out of a total of seventy-five for the entire New Testament.)
Twenty-four	Twenty-four represents the continuity between the people of God who are the twelve tribes of Israel and the new people of God who are represented by the apostles. (The number *twenty-four* in Greek *eikosi tessares,* itself a multiple of twelve, is found *exclusively* in the Book of Revelation.
A thousand	A large number, a multitude: thousands of thousands of angels (5:11); the thousand years (20:2–7); an extended period, a long time. (*A thousand* and *thousands* in Greek *chilioi-chilius,* is almost exclusively used by the Book of Revelation—twenty-eight times out of a total of thirty-four times in the entire New Testament.)

Many of Revelation's symbols are drawn from the biblical books of Daniel, Ezekiel, Isaiah, and Zechariah. Beasts, for example, represent the demonic and inhuman character of evil. A lion represents the conquering power of a king; a lamb is the animal of sacrifice; a horse stands for conquest; horns represent power (and sometimes rulers); multiple heads represent multiple rulers. When we encounter a beast with seven heads and ten horns (12:3, 13:1), we should endeavor to unpack the various symbols, sensing a demonic reality with complete power and perfect rulers (at least they might claim perfection). This demonic beast is the antithesis of the "one like the Son of Man" that symbolizes Jesus (1:13).

Colors, too, are symbolic: White symbolizes victory (not purity); black signified suffering (not evil); red is for war; pallor stands for death and decay; purple stands for royalty; white hair is for wisdom.

The author consciously informs the audience of the meaning of many of the special symbols he utilizes. He tells us that the stars and lampstands represent the churches and their angels (1:20), and that the censer with its smoke represents the prayers of the saints (5:8, 8:3–5). The meanings of other symbols can be easier to interpret: the

THE MEANING AND SYMBOLISM OF COLORS
AS USED IN THE BOOK OF REVELATION

Color	*Meaning*	*Examples*
White	Divine world Resurrection Victory—dignity, wisdom	The Son of Man and his *white* hair (1:14) *White* stone of the conqueror (2:17) *White* garments of the faithful (3:4, 4:4; 6:11; 7:9, 13; 14:14; 19:14) The twenty-four elders clothed in *white* (4:4) *White* horse (6:2, 19:11) *White* horses of the heavenly armies (19:14) *White* cloud of the Son of Man (14:14) *White* throne (20:11)
Black	Death, disaster, distress	The *black* horse (6:5); the black sun (6:12)
Red	War, violence, bloodshed	The bright *red* horse (6:4) The bright *red* breastplate of the angels who sow death (9:17) The *red* dragon (12:3)
Pale green	Death	The *pale green* horse (6:8)

Purple	Luxury or royalty	*Purple* in the cargoes of the merchants
		    of Babylon (18:12)
		The great city Babylon clothed in *purple*
		    (18:16)

Scarlet	Indicative of too much ego	The *scarlet* beast (17:3) The great city Babylon clothed in *scarlet* (18:16)
Gold	Royalty	The city of God is pure *gold* (21:18)

lion/lamb of 5:5–6 is definitely Jesus; the earthquake in 6:12 represents judgment; the birth in 12:2 is certainly that of the Messiah.

The way to understand these symbols is not to take them too literally. Always ask, What does this symbol mean? Revelation is not a book intended to be taken at face value; its meaning is to be found on a deeper level.

Heaven Above and Earth Below

The Book of Revelation forces the reader to operate on two levels at the same time. On the one level of the story, we move in a fantastic universe of angels and monsters, whores and virgins, stars and temples, dragons and warriors, Christ and Antichrist. Yet, when we consider the author's own interpretation, we find that we are also operating on the level of common ordinary experience.

We are hearing about stars, but we must understand that the real topic is the churches (1:20). John is eating a scroll, but the point is that he must prophesy (10:9–11). There is something maliciously appropriate in describing Roman imperial glory as a gaudy prostitute (17:3–14), but we must be clear that we are discussing Roman power, not gaudy prostitutes. We must constantly operate on both the level of symbol and the level of ordinary experience.

And there is another, more important sense in which the hearer is forced to think on two levels. Reality itself—the universe we live in—exists on two levels in this book. Above this world is another that is somehow correlated with it.

Notice, for example, the analogy that exists between the stars and the lamps. Lamps are earthly analogies to stars; they are on earth what the stars are above: givers of light. Also, there are angels and churches, an analogy more compelling when we recall that in Greek the word *angel* means "messenger," for churches, too, are God's messengers.

This can get quite complicated, for it results in four interrelated ideas: stars/lamps/angels/churches. Two levels of symbolism and two levels of interpretation: Each interacts with the others. Unless we are able to imagine such a two-tiered world, we will never grasp the meaning of much of what is portrayed in the Book of Revelation.

A Different Culture

We can gain some insight into how different the author's culture was from our own by considering a major problem addressed in the letters (chapters 2 and 3) in scene one: eating meat offered to idols (2:14). Such a problem seems strange to us because in our culture, religion and commerce are distinct activities. Not so in the first century, for religion permeated every sphere of life, including commerce, politics, education, sports, and entertainment.

One could procure meat offered to idols in at least three ways in John's world. First, one could go to one of the temples on a feast day when sacrifices were made and enjoy a banquet without much cost. Temple sacrifices may well have been the primary source of meat for many of the urban poor who subsisted largely on bread and fish. Second, one could be served meat while visiting another home. If the host was a devotee of the god Apollo, say, the meat would almost certainly have been offered to the god.

Third, one could buy meat at the local market when it was available. Chances were that it too had already been sacrificed to some divinity. Since nothing valuable was lost in such a sacrifice, all butchered animals were routinely dedicated to a god or goddess. If someone lived in the city and was not wealthy, sacrificial meat was probably the only meat he or she had access to.

Should a Christian eat such meat? The Book of Revelation's answer seems to be a categorical no. Any accommodation to pagan culture would be analogous to ancient Israel's idolatry which the prophets condemned as harlotry. The author of Revelation symbolizes his opponents as "Jezebel" and "Balaam," who were remembered as leading ancient Israel into idolatry through assimilation to pagan culture.

But the problem for Gentile converts to Christianity was enormous. It could easily be a choice between idol-tainted meat or no meat at all. In a similar way, every other aspect of life was tainted: Education involved reading Homer and honoring the heroes and gods; politics involved honoring the emperor and the city deities; sports involved festivals devoted to some divinity; theater was devoted to Dionysus and began with a sacrifice; holidays were almost exclusively religious; trade guilds were devoted to a patron deity viewed as the founder of the craft; the various coins used in commerce were stamped with the images of the gods; both business and social interaction depended on the social amenities of the temples; even family gatherings might be held in a temple.

To the author of the Book of Revelation, it did not appear that one could move in the world without giving some requisite honor to some false deity. Both head (worship) and hand (commerce and daily life) must be stamped with the mark of the beast (13:16–17). Much of what we read in the Book of Revelation is a call to persevere in the face of such pervasive idolatrous encounters.

The Lord's Supper

We often assume that John's audience experienced the Book of Revelation the same way we do—reading it as a book. But this is false. In those days, not all people were literate and few people owned scrolls, for they were expensive. People did not read quietly and privately as we do. Nearly all reading was done out loud, and mostly in groups. This is obviously true with the Book of Revelation since it begins with a blessing on the one who reads it out loud (1:3).

We must imagine, then, that the Book of Revelation was experienced as an oral enactment before a group, in which a public reader presented the words of John to the local churches (possibly within the context of the celebration of the Eucharist). The reader stands in John's place, so to speak, and is cautioned not to tamper with the message (22:18–19).

In other words, the Apocalypse would have been originally heard within a service of worship, thus providing the story to set the context for the receiving of the Eucharist—the Lord's Supper.

There is a remarkable similarity between the symbolic function of the supper and the story of Revelation. The supper is a meal that exists simultaneously in three times: It is a meal shared in the spirit with the risen Lord (present); it is a commemoration of the last meal Jesus had with his disciples (past); and it is a celebration of that meal to be eaten in the kingdom of God, the messianic banquet (future, see

Luke 22:14–16). The story in the Book of Revelation also participates in these three times.

The story is *past*. Clearly chapter 12 symbolically describes a past event: the birth of the Messiah. While it is a strikingly original Christmas story, it is told from the perspective of apocalyptic thinking. Everything described in Revelation, however, has already occurred. In a variety of ways, Revelation describes the conquest of evil, the overthrow of Satan's kingdom, the triumph of God — all of which happened in the death of Christ in John's view.

"The Lion of the tribe of Judah . . . has conquered" (5:5), John proclaims. But when he shows us this lion it turns out to be "a Lamb standing as if it had been slaughtered" (5:6). Even in the climactic scene where Jesus rides in on his white horse and slays all the wicked with his sword, we are told that it is "the sword that came from his mouth" (19:21). The sword is a metaphor for the word of God that Jesus uses to slay the wicked, and that word is primarily the testimony of his death. Christians believe that everything described in the Book of Revelation has already happened in the death and resurrection of Jesus.

Yet the story is *present*. Evil was not only overcome when Jesus died; it must also be overcome in the life of each believer. It is their testimony added to his that overthrows Satan (12:11). It is the prayers of the saints that bring judgment to the earth (8:2–5). In a real sense, the lives of Christians duplicate the life of Jesus so that his story becomes their own story, too.

It would be foolhardy to suppose John did not intend to speak of the *future* too. But given the highly symbolic way he describes the past and present, it would be equally foolhardy to take his symbols of the future at face value. John indeed tells a story of the ultimate and complete triumph of Christ over Satan and the elimination of evil from this world. Yet the symbolic nature of his story gives no warrant for thinking we know any details of that triumph.

It would be a mistake to think that we will see a white horse charging out of the sky some day. Both story and ritual are part of worship, and worship, by its nature, transcends time. John is in the spirit "on the Lord's day. This is a reference to Sunday on which Christian worshipers assembled. But is also refers to the Lord's day (Easter morning, when Christ conquered death, a past event). In addition, it echoes that future "Day of the Lord" of which the prophets spoke: "The day of God's coming justice."

Those who read or hear the Book of Revelation experience all three times: Jesus came to them in the past in his life death and resurrection (5:6; 11; 12:5); Jesus comes to them as prophet and in the meal they share (2:1; 3:20; 22:17, 20); and Jesus is to come to them for final vindication (6:10–11). John serves the one "who is and who was and who is to come" (1:8). The theme of Revelation is that of the eucharistic acclamation: "Christ has died, Christ is risen, Christ will come again."

The Book of Revelation Today

In brief, the Book of Revelation is truly the "revelation of Jesus Christ" (1:1). It is proclaiming the gospel of Christ no less than the four gospels. The gospels use normal language. Revelation uses highly symbolic apocalyptic language, much of which is traditional, some of which the author explains.

Revelation's two-tiered universe reveals the true meaning of Christian existence. John's fantastic journey takes us into another level of existence where we meet the risen Jesus, participate in the heavenly liturgy before the throne of God, and witness the attack of the ancient dragon.

We see the cosmic conflict and experience the overthrow of the powers of evil—conquered by the death of Christ and the faithful witness of his servants. John enacts the story of redemption before his people's eyes and ears, and invites them to commune with the risen Lord. As they gather around the Lord's table, resisting the false beauty of the idol-worshiping Greco-Roman culture, they experience the coming of Jesus. This coming is already known from the past, anticipated in the future, but also known in the present: It charges their lives with meaning.

When we read the early church's story in the Book of Revelation, we will do well to try to recapture its experience in our imaginations. The questions we must ask ourselves have nothing to do with whether some contemporary nation or group is represented by the beast in the Apocalypse or when the world will end.

Revelation asks us today: How are we called to witness faithfully to Jesus Christ in our situation? How can our faithfulness match that of these first-century Asian disciples as they struggled to live under the reign of God and not submit to the powers of darkness? How can we avoid compromising our faith to culture's demands? How is Jesus our Lord of Lords and King of Kings?

Responding to these questions will invite us to participate in God's banquet. "Blessed are those who are invited to the marriage supper of the Lamb" (Revelation 19:9).

For Discussion

1. After reading this chapter, are you better able to appreciate the Book of Revelation?
2. How is knowing that the images in the Book of Revelation are symbolic helpful to your reading? Explain.
3. Does knowing that the Book of Revelation is a drama help you to better interpret and understand it?
4. Have you ever had to face compromising your faith, as the audience of the Book of Revelation did? What did you do?
5. What does it mean for you to join in at the Lord's Supper?

For Further Reading

Beale, G. K. *The Book of Revelation*. Grand Rapids, Mich.: Eerdmans, 1999.

Collins, A. Y. *The Apocalypse*. Wilmington, Del.: Michael Glazier, 1979.

Fiorenza, E. S. *The Book of Revelation: Justice and Judgment*. Philadelphia: Fortress, 1985.

Giblin, C. H. *The Book of Revelation: The Open Book of Prophecy.* Collegeville, Minn.: Liturgical Press, 1991.

Harrington, Daniel J. *Revelation: The Book of the Risen Christ.* Hyde Park, N.Y.: New City Press, 1999.

Harrington, Wilfrid, J. *Revelation.* Collegeville, Minn.: Liturgical Press, 1993.

APPENDIX:
TRANSLATIONS
AND VERSIONS
OF THE BIBLE

Anyone WHO ATTEMPTS TO PURCHASE A BIBLE TODAY is confronted with a bewildering array of choices. The selection of Bibles at a bookstore will include at least a half dozen different translations. Participants in Bible study groups may find one member reading a passage from the *New American Bible* another from the *New Revised Standard Version,* while someone else scans the *Jerusalem Bible.*

The availability of so many different English translations can help readers discover the richness of the Sacred Scriptures, but it also can be confusing. If three different versions translate the same biblical passage in three different ways, readers may wonder if anyone really knows what it means. This appendix will look at the ways in which translations are made and at the differences between various versions.

Early Translations

Christians have read translations of the Bible almost from the beginning of the Christian movement. The earliest translation was the Greek translation of the Old Testament called the *Septuagint*. It was produced by Jewish scholars during the third century before the common era. Christians began to translate the Aramaic sayings of Jesus and other early Christian materials into Greek, which were incorporated into the writings of the New Testament.

The earliest translations of the Bible into a language other than Greek were the result of the church's missionary activity. Although Greek was the common language of most of the Mediterranean world, the Christian message traveled to places where other languages were read and spoken.

By the end of the second century, the Gospel had reached Edessa (Syria). Since the common language there was Syriac, it became necessary to translate the Greek New Testament into that language. One of the earliest Syriac translations was the *Diatessaron* of Tatian. A later Syriac version of the Bible, called the *Peshitta*, became the standard biblical text of the Syrian church.

By the end of the fourth century the church had spread throughout the Roman Empire, where the common language was Latin. As a result, Saint Jerome translated the Bible into Latin. His translation was known as the *Vulgate*. *Vulgate* means "common language" version.

Early English Vernacular Bible Translations

An English version of the entire Bible was produced by John Wyclif between 1380 and 1382. This translation was made from the *Vulgate*. Wyclif's translation encountered opposition and was condemned and its copies burned. In 1525, William Tyndale completed a translation of the New Testament from Greek. This version ran afoul of church authorities and was suppressed and its translator put to death. The first English Bible to be officially sanctioned by Sir Thomas Cromwell, secretary to King Henry VIII, was that of Miles Coverdale, which was based on the work of Tyndale. Coverdale's first edition, published in 1535, was dedicated to King Henry VIII; the next edition, in 1537, was published with the king's license.

The most influential Protestant Bible in English is the *King James Version* of 1611. On February 10, 1604, King James I of England ordered that a new translation of the Bible be made, and a group of scholars was named to begin the work. This "new" Bible was to be translated directly from the Hebrew and Greek, and its language was to follow as closely as possible the familiar usage of earlier English Bibles.

Of interest to English-speaking Catholics is the translation from the *Vulgate* completed by George Martin, under the sponsorship of William (Cardinal) Allen. The text appeared in two French cities, Douay and Rheims, in 1609–1610.

Reasons for New Translations

For over two hundred fifty years, the *King James* (or *Authorized*) *Version* was virtually the only one used by English-speaking Protestants; English-speaking Roman Catholics had the *Douay-Rheims Version*. In the late nineteenth and early twentieth centuries, a few new English translations began to appear. Then, after the Second World War, the pace accelerated dramatically. Between 1952 and 1989, at least twenty-six English translations of the complete Bible rolled off the presses. There were a variety of reasons for this.

First, because of archaeological discoveries, biblical scholars now have much better Greek, Hebrew, and Aramaic manuscripts on which to base translations. The contents of the Bible were first written down between two and three thousand years ago. These texts were all copied by hand and circulated among synagogues and churches throughout the ancient world. Originals were lost and translators had to rely on copies, which sometimes contained mistakes and changes made by those who transcribed the texts over the centuries.

Scholars subsequently discovered copies of the New Testament from the fourth, third, and even second centuries, as well as many later manuscripts. By comparing thousands of these manuscripts they have been able to establish a text of the Greek New Testament that is much more accurate than the one used for older translations.

What has helped translators with translating the Old Testament was the discovery in 1948 of the Dead Sea Scrolls. These scrolls included copies of the Old Testament that were a thousand years older than those previously available. By comparing the ancient scrolls with later manuscripts, scholars have been able to improve the quality of translations.

Second, scholars know more about biblical languages and cultures than ever before. The Old Testament contains some words and expressions whose meanings are unknown or unclear. Archaeological discoveries of ancient documents and inscriptions written in languages related to Hebrew and Aramaic have helped clarify a number of passages.

Third, the English language itself has changed over the centuries. To illustrate, let us roll back the clock to 1382, when John Wyclif published the first complete English translation of the Bible. His version of Matthew 2:16 reads: *"Thanne Eroude seynge that he has disseyued of the astomyenes, was full wrooth; and he sent and slewe alle the children that weren in Bethlehem. . . ."* The language is scarcely intelligible to us anymore.

We move ahead in time to 1611 when the *King James Version* appeared and the verse reads: *"Then Herod, when he saw that he was mocked of the wise men, was exceeding wroth, and sent forth, and slew all the children that were in Bethlehem. . . ."* The language still seems archaic, but at least we can understand it. We move ahead to 1946, when the *Revised Standard Version* translated it: *"Then Herod saw that he had been tricked by the wise men, was in a furious rage, and he sent and killed all the male children in Bethlehem. . . ."*

Finally, we fast forward to 1986, when the *New American Bible* translated it: *"When Herod realized that he had been deceived by the magi, he became furious. He ordered the massacre of all the boys in Bethlehem. . . ."* At least we feel as if the text is speaking our language.

The English language continues to change. In the 1940s and 1950s, the church used the old words *thou* and *thee* in prayers, and these words continued to appear in most biblical translations. By the 1970s, however, many people preferred to address God as "you," and the words *thou* and *thee* have been dropped from recent Bible translations. Another change has been a desire to avoid using male terminology for groups that include both women and men. Beginning in the 1980s, translators have increasingly referred to "people," or the "human race," rather than "men" and "mankind."

Techniques for Producing a Translation

People who translate the ancient Hebrew, Aramaic, and Greek texts into modern English are concerned with two things: accuracy and readability. They must accurately translate what the ancient authors wrote, yet do so in a way that reads well in contemporary English. Consider, for example, how Philippians 1:12 sounds if we simply substitute English words for the Greek ones: *"To know now you brethren I want that the things to me rather for the advancement of the gospel have come."* The sentence is unintelligible in this form and translators must decide how to turn it into a readable English sentence.

Some try to translate the text *word-for-word* (literal translation) as much as possible, adjusting the word order and making other changes only as necessary. Such a translation focuses on the form of the original and follows as closely as possible the words of the original as long as they can be understood in the receptor language. This approach works quite well for the Philippians passage quoted above. With only a *few* modifications, the sentence reads: *"Now I want you to know, brethren, that the things (which have happened) to me have come for the advancement of the gospel"* (Philippinas 1:12).

STEPS IN TRANSLATING THE BIBLE

Translating the Bible is always the result of many choices, both textual and linguistic—words chosen and grammatical contributions used. Steps followed by translators are as follows:

1. **Determine the text.** Since no original manuscripts of any of the biblical books exist, scholars examine and compare all the various manuscripts to determine as accurately as possible which text ought to be translated. This is profoundly difficult since, for example, Greek texts were written in capital letters without any breaks in words. Imagine how hard it would be to read this text GODISNOWHERE. It could be read: "God is now here" or "God is nowhere." Only the context of the words would help us decide.

2. **Determine the meaning in the original language.** Disagreements arise concerning the meaning of individual words in various literary, cultural, and doctrinal contexts. For example, did Jesus tell parables about the "kingdom" or the "reign" of God?

3. **Determine the meaning in the receptor language.** Disagreements occur concerning which words best capture and or express the shades of meaning found in the original. How one attempts to bridge the gap between the two languages depends on one's theory of translation. Is one doing a literal translation or a dynamic-equivalent translation?

Others try to translate the text's *meaning-for-meaning* (dynamic-equivalent translation). Such a translation attempts to express the original meaning in an appropriately modern form rather than word-for-word. For example, Psalm 16:7 literally says in Hebrew: *"I will bless the Lord who counsels me; even at night my kidneys instruct me."* Most English speakers would find it peculiar, if not humorous, to think of people being instructed at night by their kidneys. However, we often speak of knowing something "in our hearts." Therefore, all English translations render the passage with the word *heart* instead of *kidneys*. *"In the night also my heart instructs me"* would then preserve the meaning but not the exact words of the Hebrew text.

Translators differ, however, over a passage such as Amos 4:6. The *New Revised Standard Version* translates it word-for-word as: *"I gave you cleanness of teeth in all your cities"* as a vivid but perhaps unfamiliar way of describing hunger. Therefore *Today's English Version (Good News Bible)* translates the meaning, rather than the individual words of the text: *"I was the one who brought famine to all your cities."*

Concern for theological clarity also affects translations. This is reflected in the various translations of Isaiah 7:14, a vigorously disputed passage. The Hebrew text contains a word that often refers simply to a "young woman." Therefore the *New Revised Standard* Version and several others read, "the young woman is with child and shall bear a son, and shall name him Immanuel." Others sharply disagree with this translation, since Isaiah 7:14 is quoted in Greek in Matthew's gospel, where the word *virgin* is used, and the Isaiah passage provides vital support for belief in the virginal conception of Jesus. Therefore, the *New American Bible* and several others read, "[T]he virgin shall be with child, and bear a son, and shall name him Immanuel."

Selecting a Modern Translation of the Bible

When you select a modern English translation of the Bible, keep a couple of questions in mind. Do you want a translation that generally translates the text *word-for-word* or one that renders it *meaning-for-meaning?* Those who want to seriously study the Bible should use one of the word-for-word translations. What kind of English style do you read comfortably? Some versions are quite formal, others more simple and conversational. Try reading sample passages in two or three different translations to get a feel for their use of English. This can be done quite easily by looking at a parallel Bible. This is a Bible that is printed with various modern translations side by side, allowing the reader immediate access to the same passage in different translations. In 1993, Oxford University Press published *The Complete Parallel Bible.* It contains the *New Revised Standard Version,* the *Revised English Bible,* the *New American Bible,* and the *New Jerusalem Bible.* It is very helpful for anyone trying to decide about choosing a Bible.

Many translations come in several editions. For example, one publisher may produce two editions of the *New American Bible,* one edition containing *only* the biblical text while the other edition contains the biblical text, introductions to each book of the Bible, explanatory footnotes, and maps. Often, such editions are labeled by publishers as "study editions."

The sheer number of translations available today doesn't have to be confusing. From this brief description you can see that the particular Bible chosen depends on the likes and interests of the reader. There is no one best version. The way to determine which is appropriate for you is to sample several versions. Take a significant passage—possibly your favorite Bible passage—and see how various versions translate it. Peruse the introduction, notes, charts, maps, and articles in the translation you are examining. Then choose the one that reads and sounds best to you. The more comfortable you are with the translation you have selected, the more often you will read, reflect, study, and pray with the Bible.

COMMON ENGLISH TRANSLATIONS OF THE BIBLE

Revised Standard Version (RSV). This translation is based upon a revision of the standard *King James Version* and is still a literal translation. It remains a standard for good Bible study because of its fidelity to the original text, but it retains some antiquated expressions in English.

New Revised Standard Version (NRSV). This is a wholly redone translation in line with the *RSV* but with sensitivity to inclusive language for human beings. It retains traditional language for God. Although it is fairly literal in its translation, the English expressions have been updated to reflect current American cultural preferences.

New American Bible with Revised New Testament and Psalms (NAB-RNT). This has become the standard American Catholic edition of the Bible. It is a revision of the *New American Bible* (1952–70) done with a sensitivity to accurate yet easily understood language that can be used in public worship. This is the translation used in the Lectionary for Mass and other Catholic worship in the United States and many other English-speaking countries.

Catholic Study Bible. This is an edition of the *New American Bible* that appeared in 1990. It incorporates the text of the *NAB* with a commentary—reading guide—written by noted American Catholic biblical scholars. This edition has an excellent cross-reference system between the text and the commentary. It is a helpful, user-friendly tool for Bible study groups.

The Catholic Youth Bible. This is an edition of the *New Revised Standard Version Catholic Edition* that appeared in 2000. This unique Bible, geared primarily to youth, includes over six hundred fifty lively articles that help the reader pray, study, and live the Bible. This edition also makes connections to Catholic beliefs and traditions.

New International Version (NIV). Unlike the preceding versions, this is not a revision. This version is intended to be ecumenical and to appeal to a broad range of English-speaking people.

Today's English Version (TEV) Good News Bible. This translation was commissioned by the American Bible Society and completed between 1976 and 1979. It appears in the widely used *Good News Bible* and other editions. The purpose was to produce an accurate, original translation of the Bible in simple, clear, unambiguous English. Sentences were translated meaning-for-meaning in an able effort to make the material as accessible as possible.

Contemporary English Version (CEV). This is a new translation in "clear, everyday language," published in 1995 by the American Bible Society. A major goal of this translation is sensitivity to the hearers of God's word. It employs contemporary English that is more colloquial in nature.

Revised English Bible (REB). This is a major revision of the *New English Bible* (NEB). This version was commissioned by the Anglican churches of Great Britain and is primarily a product of British scholarship. The translators rendered the original biblical languages into contemporary English on a meaning-for-meaning basis. It is readable and useful for study purposes.

New Jerusalem Bible (NJB). First published in 1985, it and its predecessor the *Jerusalem Bible* (JB), published in 1966, were inspired by French translations of the Bible by Dominican Catholic scholars at the L'Ecole Biblique in Jerusalem. The English version is based on the original Hebrew, Aramaic, and Greek texts, but adopts the general outlook of its French counterpart. The text is the most poetic of the translations we are considering. Its poetic character lends itself to prayer. This Catholic Bible is also justifiably praised for its extensive footnotes and informative background material.

New King James Version (NKJV). Completed in 1982, this translation is an attempt to update the *King James Version* without significantly altering its renderings. Words such as *thou, thee,* and other archaic expressions have been changed and some of the longer sentences have been broken up. Words not found in the original Hebrew, Aramaic, and Greek texts are placed in italics. The editors based their New Testament work on the sixteenth-century Greek text, rather than on the evidence of older Greek manuscripts.

New Testament and Psalms: An Inclusive Language Version. This is an adaptation of the NRSV that employs radically gender-inclusive language. Some have dubbed it the "PC Bible" (for Political Correctness). For example, the title used by Jesus, "Son of man," becomes "child of the human one," and the Lord's Prayer begins with the address, "Father-mother." The result of this approach is a clumsy and at times offensive translation.

Condensations and paraphrases. Finally, mention should be made of the immensely popular *The Way,* the *Living Bible,* and the *Reader's Digest Bible.* *The Way* and the *Living Bible* are not translations but paraphrases of the biblical text. Paraphrases are not reliable for Bible study, but they can nonetheless be inspiring and easy to understand.

The Reader's Digest Bible (1982), on the other hand, is truly a condensation of the Bible. It has clipped out all repetition in the Bible. Unfortunately, the result is a distortion of the text because repetition is a vital part of the message of some biblical stories or poetry. The purpose of this condensation is to entice people to pick up and read the Bible. But using such shortcuts can cheapen the word of God.

STUDY VERSIONS OF THE BIBLE

Some of the more popular study Bibles are:

- *The Catholic Study Bible,* D. Senior et al., eds. (New York: Oxford University Press, 1990). Uses the NAB translation.

- *The Oxford Study Bible* (New York: Oxford University Press, 1992). Uses the REB.

- *The Harper Collins Study Bible,* Wayne Meeks et al., eds. (New York: Harper Collins, 1993). Uses the NRSV.

- *The Cambridge Annotated Study Bible,* Howard Clark Kee, ed. (New York: Cambridge University Press, 1993). Uses the NRSV.

The advantage of a study Bible is that it provides much more information than a standard Bible edition.

HELPFUL WEB PAGES

Note: A myriad of Web pages dealing with the Bible are available on the Internet. Those mentioned here were selected on the basis of their thoroughness and ability to be user-friendly.

Bible Words 4 at: http://www.bibleworks.com

American Bible Society at: http://www.americanbible.org

All-in-One Biblical Resources Search at
http://www.bham.ac.uk/theology/goodcare/multibib.htm

Theology Library: Sacred Scripture at:
http://www.mcgill.pvt.k12.ul.us/jerryd/cm/bible.htm

Vertical Religion Index at: http://religion.Rutgers.edu/uri/bible.html

Bible Tutor at: http://www.bibletutor.com/default.htm#OLI

INDEX
OF
SCRIPTURE

INDEX

273